Developing Thinking; Developing Learning

Developing Thinking; Developing Learning

A Guide to Thinking Skills in Education

Debra McGregor

 Open University Press

MT

Open University Press
McGraw-Hill Education
McGraw-Hill House
Shoppenhangers Road
Maidenhead
Berkshire
England
SL6 2QL

email: enquiries@openup.co.uk
world wide web: www.openup.co.uk

and Two Penn Plaza, New York, NY 10121-2289, USA

First published 2007

A catalogue record of this book is available from the British Library

ISBN-10:   033521780X (paperback) 0335217818 (hardback)
ISBN-13:   9780335217809 (pb)   9780335217816 (hb)

Library of Congress Cataloguing-in-Publication Data
CIP data applied for

Typeset by BookEns Ltd, Royston, Herts.
Printed in Poland by Oz Graf S.A.
www.polskabook.pl

The *McGraw·Hill* Companies

4|7|08

Dedication

To my two daughters, without whom
thoughtfulness would be purposeless.

Contents

List of figures and tables

Figures

Tables

Acknowledgements

I would like to acknowledge all educators and students with whom I have worked over the past 20 years. All the learning interactions with them in schools, colleges, universities and educational institutions have shaped in some way the thinking that has developed.

I would also like to thank Sara Quantock for her illustrations and proof reading and Eilish McGregor for her work on the index.

And last, but certainly not least, I would like to thank my patient family who could be forgiven for thinking that my study is a place I'd rather be.

Introduction

The human brain is made of many parts. Each has a specific function: to turn sounds into speech; to process colour; to register fear; to recognise a face or distinguish a fish from a fruit. But this is no static collection of components; each brain is unique, ever-changing and exquisitely sensitive to its environment. Its modules are interdependent and interactive and their functions are not rigidly fixed; sometimes one bit will take over the job of another, or fail, owing to some genetic or environmental hiccup, to work at all. Brain activity is controlled by currents bound together in a dynamic system of systems that does millions of different things in parallel. It is probably so complex that it will never succeed in comprehending itself. Yet it never ceases to try.

(Carter, *Mapping the Mind*)

As Carter (1998: 10) points out, the workings of the brain are complex. Teaching students how to maximize their thinking potential is therefore not straightforward. Often, in education, we become so focused on 'what' students must learn that we forget 'how' best to ensure they learn. Each individual student possesses a uniquely wired pair of cerebral cortices, which will influence, and in turn be influenced by, life experiences. Physiological studies of the brain suggest that some functions of the mind arise from differing areas of the brain. Problem solving, inferring and synthesizing, for example, have been shown to develop in the frontal lobes of the cerebral cortex. Speech and comprehension are more likely to arise within the auditory cortex, further behind the frontal lobes. The intricate neural networks that connect these areas can potentially be developed in a multiplicity of ways. The intent of education should be to stimulate the development of these kinds of networks, to develop the mind and its associated cognitive capabilities. This book is focused on suggesting what educators can do to support cognitive development while children are in school. Between the ages of 5 and 16 years, average pupils will spend more than half their waking hours at school. Educators, therefore, have significant opportunities to shape childrens' patterns of behaviour, ways of learning and thinking for life. This book attempts to set out for teachers how the interplay between thinking programmes, learning activities and teachers' pedagogy in the classroom can fundamentally affect the nature of thinking in which students engage in school. It considers the ways in which the childrens' minds respond to the 'learning' environment created by peers and teachers.

'Thinking' is defined in many ways by various educators. Dewey (1991: 12) defines it as a series of thoughts that originate from 'some perplexity, confusion or doubt'. 'It is not spontaneous', he adds, 'there is something specific which occasions and evokes it.' Probing what we mean by thinking in learning situations is an issue that merits consideration. As Robert Fisher (1990: x) explains, '...even among experts the definitions of what we call thinking vary greatly. There is much in the concept that is still in the process of being uncovered, and much still to be learned'. Therefore a review of the contrasting perspectives of prominent educators is justified.

With regard to the role of schools in thinking, Dewey (1916: 152) says '...all which the school can or need do for pupils, so far as their minds are concerned is to develop their ability to think'.

Teaching thinking in the UK

The DfES (2002) describes thinking as 'cognitive activity triggered by challenging tasks and problems' and lessons that teach thinking skills well:

- have open and challenging tasks that make pupils think hard;
- encourage pupils to use what they already know;
- offer opportunities for work in collaborative groups with high-quality talk;
- encourage pupils to talk about how tasks have been done;
- produce learning outcomes at different levels – some relating to the subject content but others to how learning can be used in other contexts.

There are examples for guidance provided in the Leading in Learning (DfES 2005) materials but teachers still need to make pedagogic decisions about when to focus on thinking in lessons and exactly how to do it to be most effective. This book attempts to guide and inform educators about the when and how.

The chapters in this book

The first chapter describes and contrasts educators' differing views of thinking. It considers how recognized experts define thinking. Clarification about the nature of thinking informs how educators perceive and subsequently nurture it.

Chapter 2 discusses the kinds of thinking we should be encouraging children to engage in. The government has extolled lifelong learning, which requires people to be independent thinkers. The thinking children need to develop to succeed in adult life to become 'wise' (Sternberg, 2002) and 'intelligent' (Costa 2002; Shayer and Adey 2002) will be considered. This discussion develops into a consideration of thinking skills needed to solve academic and life problems. So the issue and nature of problem solving and the implicit and/or explicit thinking processes required therein are explored. Reflections of these skills and abilities are contrasted with the kinds of thinking we currently demand of pupils in scholastic situations.

In Chapter 3 the relationships between thinking and learning are considered. The various views of learning and the intrinsic/extrinsic thinking required in different learning situations is examined. The nature and development of theories about how the 'mind' can be developed through argument (Aristotle and Socrates), constructivist activity (Piaget) and social constructivism (Vygotsky) and Rogoff's view of thinking as an 'apprenticeship', which is more socially and culturally aware is contrasted.

In Chapter 4 the aims, design, content and methodology of prominent thinking programmes being used by primary and secondary UK schools today are outlined. This includes the *'Cognitive Acceleration'* suite of programmes (including *CASE, CAME, CATE, Let's Think*); the *'Thinking Through . . .'* suite of programmes including geography, history, religious education; Lipman's 'philosophy in the classroom' and Fisher's 'philosophy for children'. The important components of each course are highlighted with similarities and differences contrasted.

In Chapter 5 the nature of general thinking skills programmes is outlined. Courses of this kind are frequently used with groups of children who require more support to make expected academic gains. Increasingly though, schools recognize the general advantages of all pupils participating in this kind of programme. The programmes considered include *Feuerstein's Instrumental Enrichment*; Blagg's *Somerset Thinking Skills*; De Bono's *CoRT* materials and Six Hats and Dawes, Mercer and Wergerif's *Thinking Together*. The processes and outcomes of each are considered to inform educators who must match 'needs requirements' with thinking and learning outcomes.

In Chapter 6 the nature of infused thinking is considered. The cognitive aims, content and methodology of McGuiness's 'Activating Children's Thinking' (ACTs) and 'Sustainable Classrooms' approach, based on Swartz and Park's teaching thinking approach is outlined. Techniques that de Bono has developed, which embrace the 'infusion' philosophy, are also outlined. These approaches by their very nature can be used in a wide range of lessons and can therefore be applicable throughout the curriculum.

In Chapter 7 evidence regarding success of thinking programmes will be considered. For some there is copious evidence of particular kinds of impact; for others there are less obvious indications of influence. Teachers, researchers and policy makers need to be aware of the nature and extent of the potential and actual impact of the various approaches.

In Chapter 8 the character and development of creative thinking is explored. Creativity is the ability to see things in a new way, to see problems that no one else may even realize exist, and then to come up with new, unique, and effective solutions to these problems. Standard intelligence tests measure convergent thinking – the ability to come up with a single correct answer. But creativity involves divergent thinking – the ability to come up with new and unusual answers. Creative thinking can be also be described as lateral thinking, which can be generated randomly, but can also be learned using various techniques. It can also be artistic, with aesthetic, sensitive and emotional resonance. This chapter considers which programmes or approaches could support this kind of thinking.

In Chapter 9 the nature and development of critical thinking is explored. Often described as the process to determinine the authenticity, accuracy, or value of something and characterized by the ability to seek reasons and alternatives, perceive the total situation, and base one's view on evidence. This type of thinking is frequently referred to as 'logical' or 'analytical' thinking. Ennis (1986) describes the many forms of critical thinking that are considered and expanded upon in this chapter. Most thinking programmes support development of this kind of cognition; however, some require more demanding thought than others. How teachers might support the development of critical thinking will be reflected upon.

In Chapter 10 the character and development of metacognition is explored. Definitions of metacognition range from Adey's (1997) view 'thinking about your thinking, becoming conscious of your own reasoning' to that of Schoenfeld (1985) who describes it as students learning to monitor and direct their own progress, asking questions such as 'What am I doing here?' 'Is it getting me anywhere?' 'What else could I be doing instead?' He refers to this as general metacognition that can

help students avoid persevering unproductive approaches. Some programmes employ this kind of thinking; it is, however, an approach that
could be used more widely and even more powerfully in many learning
situations. The applications of this kind of thinking will be considered.

Chapter 11 explores the nature, development and impact of problem
solving is explored. The different steps involved in problem solving are
outlined in this chapter and the various ways it could be supported
expressed. Problem solving like, thinking skills, is a term often used in a
very loose, ill-defined way. This chapter will attempt to clarify what is
meant by the thinking needed to solve problems and elaborate on its
potential in academic and lifelong learning.

In Chapter 12 various philosophies, activities and pedagogies that
appear to be successful in supporting cognitive development will be
considered. This chapter will attempt to synthesize the general from the
specific. Synthesis of the effective characteristics of various programmes
and teaching thinking approaches suggest 'what works' well. Commonalities in underpinning theories or ideology, resources, materials,
activities, lesson structure and pedagogical approaches (such as intervention, questions, questioning) will be collated to suggest strategies
teachers and educators could adopt to encourage thinking.

Chapter 13 considers professional development to support thinking
classrooms. This chapter will consider how teachers can come to
appreciate how to better support thinking and more effective learning.
Craft (2000) illustrates how teachers' views of learning (and therefore
thinking) are implicit in the way they choose to organize their
classroom. Each choice a teacher makes about – the physical layout;
the curriculum content; the structure of assignments; the availability
and use of resources; the nature of classroom interactions and relationships – reflects to some degree that teacher's view of learning. The nature
of professional development for teachers to realize 'thinking' in their
pupils will be discussed.

Chapter 14 considers school development to support thinking
communities. Organizational and management issues centred around
the development of schools as thinking communities will be discussed in
this chapter. A problem solving approach that highlights issues faced
when developing a thoughtful community of learners will be explored.
This chapter considers how strategic pedagogy may require a little
redeveloping, redefining, refocusing or even redesigning to support a
more strategic approach to support thoughtful mini- and macro-
communities of learning.

1 What do we mean by 'thinking'?

Defining thinking

Teachers often say to students 'Let's think about this ...' or 'Put on your thinking caps ...' or 'Think hard'. There is, however, little agreement about the nature of the thinking the teachers expect. Many hope for the 'right answer' that they are silently holding in their heads and some may anticipate an attempt that offers insight into their pupils' misconceptions. Very few will expect an unprompted 'I think that ... because ...' type of response. Many teachers will not know the extent or nature of the thinking most of their students engage in because, as Astington and Olson (1995) comment, 'A major problem is that ... thinking does not have any behavioural indices.' It is therefore difficult for teachers to observe it in action. Teachers can only really *infer* what kind of thinking may have taken place by listening to children's speech (through responses to questions, conversation between peers), watching their actions (through reviewing their writing), observing how they go about a practical task or judging what they produce (a work of art, a story or report or even a simple invention of some kind).

As children progress through primary and secondary school they come to understand, through experience and reflection, that teachers expect very different kinds of thinking and mean quite different things when they say 'think about it'. Just as teachers hold very different perceptions of the kinds of thinking they may wish their pupils to engage in, so do prominent and experienced educators. There are many diverse views about what constitutes thinking in an educational sense. As Bruner (1996: 25) corroborates, 'Not only are there many ways of using the mind, many ways of knowing and constructing meanings, but they serve many functions in different situations'.

The Greeks are generally regarded as the earliest teachers of thinking. Socrates would provide problem solving tasks for his students and support their learning through 'dialogue' between him the expert (knower) and his novice pupils. The dialogues allowed the novices to generate and discuss ideas amongst themselves. As Kutnick and Rodgers (1994: 2) highlight, 'this Socratic dialogue enabled two types of learning

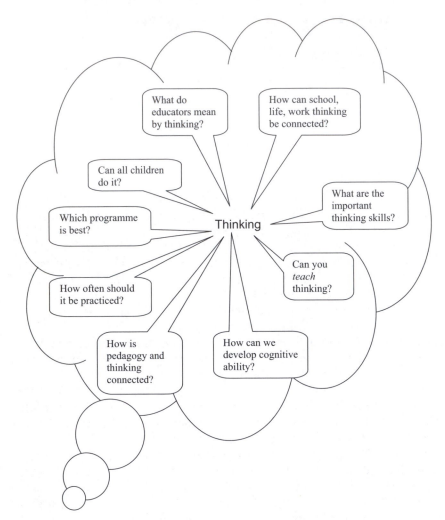

Figure 1.1 Indication of prevailing questions with regard to thinking in schools

dynamic, that appropriate answers may be confirmed by the expert and that mutually naïve novices may speculate amongst themselves and thus generate new ideas to be tested'. Socrates was also renowned for asking challenging questions of his fellow citizens of Athens. However, his probing for clear, accurate and relevant rationale to explain (the then current) Greek politics and morality, eventually led to his demise. Plato, one of Socrates' students, continued his work in questioning commonly held beliefs by seeking reasoned and logical explanations. Aristotle, Plato's student, continued the teaching and also documented ideas, current at that time, about thinking centred around 'logic', and many other aspects of philosophy, politics, mathematics and physics, described by Barnes (1984), and widely acknowledged as central tenets of critical thinking (Wheeler and Wheeler 1995). 'Critical', derived from the Greek word *kritikos* meaning to judge, arose out of the way analysis and Socratic argument comprised thinking at that time.

Direct physiological connections between logical thinking and the functioning of the brain were developed in the seventeenth century by René Descartes, the French philosopher. He argued that thinking is reasoning, and that reason is a chain of simple ideas, linked by applying strict rules of logic. His findings regarding neurological transmissions between receptors and affectors in various vertebrates led him to declare 'cogito ergo sum', which translated means 'I think therefore I am' (Gaukroger 2003). Descartes was regarded as the precursor to cognitive science, the cerebral basis of thought. English mathematician, George Boole (1854), regarded as the second precursor, invented symbolic calculus, in which logical operations like 'or', 'and', and 'if–then', are expressed as simple mathematical computations using 0 and 1 (and referred to as Boolean logic). Many current US thinking programmes apply the 'or' and 'if–then' logic approach (elaborated upon in Chapter 6). Boole hoped to translate all operations in the human mind to elementary mathematics. Swiss psychologist, Jean Piaget, with a background in biology and natural sciences, showed how elementary psychological mechanisms (mental actions and operations) gradually develop to underpin logical and mathematical thinking between infancy and adulthood.

Arguably, no other educationalists influenced the teaching of thinking so fundamentally as the early Greeks, until Piaget and then Lev Vygotsky (a Russian psychologist) contributed to the field of developmental psychology. These two very prominent educational psychologists, whose theories still inform much of educational practice today, were coincidentally born in the same year (1896). Piaget's works, which included *The Growth of Logical Thinking from Childhood to Adolescence, The Language and Thought of the Child, The Child's Conception of the World* and *The Psychology of Intelligence*, were generally published earlier. Piaget studied the evolution of children's thinking. In his studies, which involved detailed questioning of children, he argued how knowledge was constructed through the development of understanding of such things as number, time, space, velocity, geometry, chance and morality from birth to adolescence. He theorized that there was a genetic influence to higher order mental processes, in that thinking evolved from biological mechanisms, rooted in the development of an individual's cognitive structures – in the nervous system.

He also believed there was a maturational influence, that the processes of concept formation followed a pattern through several clearly definable stages (discussed further in Chapter 3), which are hierarchical and linked to age, and that each must be experienced before any subsequent stage of development is possible. Piaget also identified a way in which intellect can grow; he describes how schemata or types of cognitive functions (such as classifying things, connecting cause and effect, or sequencing events) can be applied to a problem or task to be solved. He describes intellectual development as a gradual process of self-construction, governed by what a learner already knows, which (re)develops through reflective realizations about the world.

Thinking, for Piaget, was an active process, with learners developing cognitively as a consequence of their interaction with the world around them. Vygotsky, however, conceived of the development of thinking in a more social setting. He was more concerned with the influence of societal factors on individual intellectual development. He articulated three main tenets to explain how cognition evolved. He recognized the influence of genetic inheritance and development, that social interaction with others promoted thinking and that the ways in which language was used could both stimulate *and* shape how children thought. He believed that learning and thinking were social in their origins, through interactions between peers or experts and novices, communicating about shared experiences (Crawford 1996). He indicated how the evolving nature of communications (in either written or speech form) subsequently influenced the direction and focus of thought.

Vygotsky believed that thought and language could not exist without each other. He strongly believed that articulating thoughts was an effective method to process connected thoughts in a conscious way, to raise the awareness of mental activity and subsequently to create organized logic and meaning for oneself and others from these utterances. He perceived that dialogic exchange in learning was thus essential because it can transform the way in which children learn, think and understand in social contexts.

John Dewey describes everything that comes to mind, that goes through your head as a 'thought', and that to think of a thing is just to be conscious of it in any way whatsoever.

Dewey (1910: 5) uses the example of 'Men *thought* the world was flat until Colombus *thought* it to be round' to illustrate how thought and belief are interrelated. He argues that we may engage in thoughts that often prepare the way for developing beliefs (for example, often when listening to a story or a report of some happening, a complex movie plot or unexpected weather causing life trauma, one might respond with

'I never thought of that'). Thoughts can also induce belief at an indirect or direct level. Through communication you may accept that 'men used to think the world was flat' or that 'birds migrate south in winter' without needing the direct evidence.

He highlights how thinking is 'that operation in which present facts suggest other facts (or truths) in such a way as to induce belief in the latter upon the ground or warrant of the former.' He further describes how thinking at its best is 'active, persistent, and careful consideration of any belief or supposed form of knowledge in the light of the grounds that support it, and the further conclusions to which it tends' (Dewey 1910: 6).

He extends his ideas to those 'correct habits of reflection' whereby reflective thought involves consideration of the significance of some-thing – in other words, the quality of evidence to support or refute a suggestion. He elaborates on reflective thinking to suggest that, once a belief is proposed, enquiry should proceed to test the proposition and engage in critical evaluation and thinking about the original belief. Dewey highlights that 'bad' thinking is the acceptance of a 'plausible' suggestion and no subsequent mental concern about the evidence; 'good' thinking is always

> more or less troublesome because it involves overcoming the inertia that inclines one to accept suggestions at their face value; it involves willingness to endure a condition of mental unrest and disturbance ... To maintain the state of doubt and to carry on systematic and protracted inquiry – these are the essentials of thinking.
>
> (Dewey 1910: 13)

Edward Glaser (1941: 6) expanded on Dewey's thinking to list what he perceived as essential skills for good critical thinkers. He described these as the ability to: a) recognize problems; b) find workable means for meeting those problems; c) gather and marshal pertinent information; d) recognize unstated assumptions and values; e) comprehend and use language with accuracy, clarity and discrimination; f) interpret data; g) appraise evidence and evaluate statements; h) recognize the existence of logical relationships between propositions; i) draw warranted conclu-sions and generalizations; j) test the generalizations and conclusions at which one arrives; k) reconstruct one's pattern of beliefs on the basis of wider experience; and l) render accurate judgments about specific things and qualities in everyday life. This listing of attributes of good critical thinking has since been much extended (Ennis 2001; Fisher 2001) indicating the scientific influence and nature of reflectivity brought to the conceptualization of thinking.

Robert Ennis extends Dewey's perspectives to include action with respect to thinking. He describes critical thinking in a very comprehensive way. Ennis (2001: 44) describes how it means reasonable and reflective thinking focused on deciding what to believe or do. He describes three broad dispositions that are desirable and 15 key abilities that they should possess. His extensive work on defining critical thinking is considered further in Chapter 9.

Alec Fisher (2001) is also an advocate of critical thinking. He highlights how teachers *may* develop children's thinking skills through teaching their subject content in an implicit or indirect way but this does not develop the competencies in 'how to think'. He explicates how thinking should be taught explicitly and directly so that the thinking skills are transferable to other subjects and contexts. Unlike many US educators, he recognizes the connection between creative *and* critical thinking, which he describes as critico-creative thinking. Critical thinking tends to be 'negative' and to be truly evaluative. Good thinking, he explains, will also produce alternative suggestions, which can be imaginative and *creative* to improve whatever is being critiqued.

Jerome Bruner (1966), writing about the process of education, adds that we do not have much of an idea of what thought is, either as a 'state of mind' or as a process. Indeed 'thought' as it is usually discussed may be little more than a way of talking and conversing about something we cannot observe. Talking functions to give 'thought' some form that is more visible, more audible, more referable and more negotiable. As Bruner (1986: 72) goes on to describe: 'Language is (in Vygotsky's sense as in Dewey's) a way of sorting one's thoughts about things. Thought is a mode of organizing perception and action'.

Bruner describes how thinking is essential in education, it:

> Should be an invitation to generalise, to extrapolate, to make a tentative leap, even to build a tentative theory. The leap from mere learning to using what one has learned in thinking is an essential step in the use of the mind. Indeed, plausible guessing, the use of the heuristic hunch, the best employment of necessarily insufficient evidence – these are the activities in which the child needs practice and guidance. They are among the great antidotes to passivity
>
> (Bruner 1996: 126)

He also suggests that teachers should perceive children as thinkers (Bruner 1996: 57) so that, 'The child, in a word, is seen as an epistemologist as well as learner'. He explicates further by adding

'Knowledge (in the child's world) is what is shared within discourse ... truths are the product of evidence, argument and construction rather than authority, textual or pedagogic'. Bruner (1986: 130) describes how learners should engage in some kind of activity (actional or dialogic) to construct or construe their meaning of the world.[1] He also recognizes that context of learning and social and cultural influences are important in developing children's thinking and 'ways of knowing' and understanding.

Barbara Rogoff (1990) describes children's intellectual development as an apprenticeship. She describes this apprenticeship as arising through guided participation in social activity with others who support and stretch children's understanding of and skill in using the tools of culture. She illustrates how the socio-cultural basis of human skills development is inseparable from the biological and historical basis of humans as species. She recognizes how the nature and development of conceptual understanding can arise through the naturalistic interaction between peers in learning tasks who might 'teach each other'. She also speculates that the nature of thinking and learning will differ when children are taught under the direction of adults and participate in tasks in which adults are more skilled.

Reuven Feuerstein also rejects the idea that intelligence is fixed. His view is that thinking skills can be directly taught and learned and that these skills are transferable and usable in all areas of life. 'Except in the most severe instances of genetic and organic impairment the human organism is open to modifiability at all ages and stages of development' (Feuerstein et al. 1980: 9). To improve the quality of thinking, his philosophy is to focus on what constitutes 'deficient cognitive functions'. Providing learners with tasks that are designed to improve these particular thinking skills will improve their cognitive performance. The focus on specific types of thinking, in his programme, develops thinking processes. He believes that interventional mediation techniques can be used to improve students' cognitive resources, including flexible thinking to become more socially adaptable and subsequently better *life* problem solvers. Most informatively, Flavell et al. (1995) describe how children conceive of thinking as an effortful, voluntary process associated with problem solving. The tenets of *Feuerstein's Instrumental Enrichment* programme (FIE) have been adopted by Nigel Blagg, who has grouped, categorized and extended the cognitive skills into the *Somerset Thinking Skills* (STS) course. This course, widely used in

---

[1] 'Constructivism' in this context is about children construing their personal understandings of something.

the UK, is developed from Feuerstein's original cognitive resources and mediational philosophy.

Michael Shayer recognizes important tenets of the FIE and indicates how it is metacognitive (Shayer and Beasley 1987) and teaches 'thinking about thinking'. This is because the problem solving strategies developed by the learner have to be explicated so that they become more consciously aware of their processing involved in reaching a resolution. Shayer also illustrates how the FIE elucidates three phases of problem solving: information-gathering, elaboration or solution finding and finally output. Each involves students communicating about their solutions. Shayer refers to Piaget as the Galileo of cognitive development (Shayer 1993), extolling his notions about constructivism (children developing their own understandings about the world around them), phased development of learners *and* the interventional role of mediators in learning. He further describes how psychological insights into how learners perceive 'given facts' from a teacher and hold alternative concepts (Driver et al. 1985) can offer suggestions about the way mediational methodology could support learning.

Philip Adey describes thinking as:

> something we do when we try to solve problems; it involves processing the information that we have available to us – either from the external world or from within our own memories. Thinking allows us to take things we know or observe and turn them into new ways of understanding.
>
> (Adey et al. 2001: 2)

He highlights how an interventional approach can bring about long-term effects on the development of thinking and general academic ability (Adey 1991). He describes important features influencing the development of high-level or formal thinking, such as readiness or preparation for cognitive engagement, focus on particular kinds of thinking, presenting problems that cause conflict and transferring thinking strategies developed through problem resolution. He emphasizes, like Shayer, that metacognition or 'thinking about your thinking' is important.

Philip Adey and Michael Shayer have collaborated and integrated their perspectives on the teaching of thinking to develop various interventional 'thinking skills' programmes, intending, like Feuerstein to improve students' cognitive processing capabilities.

Robert Sternberg is probably best known, in the UK, for his theory of triarchic intelligence. He has, however, also focused on development of creativity and wisdom too. In his triarchic theory he proposes that 'successfully intelligent people are those who have the ability to achieve success according to their own definition of success, within their socio-cultural context.' He elaborates that success requires a balance of analytical, creative and practical skills. He views intelligence as a form of developing competencies, and competencies as forms of developing expertise. He perceives that intelligence (and the accompanying thinking required to develop it) is modifiable and not fixed. His balance theory of wisdom is that someone who is wise uses his or her successful intelligence in order to seek a common good. Sternberg also proposes a theory about thinking styles, based on how people use their abilities in their life. He describes how thinking styles (Sternberg 1999) are probably more important than abilities. Thinking styles describe the *ways people prefer to think*, which can explain, when in particular environments, how students thrive and succeed *or* struggle.

Robert Swartz describes how good thinking is 'skilful'. He categorizes (see Figure 1.2) the kinds of thinking to be developed as 'generating ideas', 'clarifying ideas', 'assessing the reasonableness of ideas' and 'complex thinking' (problem solving and decision making). Generating and clarifying ideas, he states, are relatively easy for teachers to develop through restructuring their content lessons but more complex tasks involving decision making and problem solving may need much more practice to be *carefully* and *skilfully* applied. He also believes it is most efficacious to teach thinking skills within a subject context and not through direct instruction in a non-curricular context. He believes that to 'infuse' thinking in teaching is a natural way educators can teach students how to think 'skilfully' as they live their lives.

Bloom et al. (1956) have also extensively categorized cognitive abilities. His hierarchical taxonomy of cognitive processes is often used to evaluate whether higher levels of thinking are being developed in classrooms. Teachers are encouraged to apply the classification (outlined in Figure 1.3) to the questions asked or the types of tasks pupils are engaged in (DfES 2002: 208) to assess whether higher order thinking is being addressed. Questions or tasks involving analysis, synthesis or evaluation are deemed to be more challenging and demanding than those that require only recall or comprehension.

Art Costa (2001) recognizes how, with the increase in knowledge and information that is available in the world, education needs to focus on the ability to solve problems, apply cognitive processes and develop good habits of mind. He describes how we can think when we are born, but to do it effectively and skilfully requires practice, concentration, reflection and coaching. However, unlike athletics, thinking is often

1. Generating ideas
i. **alternative possibilities**
  • multiple ideas
  • varied ideas
  • detailed ideas
ii.**composition**
  • analogy and metaphor

2.Clarifying ideas
i analysing ideas
  • compare/contrast
  • classification/definition
  • parts/whole
  • sequencing
ii **analysing arguments**
  • finding reasons/developing conclusions
  • uncovering assumptions

3 Assessing the reasonableness of ideas
i **assessing basic information**
  • accuracy of observation
  • reliability of sources
ii **inference**
A Use of evidence
  • casual explanation
  • prediction
  • generalization
  • reasoning by analogy
B Deduction
  • conditional reasoning (if ... then ...)
  • categorical reasoning (some ... all ...)

4 Complex thinking tasks
  • decision making
  • problem solving

Source: Summarized from Swartz et al. (1996) and Swartz (2001)

Figure 1.2 Important types of thinking that should be taught to students

idiosyncratic and covert. Awkwardness and agility are not as easily distinguished as they are in athletics. Which is why he explains, 'definitions of thought processes, strategies for their development and assessment of the stamina required for their increased mastery are therefore illusive' (Costa 2001: 80). He does, however, highlight that there is a need to develop clarity of what characterizes effective thinkers and problem solvers. He also proposes that infusing thinking within subject content should be perceived as 'a vehicle by which the mind is activated and engaged to experience the joy ride of learning'. Costa's view of intelligent behaviours are emphasized in his descriptions of the characteristics or 'habits of mind' to which good thinkers should aspire (see Figure 14.1). These thoughtful habits are key because, as he elaborates, when humans experience dichotomies, are confused by dilemmas, or come face-to-face with uncertainties the most effective

BLOOM'S TAXONOMY

KNOWLEDGE – includes those behaviours and test situations which emphasize remembering.
• Define, recognize, recall, identify, label, understand, examine, show, collect.

COMPREHENSION – emphasis is on the student grasp of the meaning and intent of the material being communicated.
• Translate, interpret, extrapolate, explain, describe, summarize.

APPLICATION – applies comprehension in a situation new to the student without prompting, requires transferring of knowledge and comprehension to a real situation.
• Apply, solve, experiment, show, predict

ANALYSIS – emphasis is on the breakdown of the material into its constituent parts and detection of the relationship of the parts and of the way they are organized and connected.
• Connect, relate, differentiate, classify, arrange, check, group, distinguish, organize, categorize, detect, compare, infer.
• Not to be confused with comprehending the meaning of something abstract (Comprehension).

SYNTHESIS – putting together elements and parts so as to form a whole, to a pattern or structure not clearly there before.
  Produce, propose, design, plan, combine, formulate, compose, hypothesize, construct.

EVALUATION – making of judgments about the value, for some purpose, of ideas, works, solutions, methods, material, etc. Involves use of criteria as well as standards. May be quantitative or qualitative. Are not opinions but judgements based on criteria.
• Appraise, judge, criticise, decide.

Note: These cognitive abilities are hierarchically classified. Evaluation is deemed the most demanding and remembering knowledge the least.
Source: Adapted from Bloom et al. (1956).

Figure 1.3 Description of the associated kinds of thinking in each of the Bloom et al. (1956) cognitive categories

actions require drawing forth certain patterns of intellectual behaviour. Practising intelligent behaviours when solving problems could therefore, he suggests, result in wise decision making.

David Perkins contrasts the notion of intelligence, defined as 'abilities centric' (Perkins et al. 1993; Perkins 1995) with traditional measures of IQ or mental ability (including Spearman's (1904) 'g') to how to think appropriately in daily life. He describes how in day-to-day life we have to solve problems and deal with complex incoming streams of stimuli imposing constant demands and distractions. He argues that thinking is not just a matter of engaging our intellect when a peak performance is demanded, but also a 'matter of sensitivity to occasions and our inclination to invest ourselves in them thoughtfully'. He also emphasizes how good 'habits of mind' (Costa and Kallick 2000) represent intelligent behaviours and can implicitly develop an appropriate disposition for critical thinking (Ennis 1986) and mindfulness (Langer 1989). He discusses the nature of the end point of thinking rather than the process of thinking itself. He connects the nature of learning and understanding to an epistemic type of study and talks about making 'thinking visible'. He relates the visible nature of thinking to levels of understanding and highlights that attention should be paid to context and transfer. He highlights that 'thinking on paper' does not solve the issues of students thinking beyond classroom constraints and not being able to recollect their threads of thought (Perkins 1991: 111). In a study of high-school, college and graduate students he investigated the longevity of education and the ability to construct valid arguments in informal contexts. The students were asked to consider ideas such as 'does violence on TV influence the likelihood of violence in real life?' or 'would a refundable 20 cent deposit on soft drink cans and bottles reduce the amount of litter?' Surprisingly the length of time in school made little difference to the quality of arguments. Eleven-year-olds, on average, produced fewer than two different lines of argument; after ten or more years of education, this average increased to just over three! It appeared that adept specialist reasoning within school curricula was not transferred to everyday thinking. What Perkins proposes is that we should consider another kind of curriculum, 'the knowledge arts' (Perkins 2004). This kind of curriculum focuses on how we think about, understand, use and develop action from the knowledge that we have beyond the boundaries of the subject content. A curriculum of this kind would support thoughtful learning and include making thinking connections across subject matter.

Matthew Lipman defines thinking skills as ranging from

> very specific to very general abilities, from proficiency in logical reasoning to the witty perception of remote resemblances, from the capacity to decompose a whole into parts, to the capacity to assemble random words or things to make them well-fitting parts of a whole, the ability to explain how a situation may have come about to the ability to foretell how a process will likely eventuate, from a proficiency in discerning uniformities and similarities to a proficiency in noting dissimilarities and uniqueness, from a facility in justifying beliefs through persuasive reasons and valid arguments to a facility in generating ideas

and developing concepts, from the power of discovering alternative possibilities to the power of inventing systematic but imaginary universes, from the capacity to solve problems to the capacity to circumvent problems or forestall their emergence, from the ability to evaluate to the ability to re-enact – the list is endless, because it consists of nothing less than an inventory of the intellectual powers of human kind.

(Lipman 2003: 162)

Lipman (2003) defines the nature and characteristics of various forms of thinking (particularly critical, creative and caring) and suggests how education should amend its focus and restructure practice to promote a more reflective, educative paradigm to invoke pupils' consideration of social, moral, ethical and philosophical issues. He highlights the importance of conversation and underpinning dialogic exchange of experiences to negotiate understandings, deliberate about reasons or options and examine interpretations. He argues that this kind of approach develops children's ability to make informed and discerning judgements. He also recognizes how emotions can affect thinking and how thinking should be developed about emotions and that a relevant lexicon of words should be developed to enable thinking, discussion and learning about emotions so that children can be educated to understand *values*. He expounds the view that 'just as the perfection of the thinking process culminates in philosophy, so too philosophy, *par excellence*, is the finest instrument yet devised for the perfection of the thinking process'.

Robert Fisher (2000: 2) builds on the work of Matthew Lipman's philosophical perspective regarding the teaching of thinking. He perceives that 'philosophy is the only discipline which has, as its subject matter, *thinking and the improvement of thinking*'. He recognizes that children cannot be taught *how to think*, but rather engage in philosophical discussion. In other words, he says they can be taught how to philosophize, the heart of which, he describes as, 'the challenge to improve children's thinking, learning and language' (Fisher 2000: 1).

He emphasizes that what makes 'the human mind so powerful is the use of speech for learning, and in particular an elaborate syntax linked to a powerful symbolic memory which enables humans to elaborate, refine, connect, create and remember great numbers of new concepts'. He argues, therefore, that a key aim of any thinking programme should be to develop linguistic intelligence, through enhancing students' powers of communication and concept formation. He continues to argue (Fisher 1990: x) that 'thinking is the source of human capability and key to human survival. It is this human capacity which separates us from animals (and computers)'.

Edward de Bono (1993: 6) compares intelligence, thinking and driving a car. He describes intelligence as the horsepower of a car and thinking as the skill with which the car is driven. A powerful car can be driven badly and a less powerful car driven well. The power of the car is the potential of the car just as intelligence is the potential of the mind. The skill of the car driver determines how the power of the car is used. The skill of the thinker determines how intelligence is used. He argues that thinking, like driving, can be taught and developed. In his book *Teach Your Child How to Think* he describes the different kinds of thinking that are needed in schools. He emphasizes the difference between information and thinking and highlights how educational systems have been focused on and deeply concerned with knowledge and information rather than thinking. He indicates how, in dealing with the future, thinking is a skill needed to avoid being overwhelmed and confused by all the (albeit valuable) information. He considers the challenge of thinking by describing how, if we give children something too difficult to do, they don't succeed, but conversely if it is too easy they do not have to think. Tasks of moderate difficulty are appropriate to develop competency and confidence.

De Bono also challenges intellectualism and thinking and highlights how many folk equate 'intellectual' with 'complex' and mistakenly 'thinking'. He argues that many intellectuals are not good thinkers. In scholastic contexts he describes how thinking is often reactive. Texts, works-sheets, notes, instructions are all placed in front of a student and they have to reactively 'think about them'. Conversely, life is arguably more about proactive thinking, because in real-world situations information has to be sought and life is about going out, doing and making things happen.

De Bono (1993) also acknowledges the role of emotion, feelings and intuition in thinking. He has developed strategies for thinking about everyday issues, from a variety of perspectives, by applying different kinds of thinking when metaphorically 'wearing' a hat. He also connects 'thinking in action' by using six shoes (De Bono 1991) as a metaphor for types of action anyone could take in a particular problem situation.

Neil Mercer extends many Vygotskian notions on language and thought. He highlights how discussion is important in a social sense for children thinking together (Mercer 1995). He elaborates on the social-ness of meaning-making and describes how different kinds of talk can illustrate whether pupils are engaged in effective social construction. In his analysis he clarifies how one pupil building positively on another's utterance is cumulative talk, but engaging critically and constructively with another's idea is exploratory. He clarifies how different types of talk are distinctive social modes of thinking, because 'knowledge is made more publicly accountable' and 'reasoning is more visible in the talk' (Mercer 1988: 104). He has collaborated with Lyn Dawes and Rupert Wegerif to develop *Thinking Together*, a programme of activities for developing thinking skills at KS2. Their programme of *talking lessons*, creates an understanding of ways in which children should work more effectively together in small groups to develop creative and critical inter-thinking.

Carol McGuinness (1999: 3) reflects that students being supported in 'learning how to think' and being able to independently 'think how to learn' is important. That to become better thinkers they have to learn meaningfully, think flexibility and make reasoned judgments. Learning how to think, she explains (McGuiness 2000), has to be 'taught explicitly' and infused across the curriculum. She believes that students should develop a thinking disposition and actively create their own knowledge, through challenging activities that involve metacognitive reflection through dialogue. She highlights six kinds of thinking that are important for students to learn (1) Searching for meaning and understanding, which focuses on uncovering patterns in information including comparing contrasting, sorting, classifying and sequencing; (2) Thinking critically, where students learn to scrutinize, examine their personal thinking and adopt sceptical stances; (3) Developing flexible and creative thinking through encouragement to look for alternatives and generate new ideas; (4) Problem solving; (5) Decision making. 6. Metacognition, which is about reflecting and evaluating the five previous kinds of thinking. This cognitive framework adapted from Swartz and Parks (1994) outlines the types of cognitive processing, involved in sustainable thinking in classrooms (McGuinness et al. 2003).

David Leat (2000) describes how developing thinking is predicated on motivating and challenging learning activities, within which teachers apply their professional prowess to mediate the nature of thinking. He has developed the *Thinking Through* series, to be used within a subject teaching approach. The first series of activities developed was initially within geography, but the ideas have since been transferred to various other areas of the curriculum. He perceives that pupils should be supported in actively creating individualized understandings by working in groups, for teachers to develop learning through questioning (who, what, why, where and when), and discussing reflectively the thinking that has taken place during the lesson. The lesson activities provide the opportunity to elucidate reflectively when 'classification', cause and effect', 'decision making', 'handling data' and other processing outcomes have been operationalized to tackle the learning task. His general view is that thinking should be developed within the curriculum context at the discretion of the teacher (Leat 2000: 3).

Conclusion

Thinking can be random, a little like day dreaming, where disconnected ideas, facts, fancies or recollections drift in and out of our consciousness. This kind of purposeless, almost effortless but not driven thinking can sometimes result in creative ideas. It is the kind of thinking you might engage in during the morning shower, or relaxing evening bath or even while travelling or on vacation. Such reflective brain activity is personalized, determined by your own neural connections, not necessarily intended for a specific purpose or outcome. It is not the kind of thinking we can directly affect and influence in schools. It does not *have to be* communicated, it is driven through personal interest and originates within oneself (and may be unconscious or innately reactive).

Extrinsically motivated thinking is that which can be encouraged through purposeful and meaningful learning experiences. Educators should purposely strive to support development of this thinking in their teaching. Teachers cannot *enforce* thinking. Just directly instructing students to think this way or that way is as didactic as 'transmission' teaching. Nurturing the development of thinking capability involves interaction with motivating learning opportunities and frequent invitations for students to reflect on progress in tasks or challenges that entice them to cogitate.

As educators, it is essential to recognize the range of thinking skills it is possible to nurture, to realize how important they are, and then to plan how they should be extrinsically encouraged in school.

There is currently no consensus on what constitutes good quality, skilful and effective thinking. There are however, some common characteristics that educationalists agree on. They are summarized below.

Key ideas

Many cognitive functions contribute toward the accomplishment of thinking skills.

There is no common taxonomy of thinking skills.

Language and social interactions are recognized as important in developing thinking.

Simply, extrinsically stimulated thinking, is any cognitive processing that is purposely invited by question, task or challenge.

Critical thinking could be defined as the cognitive process(es) by which information (of a visual, olfactory or auditory nature) or data of any kind, (that can be gathered through sensory perception) are transformed or mentally operated upon in some effortful and purposeful way. It is the analysis, processing or transforming of *given* information, data or ideas.

Creative thinking could be defined as the *original creation*, development or innovation of an idea, product or process.

Metacognitive thinking could be defined as the reflective thinking concerned with describing or reviewing either the process or outcome of any activity (mental or physical).

Socially aware thinking which considers (others') personalized perspectives as well as moral, ethical, religious and cultural and wider societal implications can be described as maieutic.

Good thinking:
- is effortful
- challenging
- not easy
- requires practice

Skilful thinking:
- is not spontaneous
- is through application of practised cognitive techniques (types of thinking)
- is effective in developing quality solutions
- can be significantly improved through conscious reflection

Good quality thinking should:
- be skilful
- be flexible
- be meaningful and purposeful
- be developed through the *application* of thinking skills
- arise in authentic learning situations
- support effective learning
- illustrate social responsibility for actions
- be personally fulfilling
- be useful (academically *and* socially)
- be transferable to other contexts and situations (in and out of school)
- continue to be developed throughout life, not just in school
- be more widely acknowledged in schools

Educators can make judgments about the thinking their learners have engaged in through what they communicate (verbally or in written or symbolic form) and do (action as a result of thought).

2 What kind of thinking should we encourage children to do?

> What avail is it to win prescribed amounts of information about geography and history, to win ability to read and write, if in the process the individual loses his own soul; loses his appreciation of things worth while, of the values to which these things are relative; if he loses desire to apply what he has learned and, above all, loses the ability to extract meaning from his future experiences as they occur?
>
> (Dewey, *Experience and Education*)

As Dewey (1938: 49) quite appropriately highlights, if we teach children to read and write, provide them with factual information, but do not equip them with the cognitive skills to understand, appreciate and transfer or connect ideas, then the information they have may be meaningless in future. Nurturing skills that enable children to synthesize meaning or apply ideas to other contexts and other situations are key, especially for life after school.

This chapter begins by exploring connections between thinking and intelligence. The nature of thinking encouraged in schools, through National Curriculum policies, is then briefly described and contrasted with the associated problem solving skills conceivably useful in a pupil's future world of work. Contrasts and connections are then drawn to make suggestions about thinking skills and problem solving to highlight what we need to emphasize currently in our development of the curriculum and pupils' thinking abilities.

Thinking about intelligence

There are confusions and contradictions around ideas about intelligence and thinking. Nigel Blagg (1991) has suggested we could 'teach intelligence' and Shayer and Adey (2002) suggest we can 'learn intelligence'. Edward Boring (1923) proposed that 'intelligence is nothing more than what tests of intelligence measure'. However, there is increasing evidence that what psychological tests measure is only a part of the entire portrait of what intelligence is (Sternberg 2003).

As thinking is an abstract concept, so is what constitutes intelligence. There are numerous theories regarding the nature of intelligence. Some ideas are briefly described here to provide context to the perspective of thinking in this book. Arguably one of the most influential theorists suggesting a psychometric model of intelligence is Charles Spearman (1927). He proposed a two-factor theory of intelligence. He suggested that any intellectual act requires a combination of general intelligence ('g') and specific intelligence(s) ('s'). He argued that different tasks will vary in the proportion of 'g' or 's' required to solve them. He suggests that 'g' is a core or common level of intellect required for any task. The 'g' or innate general intelligence is much more easily measured, by psychometric means, than 's', which will vary in every task. Thurstone (1935) developed from this a more comprehensive description of 'g'. He didn't think 'g' was a general capability. He argued that there were seven primary mental abilities:

- Verbal comprehension. The ability to understand verbal material. Measured by vocabulary tests and reading comprehension tasks.
- Word fluency. The ability to produce words rapidly. Measured by timed word tasks.
- Numeracy. The ability to rapidly compute numerically. Measured by timed arithmetic tasks.
- Memory. The ability to remember strings of words, letters, numbers, symbols or objects. Measured by serial or free recall tests.
- Spatial visualization. The ability to 'see' shapes, rotations of objects and how pieces of a puzzle would fit together. Measured by tests requiring mental manipulation of geometric objects.
- Perceptual speed. The ability to recognize letters, numbers or symbols rapidly. Measured by timed proofreading or identifying the odd one out.
- Inductive reasoning. The ability to reason from the specific to the general. Measured by predicting the final number or letter of a given sequence.

More widely accepted today, however, is Raymond Cattell's theory that there is general innate intelligence ('g'), deemed most important, but also fluid ('gf') and crystallized intelligence. Fluid intelligence is the ability to think flexibly and to reason abstractly. Cattell proposed that this increases during childhood and adolescence as the nervous system matures, then levels off during adulthood and then begins to decline. He suggested that crystallized intelligence increases throughout the life span and is primarily a reflection of accumulated learning experiences. It involves understanding relations or solving problems that depend on knowledge acquired as a result of schooling and other life experiences (general knowledge, work comprehension and numerical abilities). However, measuring fluid intelligence remains a challenge. Often the tests developed to assess it are similar to ways of measuring 'g' (Gustafsson 1984, 1988).

John Carroll (1993) studied human cognitive abilities and proposed a three-tiered model. The highest level (or stratum) comprised general intellectual ability, similar to 'g'. The second stratum was broader and consisted of eight factors, including fluid intelligence, crystallized intelligence, general memory and learning, broad visual perception, broad auditory perception, broad retrieval ability, broad cognitive speediness, and processing speed. The final stratum identified 2850 specific factors, which he grouped into similar abilities. Carroll's comprehensive list of human abilities informs current research in Indiana, US. These descriptions of intelligence can be assessed by means of a huge variety of tests (Nickerson et al 1985: 23) and focus on intellect as a measurable, quantifiable characteristic.

Piaget, however, directed attention to the evolution of children's thinking. In his studies, which involved detailed questioning of children, he argued how knowledge was constructed through development of understanding of such things as number, time, space, velocity, geometry, chance and morality from birth to adolescence. He theorized that there was a genetic influence to higher order mental processes in that thinking evolved from biological mechanisms, rooted in the development of an individual's cognitive structures – in the nervous system. Piaget (1950, 1973) viewed intelligence as arising from cognitive schemas (particular types of mental acts or actions), or structures that mature as a function of the interaction of the learner with the environment.

He believed that, through adaptation, individuals learned from the environment and changed in response to it. These adjustments consisted of two complementary processes: assimilation and accommodation. Assimilation is the process of absorbing new information and fitting it into an already existing cognitive structure about what the world is like. Accommodation involves forming or restructuring the cognitive connections in order to understand or resituate the new information. He also believed there was a maturational influence and that the processes of concept formation follow a pattern through several clearly definable stages, (see Figure 2.1) which are hierarchical. He thought that each must be experienced before any subsequent step in development is possible.

Period	Stage	Mental age range in years
Sensori-motor	I Sensorimotor	0–2
Preparation for,	II Preoperational	
and use of,	(A) Preconceptual	2–4
concrete operations	(B) Intuitive	4–7
(or latency)	III Concrete operations	7–11.5
Formal operations	IV Formal operations	11.5 onwards

Source: Adapted from Brown and Desforges (1979).

Figure 2.1 The Piagetian stages of development

Piaget described concrete operations as those where children can reason, but largely based on the perceptual facts or happenings visible before them. Thornton (1980) elaborates on this to illustrate how an individual operating at a concrete level could 'order a collection of sticks' but not 'decide who is tallest if told that Bill is taller than Tammy and shorter than Shelia'; or could 'list all possible outcomes of flipping two coins' but could not 'easily list the outcomes for three and certainly not for four coins'. Piaget describes more complex thinking as 'formal operations' the highest level of thinking. Understanding and developing a mental model to explain, for example, volume, density, dissolution, justice or cruelty requires higher level *abstract* thinking capability without needing the concrete materials to provide substance to the argument.

Vygotsky, also concerned with development of intellect, focused on the influence of societal factors on individual's capabilities. He postulated that children's cognitive development could not be understood without regard to the social interaction with others. Leont'ev (1981: 55) highlights Vygotsky's view of the importance of social interaction in the development of thought: 'higher psychological processes unique to humans can be acquired only through interaction with others, that is, through interpsychological processes that only later will begin to be carried out independently by the individual.

In contrast with Piaget's more individualistic perspective of cognitive development, Vygotsky (1978, 1986) regarded higher mental functions such as thinking, reasoning and understanding as social in their origin. Vygotsky's perception was that the child's interactions with other people served to mediate between the child and the world-to-be-learned-about. He viewed cognitive development as subject to dialogic interplay between nature and history, biology and culture, the lone intellect and society. He believed that language and communication (and hence, instruction) promoted intellectual and personal development. He thought that instruction lay at the heart of development, enabling a child's potential for learning to be revealed when working with more knowledgeable others. Central to his notions of learning is the concept of the 'zone of proximal development' (ZPD), the region within which a child could be sensitively guided to complete a task. Vygotsky argued that to mediate 'higher mental functioning' – to enable learners to move into their ZPD – would require 'psychological tools', particularly speech (Daniels 1996: 7). Vygotsky claimed that a defining feature of human mental functioning (on both the intermental and intramental planes) is mediated by tools and signs.

In rather stark contrast to Vygotsky's ideas about intellectual development Hernstein and Murray (1994) developed understandings about the normal distribution of intelligence. They studied the distribution of intelligence in American society and produced a Bell curve. Their analysis and interpretation of findings has been extremely controversial in suggesting that intelligence cannot be significantly changed through societal interventions.

More recent conceptions of 'intelligence' have broadened to embrace more practical and social abilities, perhaps catalysed by studies and proposals from Sternberg et al. (1981) that recognized practical problem solving; verbal ability and social competence. Sternberg's (1983) early work built on the standard psychometric conception of intelligence as a single, general trait (Spearman's 'g'). His componential theory broke 'g' down into its underlying information processing components, but Sternberg found that even this theory and the tests he developed to measure the component processes still missed a lot. Individuals who scored highly on Sternberg's early test still were not guaranteed success and many individuals who did not score as well went on to have a better record of real life accomplishments than did those who scored well on his or on other traditional tests.

Sternberg (1985) has developed his ideas beyond the componential theory to what is now known as the triarchic theory of intelligence. In his view, this theory does not disprove either 'g' or his earlier componential theory, but rather subsumes them under a larger framework. The triarchic theory regards intelligence as comprised of

1   Analytical intelligence, which is similar to the standard psychometric definition of intelligence and corresponds to his earlier componential intelligence. It is measured by analogies and puzzles and reflects how an individual relates to his internal world.

2   Creative intelligence, which involves insight, synthesis and the ability to react to novel stimuli and situations. This is the

experiential aspect of intelligence and reflects how an individual connects the internal world to external reality.

3   Practical intelligence, which involves the ability to grasp, understand, and solve real-life problems in the everyday jungle of life. This is the contextual aspect of intelligence, and reflects how individuals relate to the external world about them. In short, practical intelligence is 'street smart'.

The Sternberg Multidimensional Abilities Test measures all three (on separate scales). He has now developed his perception of intelligence into wisdom, as a value-laden application of tacit knowledge not only for one's own benefit (as can be the case with successful intelligence) but also for the benefit of others, in order to attain a common good. He describes a wise person as one who realizes that what matters is not just knowledge, or the intellectual skills one applies to this knowledge, but how the knowledge is used.

Howard Gardner (1993) proposes a theory of multiple intelligence. He recognizes the multifarious nature of human intelligence and initially proposed that humans have a family of seven intelligences that can be divided into three main groups: object-related intelligence, which includes mathematics and logic; object-free intelligence, including music and language; and personal intelligence, or the psychological perception we have of ourselves and others. These intelligences include:

1   Linguistic intelligence. This refers to an individual's capacity to use language effectively as a vehicle of expression and communication. Includes skills involved in reading, writing, listening and talking. Linguistically intelligent people would include poets and writers.

2   Logical-mathematical intelligence. Refers to an individual's capacity to think logically, use numbers effectively, derive proofs, solve logical puzzles and discern relationships and patterns between concepts and things. Mathematicians and scientists display this kind of intelligence.

3   Spatial intelligence. This refers to the capacity to think visually and to orientate oneself spatially. Used in marine navigation, piloting a plane, driving a car, working out how to get from A to B, figuring out one's orientation in space. Spatially intelligent people are also able to graphically represent their visual and spatial ideas. They include artists, decorators, architects, surveyors, inventors and guides.

4   Musical intelligence. This refers to the capacity to appreciate a variety of musical forms in addition to using music as a vehicle of

expression. Musically intelligent people are sensitive to rhythm, melody and pitch – for example singers, musicians or composers.

5   Bodily-kinaesthetic intelligence. Refers to the ability to use one's own body, or parts of it, skilfully as a means of expression or to work skilfully to create or manipulate objects. Dancers, actors, athletes, sculptors, surgeons, mechanics and craftspeople illustrate this kind of intelligence.

6   Interpersonal intelligence. This refers to the ability to respond appropriately and effectively to other people, to understand their feelings and to act upon that understanding of others, noticing differences between people, reading their moods, temperaments and intentions. Politicians, sales people, psychotherapists, travel agents and teachers display interpersonal intelligence.

7   Intrapersonal intelligence refers to the capacity to know oneself accurately, including knowledge of one's own strengths, motivations, goals and feelings. Entrepreneurs and therapists might exemplify this.

Gardner has, since 1999, considered at least three more intelligences, including naturalist, existential and spiritual. Gardner also argues that if the idea that intelligence includes the knowledge of human beings, then moral intelligence is also plausible. Described as the ability to distinguish between right and wrong, moral intelligence represents the ability to make sound decisions that benefit not only yourself, but others around you (Coles 1997; Hass 1998).

Parallels can be drawn between social intelligence and interpersonal intelligence. Interpersonal intelligence is the ability to understand other people: what motivates them, how they work and how to work cooperatively with them. Successful salespeople, politicians, teachers, clinicians and religious leaders are all likely to be individuals with high degrees of interpersonal intelligence. At the same time, social intelligence probably draws on specific internal (Gardner would say intrapersonal) abilities. For example, in a recent study of incompetence, Kruger and Dunning (1999) found that incompetent people assessed themselves as being highly competent. This lack of ability to self-assess may be due to a combination of internal (poor metacognition) and external factors (poor ability to compare oneself to others). Social intelligence appears to be receiving the most attention in the management and organizational psychology literatures (for example, Hough 2001; Riggio et al. 2002).

Emotional intelligence, on the other hand, 'is a type of social intelligence that involves the ability to monitor one's own and others' emotions, to discriminate among them, and to use the information to guide one's thinking and actions' (Mayer and Salovey 1993: 433).

According to Goleman (1995), 'Emotional intelligence, the skills that help people harmonise, should become increasingly valued as a workplace asset in the years to come'. This overlaps somewhat with Gardner's view of interpersonal and intrapersonal intelligence. Goleman claims that emotional intelligence can matter more than IQ or 'g' because it recognizes skills and abilities in dealing with people and emotions. He describes how it relates to:

- recognizing your own emotional life;
- regulating your own feelings;
- understanding others' emotions;
- being able to work with others;
- having empathy for others.

He argues that if education promoted emotional intelligence as much as cognitive intelligence, the world would be a more 'hospitable place to live'.

It appears that there is no generally agreed definition of intelligence, but capabilities that illustrate intelligent behaviours can be identified, described and improved upon appropriate and focused practice.

Thinking in the school curriculum

The KS3 National Strategy defines intelligence as 'the capacity to learn'. In the introduction to each subject document, the Minister for Education, states that 'An effective National Curriculum ... gives teachers, pupils and parents, employers and their wider community a clear and shared understanding of the skills and knowledge that young people will gain at school' (DfES 2004). It goes on to explain that the focus of the National Curriculum is to ensure that

> pupils develop from an early age the essential literacy and numerical skills they need to learn; to provide them with a guaranteed, full and rounded entitlement to learning; to foster their creativity; to give teachers discretion to find the best ways to inspire in their pupils a joy and commitment to learning that will last a life time

and 'by using thinking skills pupils can focus on *knowing how* as well as *knowing what*, ultimately learning how to learn'. Thinking skills (see Table 2.1) are listed with the other key skills (communication, application of number, information technology, working with others, improving one's own learning and performance and problem solving) that are embedded in the National Curriculum.

Barber (2000) emphasizes how 'raising standards' involves focusing 'beyond what children learn to how they learn *and* how teachers intervene in this process'. Various DfES materials have been written to guide teachers in the development of thinking. The school training manual (DfES 2005) suggests how focusing on these skills should enable independent thinking to develop. Thinking opportunities are identifiable

Table 2.1 Department for Education and Skills (DfES) categorization of thinking skills in the KS3 National Strategy

Thinking skill descriptor	Specific constituent cognitive functions
Information processing skills (developed by locating and collecting relevant information)	• Finding relevant information • Sorting/classifying/sequencing information • Comparing/contrasting information • Identifying and analysing relationships
Reasoning skills	• Giving reasons for opinions/actions • Inferring • Making deductions • Making informed judgements/decisions • Using precise language to reason
Enquiry	• Asking questions • Defining questions for enquiry • Planning research • Predicting outcomes • Anticipating consequences • Drawing conclusions
Creativity	• Generating ideas • Developing ideas • Hypothesizing • Applying imagination • Seeking innovative alternatives
Evaluation	• Developing evaluation criteria • Applying evaluation criteria • Judging the value of information and ideas

in various places in the National Curriculum. For example, in the KS2 Science (Sc1 strand), one learning objective is:

a   **ask questions** *that can be investigated scientifically and decide how to find answers*

Asking questions is classified as 'enquiry' thinking. For older students at KS3 (Sc1 strand), another learning objective is:

p   **suggest improvements** *to the methods used, where appropriate*

Suggesting an improvement is classified as 'creative thinking'. In English, at KS2, students are expected to 'evaluate':

d   **evaluate** *how they and others have contributed to the overall effectiveness of performances (in Drama)*

Older students at KS3 are expected to:

2d **distinguish features** *of a presentation where a speaker aims to explain, persuade, amuse or argue a case*

which involves inferring or 'reasoning' what a speakers' intentions are. In mathematics, at KS2, students are expected to:

k   **search for a pattern** *in their results; develop logical thinking and* **explain their reasoning**

which involves 'information processing' and 'reasoning'. Older students at KS3 are expected to:

c   *use* **alternate approaches** *to overcome difficulties and* **evaluate** *the effectiveness of their strategies*

This could involve both creative thinking and critical thinking in the form of 'evaluation'.

Within the *subject* National Curriculum documents there is little or scant *direct* reference to 'thinking'. Teachers need to interpret Programme of Study (POS) descriptors to ascertain what kind of thinking could occur where. A quick textual analysis indicates the term *think* or *thinking* was included approximately 15 times in the English and maths documents, was much less frequent in science and was almost absent in physical education and music. Teachers can be forgiven, then, if they do not easily recognize where to develop good quality thinking, or indeed how to devise and implement a co-ordinated and progressive pedagogy that encompasses development of the wide range of cognitive skills outlined in Chapter 1. Policy documents suggest that thinking within the National Curriculum is expected to arise within specific subject contexts (DfES 2005).

The search facility provided at www.nc.uk.net allows teachers to search their subject areas for key terms related to the thinking skills identified above. The search outcome provides a listing of incidences of thinking skills in the curriculum documents, but this does not yet suggest how teaching and learning should proceed.

A further textual analysis of the English, mathematics and science POS for KS2 suggests that in English a wide range of cognitive processes *could* be developed, exemplified by the plethora of key phrases that describe where thinking could naturally arise, for example, 'respond flexibly and imaginatively'; 'engage with challenging and demanding subject matter'; 'convey meaning, emotion, theme and story'; 'use persuasive language'; 'deduce'; 'clarify'; 'qualify'; 'reflect'; 'identify gist'; 'explore'; 'anticipate consequences'. There are also many phrases that suggest information processing and enquiry (problem solving) should be prominent within mathematics, such as the request to 'identify information' needed for a task; 'solve simple' problems; 'think about' the context of the problem; break down complex problems; approach problems flexibly; find different ways or alternative approaches to a problem. In science, references to critical and creative types of thinking appear to be significantly fewer. This brief analysis suggests that, within subjects, there are particular kinds of cognitive processes that can naturally arise in teaching, through the nature of the subject itself. An analysis of this kind within all of the National Curriculum subjects could also suggest for teachers:

- whether certain types of cognitive processing naturally arise (and should be encouraged) or are absent (and more challenging to nurture) in particular curricular areas;
- where 'thinking skills' or 'problems to solve' (requiring a raft of cognitive processes) should be explicitly developed or just implicitly experienced by the learners;
- where 'transfer' (elaborated upon in Chapter 10) of thinking (across the curriculum and beyond) in various subject content areas *could* and *should* be made.

Curriculum designers could highlight which cognitive processes it is possible to include in teaching subject content to ensure that a comprehensive range of cognitive skills is developed appropriately, progressively and connectedly. Applying the nature of the thinking involved in learning to a variety of contexts is paramount. More specific guidance is needed about this.

The issue of reflecting to connect similar thinking in different contexts is considered below. The National Numeracy Strategy (NNS) and National Literacy Strategy (NLS), originally intended to improve teaching and learning (Stobart and Stoll 2005), offer some guidance about teaching thinking. The NNS suggests when to 'use groupwork', 'question pupils', 'give them time to think', ask them to 'explain their methods and reasoning' and 'explore reasons for wrong answers' and include 'non-routine problems that require them to think for themselves'. In the NLS teachers were also guided regarding when and how to carry out group and independent work, and they were reminded not to return to 'transmission' teaching. They were encouraged to engage in 'discursive', interactive' teaching that involved explanation to clarify and discuss, question, investigate ideas, argue to justify a view and evaluate presentations. The success in raising standards was generally accepted (Earl et al. 2003), but Alexander (2003) suggested that further attention to pedagogy was still required. *Leading in Learning* (DfES 2005) provides much advice about the kinds of pedagogic strategies that can be used to develop particular kinds of thinking (DfES 2005: 31). However, even with this additional guidance, teachers are still required to make professional judgements about where, when and how exactly to employ the suggestions offered. Key message leaflets (DfES 2003a) have subsequently been written to convey further advice and guidance about thinking. This centrally devised and driven strategy is part of the government's 'informed prescription' (Barber 2000) to improve students' learning. 'Leading in learning' within the KS3 National Strategy (DfES 2005) has since elevated 'thinking skills' to a whole-school initiative, but still rather as an additional layer to lessons or an intermittent intervention. Clarity about the nature of thinking within each subject and how to nurture it logically, has to be *understood* by teachers, otherwise, under time pressure to deliver a content laden curriculum (Parkinson 2002; Leat and Lin 2003) they will revert to established methods of instruction (which are more transmission or didactic in nature).

The Department for Education and Skills (2002) describes thinking as 'cognitive activity triggered by challenging tasks and problems'. Teachers are informed that where thinking skills are taught well the lessons:

- have open and challenging tasks that make pupils think hard;
- encourage pupils to use what they already know;

- offer opportunities for work in collaborative groups with high-quality talk;
- encourage pupils to talk about how tasks have been done;
- produce learning outcomes at different levels – some relating to the subject content but others to how learning can be used in other contexts.

It describes how to develop the above thinking opportunities through ten different kinds of teaching strategies (advance organizers, analogies, audience and purpose, classifying, collective memory, living graphs and fortune lines, mysteries, reading images, relational diagrams and summarizing). It is, however, still unclear as to how cognitive skills should be *progressively and incrementally* nurtured. It is not clear how teachers should plan for *systematic* introduction, development and enhancement of a range of cognitive skills that can then be applied or transferred to real-world problem solving situations.

Barber (2000) describes how the introduction of 'citizenship provides specific opportunities to enhance the teaching of thinking skills'. The debates, discussions and the use of evidence involved in addressing the range of moral, social, political and environmental issues are 'ideal contexts for using enquiry, information processing, reasoning, problem solving and evaluation'.

The modules for 'Teaching thinking' in the training materials for the foundation subjects (DfES 2002) include *thinking together, reflection* and *big concepts and ideas*.

Thinking together

This module aims to develop teachers' appreciation of the nature and use of talk in the classroom. It emphasizes 'ground rules' for talking in groups and highlights that two people can often solve problems more effectively together than working alone. It emphasizes how talk should be used as a tool for thinking and learning. It uses much of Mercer's (1995, 2000) work on how to guide teachers to encourage students to develop 'exploratory talk'. Exploratory talk is described as talk in which:

- pupils and teachers engage critically but constructively with each others ideas;
- contributions build on previous comments;
- relevant information is offered for joint consideration;
- there is speculation;
- pupils give reasons for their views and seek them from others.

Reflection

This module aims to highlight why students should reflect on their learning and it intends to help them develop a vocabulary to describe their thinking and learning processes. This is potentially useful to help teachers support development of metacognitive capability in their students.

Big Concepts and Ideas

This module aims to emphasize principal concepts and skills, which underpin thinking and learning. One technique that is exemplified is the reading out of a passage of text to pupils while having them draw pictures that illustrate the information given. Discussion and reflection after completion of the task provides learners with shared insights about how they tackle a learning task differently. Transfer of the learning process is promoted through thinking about where they could use similar strategies in other subjects.

Pupils are encouraged to work in groups and reflect on where else in their learning similar cognitive processes and strategies would be applicable and useful.

The materials for these three modules have since been somewhat subsumed into the *Leading in Learning* materials (DfES 2005).

Thinking in life

De Bono presents various arguments about why children (and even adults) should develop their thinking prowess. He argues (De Bono 2000) that 'in a rapidly changing world we are finding that our thinking is inadequate to meet the demands put upon it.' As Bentley (2000) argues, if education is to meet the emerging challenges of the twenty-first century, educators must recognize that learning within the formal setting must connect with life after school. In the preparation of children for successful and fulfilling adulthood, 'our conventional conception of schooling, its purposes, methods and scope are in fact limited to a relatively narrow range of capacities, outcomes and types of challenge.' He describes how two-thirds of people aged 16 to 25 believe that schools *do not* prepare them for everyday life. He elaborates about how over the last two decades, the ways people live, work and communicate have been transformed through information technologies. In this ubiquitous environment of information and knowledge, evidence suggests (Stobart and Stoll 2005) that although numeracy, literacy, basic skills and qualifications achieved by students have improved, there are many other issues to address such as behaviour, values and workforce skills (DfES 2002). Bentley describes how societal pressures developed from a variety of sources, including more readily available drugs, access to more questionable Internet resources, and family breakdown require that young people learn the values and obligations of citizenship, that they know right from wrong and, most importantly, understand what is valuable in a world increasingly characterized by diversity, mobility and choice. In the twenty-first century computer technology can collect, synthesize and communicate information more rapidly, precisely and powerfully than ever before. What are needed are the cognitive skills to use these evolving technologies to benefit society and individuals' lives. Innovative technology influences every sphere of our lives, from personal relationships to the structure and content of work, economic investment to leisure, human reproduction, disease and illness to patterns of transcontinental migration. How to continue to use these technologies and the vast knowledge bases they provide in a useful and meaningful way is arguably more important than gathering and storing yet more data (De Bono 2000).

Children must be guided and taught how to sort and synthesize the meaningful from the useless, discern connections between pieces of relevant information, analyse detail while recognizing the whole, strategize how to solve problems and distinguish what matters in life situations.

The cognitive processes described here and in Chapter 1 need to be systematically and progressively developed within and across subjects but related, connected and meaningful for life outside school in a coherent and relevant way.

As Fisher (2000) argues, a successful society will be one in which the capacities for lifelong learning of its citizens are most fully realized. If thinking is how we make sense of experience then being helped to think better will help children learn more from what they see, say and do.

Exercising the mind through intellectual challenge is not only a means for enjoyment and for success in a rapidly changing world but can also promote moral qualities and virtues. Intellectual virtue can be seen as a complex set of attributes including curiosity, thoughtfulness, intellectual courage and perseverance in the search for resolution, a willingness to speculate and analyse, to judge and reflect, an openness to the views of others and other elements, developed through practice. These are qualities that need to be practised through thinking for oneself and thinking with others. Thinking in social contexts could also, as Lipman (2003) argues, 'develop thinking that could potentially reduce violence in our society'. Smethurst (1995: 33) supports this, emphasizing how, in order to succeed in life, in the world, in history, you need not just academic skill but personality, independence of mind, and autonomy of spirit.

Teaching for thinking and teaching about thinking

Thinking is not always purposeful and constructive, working towards an objectified goal. It can be effortless. Thoughts can drift in and out of our minds when not concentrating in a focused way on some task. This kind of freewheeling thinking is not extrinsically motivated (as intended through teaching thinking) but can sometimes result in creative ideas. This kind of reflective, personalized or intrinsic brain activity determined by your cerebral connections (arguably reflecting your 'g') but not carried out for a specific purpose or outcome is not the kind of thinking educators can directly influence in schools. This is an argument that the philosopher Stephen Johnson (2000) uses to protest that we cannot 'teach thinking'. He is referring to the kind of thinking that could be defined as intrinsically driven: that which is intrapersonal and originates within oneself (and may be unconscious or innately reactive). Educators *can* purposely strive to *support development of* thinking in their teaching through presentation of provoking information or invitations to question. Learners can be encouraged to engage in purposeful thinking through appropriately designed learning tasks and can be supported in developing a repertoire of cognitive or thinking skills. Reflection on learning progress can provide opportunities for pupils to think *about thinking*. If learners are also motivated to think after lessons and begin to make more lateral, multiple or varied neural connections, then perhaps schools may also be able to influence intrinsic thinking too. As Kirkwood (2001a) and Costa (2001) suggest, students can already think but in teaching about thinking, reflecting on thinking processes and modelling good thinking, educators can help learners develop better quality thinking. Educators and practitioners can influence the nature of the thinking engaged in through various means (not just thinking programmes), designing activities with cognitive outcomes in mind; intervening to engage cognitively; presenting intriguing ideas; asking thought-provoking questions or reflecting on task outcomes are all pedagogical tactics that can support development of cognitive skills and ways of thinking (Costa and Liebmann 1997; McGregor and Gunter 2006). The DfES materials certainly suggest a range of pedagogical strategies that teachers can use to develop teaching that encourages pupils to think and reflect on learning processes.

Developing thinking for life

Thinking for life involves developing independent thinkers. Kirkwood (2001b) argues that children use a variety of types of thinking in their everyday lives and they do not have to be taught to 'do thinking'. However, she elaborates that they do need support in improving the quality of their thinking.

There are ways of thinking within subject disciplines that are important for developing understanding and learning. As Claxton (1999: 331) claims:

> throughout life, tomorrows learners will be called upon to master a wider range of skills, to solve a broader range of problems, to craft satisfying personal responses to a deeper and more complex set of freedoms and responsibilities, than probably any other generation in the history of the world. To do that well, they will need to be playing with a full deck of learning strategies and sensitivities.

A narrow conceptualization of learning, which focuses on content over process, comprehension over competence, ability over engagement, teaching over self-discovery will constrain the nature of pedagogy teachers employ. Arguably, many current attempts to create learning communities are somewhat hamstrung by a tacit acceptance of this view that values *knowing what* rather than *knowing how*. As David Perkins (1991) argues, we need schools that are full of thought, that focus not on schooling memories but on schooling minds. We want what policy analyst Rexford Brown in an extensive study of schools called 'a literacy of thoughtfulness' (Brown 1991: 233). We need educational settings with thinking-centred learning, where students learn by thinking through what they are learning about. As he says: 'learning is a consequence of thinking'.

Retention, understanding, and the active use of knowledge can be brought about only by learning experiences in which learners *think about* and *think with* what they are learning. Conventionally, students first acquire knowledge (usually through transmission from the teacher), then they apply the knowledge they have absorbed to answer further questions within the same subject domain. What has been lacking is thinking through the learning, reflecting on the learning process and subsequently considering how the process *and* content are useful *and* applicable in other learning, life settings and problem solving situations.

Thinking skills and preparation for work

Thinking and learning in school cannot substitute for real work experience and life, however, developing relevant cognitive skills and bridging to real-world situations could better prepare today's learners for tomorrows workforce. Developing the capability to:

- clearly contribute and communicate ideas, proposals, suggestions and reflections in a variety of electronic, written and graphical forms;
- work as an effective team member, contributing sensitively and imaginatively, but critiquing in a supportive way while applying intra-emotional intelligence;
- reflectively identify strengths and weaknesses and recognize how to develop a plan to improve weaknesses and appropriately use strengths.

Cleverdon (2005) Chief Executive Officer of Business in the Community (BITC) describes how she doesn't think the needs of business have changed much since the mid-1980s: 'they need people with good communication skills – the ability to persuade and explain – who are good at team-work and problem solving'. McDonald (2005), quoting Bob Wigley of Merrill Lynch, recognizes that although 'concentrating on studying and passing examinations in school are very important, alongside that it is equally important to prepare young people for the world of work ... teachers are very experienced in the former area, but not necessarily experienced enough to be able to impart the life skills that are needed for the latter – and that is where business knowledge can help'. Wigley explains how he had the opportunity at school to take part in an enterprise programme. With an explanatory kit and a mentor from the company sponsoring the challenge, he set up and ran a real company, as a managing director, appointing school friends as senior managers. He was successful and maintains that one-to-one personal interaction is key. He also suggests that business should be involved at primary level and not just for 14–19-year-olds, as governmental policies suggest. His thoughts are that disaffected students can be educated to understand the state cost implications if they are eventually convicted of crime and detained (complementing the *Philosophy for Children* approach described in Chapter 4). McDonald (2005) reports on the collaboration between both business and government that links work done in school with work students will be doing when they leave education. Students should engage in tasks that provide a work-like context to simulate real-life problems they may face in future. These learning opportunities offer authentic complex problem solving situations, which is crucial for applying cognitive skills from one domain to another. 'For too many people, learning is something that stops when they leave school. Learning new skills, at work and for pleasure, must become a rewarding part of everyday life' (DfES 2003c).

Transfer of thinking

Key skills for success in the workplace, such as good communication, working with numbers, information technology, problem solving and working with others, are potentially developable through application of cognitive processes. As the Twenty-first Century Skills (DfES 2003b) and Skills for Success (DfES 2003c) documents describe 'young people are doing better in international literacy, numeracy and science' and our 'university graduates are educated to a high standard', but 'too many adults still lack the right skills for work'. As 'every one has a role to play' in the workplace, from basic employability to management, some of the skills identified above can be improved through appropriate pedagogic emphasis on metacognition involving *transferable reflective 'thinking'* from school to life. Lifelong learning requires learners to become informed learners. When solving problems they need to reflect on their experience of learning and not just what they came to understand or produce at the end of a task. Using learners' experiences of learning to reflect consciously on their process of learning is key in schools, and recognizing that explaining 'how they got there' is a transferable approach that can be used at work. Connecting reflections of the learning process in a formal context, in school, to life out of school and after school will help pupils develop awareness of transferable problem solving skills.

As Tight (1996) explains, lifelong education should be seen as 'building upon and affecting all existing educational providers, both schools and institutions of higher education'. It should also 'extend beyond formal education providers to encompass all agencies, groups and individuals involved in any kind of learning activity' and should enable 'individuals to become self-directing, and that they will see the value in engaging in lifelong education'. In general a wider recognition of when and where particular cognitive processes are useful and applicable can begin to stimulate children to think 'out of the box'. The changing nature of the skills needed in contemporary society is emphasized by Rose (1997) and Abbott and Ryan (2000). They indicate how international curricular prescriptions are reducing emphasis on content knowledge and increasing emphasis on transferable skills such as creative and critical thinking and collaborative problem solving (MacBeath 1999; Scottish Executive Education Department 2000), both as a means to facilitate more meaningful and relevant learning and support the development of important life skills. These social and cognitive skill sets are not only required by employees and employers (Abbott and Ryan 2000; Powney and Lowden 2000) but are also seen as key for educational managers themselves.

Problem solving and thinking

Bentley (2000) describes how learners need to be flexible thinkers, Sternberg (2003) highlights how to be wise in the context of problem solving, Costa (2001) discusses how developing particular approaches to thinking is intelligent behaviour. All of these recognize how good thinkers need to adapt to the situation in which they find themselves. Inviting pupils to solve authentic problems with multiple possible solutions can offer opportunities to develop key cognitive skills that underpin skilful thinking. Polya (1948) has simplified the steps that can inform problem solving approaches. He suggests a simple framework for tackling problems, which highlights four phases (considered further in Chapter 11). The first phase is about understanding a problem; the second about devising a plan; the third carrying out a plan and fourthly to examining the solution.

It is possible to develop more than just the cognitive skills listed in Table 2.1. Discussion later in this book indicates how collaborative open-ended problem solving can offer more extensive opportunities for a wider range of cognitive skills to be developed.

Problem solving appears to offer excellent potential for nurturing thinking skills. If the problems are approached collectively in small groups, then many social skills can also be encouraged and developed to enhance collaboration. As McGregor (2003) suggests, effective collaboration centred on solving open-ended problems can provide excellent opportunities to develop cognitive and social skills. The skills enhanced could extend to include clarifying, extrapolating, rationalizing, explaining, elaborating, exploring, deliberating, justifying, prioritizing, negotiating (not present in the DfES skill descriptors), which are essential for solving social as well as conceptual problems in the future world of work. More collaborative problem solving opportunities, set in a variety of contexts that can connect with real-life or the world of work, could support development of the social and cognitive skills that employers appear to value.

Conclusion

Intelligence on its own is not sufficient to prepare students for life after school. A wide variety of cognitive skills are needed to solve problems, including discerning the relevant from the irrelevant, recognizing connections, understanding when bias might be involved, empathizing with societal pressures of others, deliberating in an objective and systematic way all plausible options to reach an agreeable, workable solution. Pupils need to develop experience in the use of these *and* to be able to recognize when it is appropriate to apply them. Schools need to introduce and develop in learners a range of cognitive skills that are critical, creative, socially cognizant and metacognitive. Educators need to support development of expertise in applying these skills by providing extrinsically provoking and focused problem solving opportunities in a wide range of subject contexts. The problems to be thought about should be connectable to life *out of school* and *life after school*. The thinking processes and outcomes should become explicit to the learners through reflection by either discussion with the teacher and/or peers. Thinking purposefully should be practised and developed over time, in contrasting situations, offering open-ended resolution possibilities. Preparing children for success in a rapidly changing world requires many types of thinking: planning ahead, reflecting on success and failure, consideration of others' views, analysing why things happen the way they do. All these contribute to the pupil's cognitive skills for solving future problems. In the knowledge revolution of the twenty-first century, the emphasis in education must be on using ingenuity, creativity and intellectual prowess (Costa 2001: 2). As Tom Bentley (2003) says, 'the future is, by definition created today. The seeds of tomorrow's successes or failures are around us now'.

Key ideas

Intellectual capability is developable.

Thinking skills required for school education include:
- information processing skills
- reasoning skills
- enquiry Skills
- creative skills
- evaluation skills

Types of thinking capabilities needed for the future and work include:
- processing and searching information to
  - discern relevance
  - consider what matters and distinguish importance
  - explore connections
  - speculate about possibilities
  - recognize bias
- thinking creatively to
  - innovate and solve problems
- thinking critically to
  - synthesize, generalize and summarize from information
  - judge accuracy, value and authenticity in information
  - become systematic in analysis
- flexible thinking
- perseverance in thinking
- developing societal empathy
- reflective thinking to elucidate problem solving approaches

3 Thinking and learning

> A person in pursuing a consecutive train of thoughts takes some
> system of ideas for granted (which accordingly he leaves unex-
> pressed, unconscious) ... we have to turn upon some unconscious
> assumption and make it explicit.
>
> (Dewey, *How We Think*)

Dewey (1910: 215) indicates that thoughts involved in developing ideas
and understandings are often assumed and implicit. To develop
thoughtful learning these processes need to become more explicit and
connected with the processes of coming to know or understand
something. This chapter is intended to provide the reader with an
overview of prominent learning theories and how they are related and
connected to the implicit and explicit development of thinking
capability. The nature and development of theories about how the
'mind' can be developed through different kinds of learning, including
constructivist activity (based on Piagetian ideas), social constructivism
(based on Vygotskian notions) and Rogoff's (1990) view of an
'apprenticeship in thinking' will be considered. Reflecting upon these
theories can reveal how learning and thinking approaches are informed
by a sound theoretical basis. The chapter will end by reconsidering how
thinking for learning and thinking about learning are interconnected.

Theories of learning

Learning is a highly complex aspect of human activity and many
theories have been developed to try to generalize about how it arises.
Although many theorists agree that the child is the 'constructor' of
knowledge (or the agency of learning), there are disagreements about
how learning occurs (the processes involved) and where it occurs (solely
in the mind, or combinationally through bodily engagement and the
mind, or simply through language), what influences might have a
greater or lesser bearing (context, structure, historical, social, cultural)
and what outcomes are a sign that learning has occurred (knowledge,
'expertise', skill, reality, understanding). As Phillips and Soltis (2004)
indicate, these are issues about which there is much discord. This chapter

Table 3.1 Brief description of some prominent features and implicit assumptions in various theories of learning

Theoretical perspective:	BEHAVIOURIST	CONSTRUCTIVIST (Premised mainly on Piagetian ideas)	SOCIAL CONSTRUCTIVIST (Premised mainly on Vygotskian ideas)	SOCIO-CULTURAL (Arising out of and extending beyond Vygotskian notions)
Prominent features:	Transmission of knowledge. Modelling of skills. Passive learner. Absorption of knowledge. Extrinsically motivated	Disequilibrium brings about: • Assimilation • Accommodation. Developed cognitive structures into schema(s)	Zone of proximal development (ZPD). Mediation and scaffolding. Social origins of mental development. Understanding social developing on an individual plane	Communities of learners • Intersubjectivity • Situated cognition • Guided participation • Apprenticeship
What is knowledge?	New behaviour(s), observable actions and transmitted information.	Schemata (kinds of thought processes/capability). Acquiring knowledge that is scientific reality. Concrete -> Abstract.	Intrapsychological construct(s) or internalization derived through social interaction. Has historical, social and cultural influence.	Situated cognition within a real-life community. Seamless connection between individual, social, historical and cultural processes. Evolving apprenticeship in becoming knowledgeable.
Characteristic teaching	Transmission of information. Modelling of new skills. Systematic reinforcement of correct behaviours.	Teacher providing opportunities for learners to develop their own individual understandings. Reflective questioning of learners. Language and interaction with learners not as significant as social constructivists.[1]	Teacher mediation and scaffolding. Social interaction and negotiation between expert and novice. Dynamic process between teachers and learners.	Guided participation in learning with more experienced or expert other. Gradual reduction of scaffold. Learner initially legitimate peripheral participator, gradually full participator in learning community. Dynamic process within.
How does learning happen?	Uncritical retention of information. Mimicking or copying new skills and behaviours. Teacher rewards correct behaviours and chastises incorrect behaviours.	Actively experimenting with materials, objects and ideas. Developing own personalized understandings of world around them. Accomodation and assimilation into cognitive structures.	Through social interaction while engaging in problem solving or task resolution. Actions = speech (inter and intra) and other physical activity. Scaffolded, teacher/expert most important initially, gradually	Appropriating understanding through contextualized and interactive participation. Mind arises through the interactive social processes as apprenticeship develops in learning with a more expert other. Gradual shift from peripheral participation, with more expert others in learning

| Implications for thinking? | Opportunities constrained. Implicit thinking illustrated through behavioural outcomes. | Implicit thinking through assumed processes. Interpsychological reflection. Thinking outcomes shared overtly by task resolution. Particular types (schemas) of thinking encouraged; cognitive outcomes valued. Constrained view of explicating cognitive processes required to problem solve. | dependence decreased. Discourse essential to verbalize activity (action and thought). Explicating thoughts to collaborate underpins more overt sharing of cognitive processes and strategies required to reach resolution. Wider cognizance of collective contributions to enrich the problem solving process and resolution. | community, to full participation as become more knowledgeable. Recognition of the socio-historical and cultural influences on the nature of the thinking required in an authentic problem solving situation. Naturalistically a more comprehensive array of cognitive, social and practical skills would be involved. |

Note: [1] Although there are psychological theorists who would argue that language is important in a social sense in Piaget's work (Tudge and Rogoff 1989)

attempts to summarize for readers the *basic* premises upon which behaviourist, constructivist, social constructivist and socio-cultural views of learning are based and the implicit or explicit cognitive activity implied. Characteristic pedagogies implied by these views can influence the nature of learners thinking. Consideration of these views suggests potential associations between pedagogy, learning and thinking, because the ways in which teachers guide and support participation in, engagement with, and development of, learning will influence both the nature and extent of cognitive development.

Behaviourism

Behaviourist theory in education has developed from Thorndike (1911) whose 'law of effect' indicated how the nature of a response (rewarding or punishing from a teacher) in particular situations can affect the strength or weakness of an association 'bond' between a learner's experience, thought or behaviour. He also developed the 'law of exercise' which highlighted how the probability of particular responses (for example, from a teacher) in certain situations can influence a learner's behaviours and thinking. Skinner's (1968) work built upon this when he further demonstrated how rats' could be 'conditioned' to push a lever to find food. He illustrated how a response can positively reinforce particular behaviour(s). He called this operant conditioning. He developed his theory about learning, which included stimulus, response, reinforcement and consequence. He also illustrated how pigeons' behaviours could be changed so that they could 'habitually' perform particular acts (Skinner 1953). In the early part of the twentieth century behaviourism was influential in providing the 'science of teaching' based on whole-class, didactic approaches through which knowledge and skills were transmitted (Pollard 2002). The 'law of effect' was reflected in elaborate systems and rituals for the reinforcement of correct pupil responses. The 'law of exercise' was reflected in an emphasis on practice and drill. There are variations on the view of behaviourism but, in essence, it is centred around reinforcing 'correct', repetitive, observable behaviours deemed to illustrate the learner has mastered a skill or recital of information (spellings, mathematical tables and so forth). Behaviourist perspectives do not take sufficient account of mental activity, as learning is perceived as the acquisition of new behaviour(s).

Constructivism

The theoretical underpinning of constructivism is based on Piagetian notions of how children learn. Piaget describes how when children encounter a new 'experience' they cognitively adapt. The process of intelligent adaptation (Piaget 1950) includes both 'accommodation' of their existing thinking and 'assimilation' of aspects of the new experience. The development of children's thinking arises in accruing steps, after successive experiences with the world around them. Over time they gradually restructure their understandings to explain phenomena. Piaget described how children's cognitive abilities followed a pattern through several hierarchical stages (see Figure 2.1). The schemata or types of thought (Rommetveit 1985: 193) or mental understandings, that Piaget highlights children can or can not possess at particular stages of development, are classified into distinct patterns of cognitive behaviour. For example, recognizing how sample size can affect measured outcomes, proportionalistic thinking, recognizing the ratio of one thing to another, like, for example, gearing ratios of differently sized cogs (Adey et al. 2001).

The sensorimotor stage describes the progressive development from innate reflex systems to the onset of language use. The preconceptual stage describes how children use transductive reasoning in order to form preconcepts. A young child sees her mother combing her hair. She says 'Mummy is combing her hair. She is going shopping'. The child links the two actions, although both are carried out at other times linked with other activities. Egocentricism also predominates because the child is unable to view things from another person's point of view.

The intuitive stage is very much superficial perceptions of the environment. This is because the child appears to be unable to consider all aspects of a situation simultaneously. A child will usually fixate on one dimension of an object or event to the exclusion of all others, which Piaget calls *centring*. Concrete operations are those where a child can reason, but largely based on the facts or happenings before them. They can identify and qualitatively describe relationships between variables, but not necessarily explain them. They can classify at this stage, (group things together with similar characteristics) unlike the preconceptual stage, sorting between similar (and dissimilar) relevant properties.

Formal operation or abstraction is the highest level of thinking. Developing an explanatory model of, for example, dissolution, particle theory, cruelty, justice or responsibility requires this *abstract* thinking capability without needing the concrete materials to provide substance to the argument. Active manipulation and practical experimentation has a crucial role in the assimilation process at each stage (Piaget 1951) and has been acknowledged as useful by many early childhood educators (Anning 1991; Dowling 1992; Moyles 1994; Parker-Rees 1999).

The Plowden Report, published in 1967, proclaimed Piaget's view that 'at the heart of the educational process lies the child' and the empirically worked out theory of developmental sequence appeared to fit observed facts of children's learning more satisfactorily than any other at that time (Donaldson 1987). The idea of staged development or achievement, linked to age, is a concept we still apply to the four key stages of the English National Curriculum. Pollard (2002) claims constructivism can be seen in all schools and is reflected in the provision of a rich varied and stimulating environment, in individualized work and creative arts, the manipulation of practical apparatus, the role play of historical or political characters and more recently the development of a myriad of MI[1] approaches to stimulate learners (Armstrong 2000). A simple model of constructivism, indicated in Figure 3.1, illustrates how a constructivist teacher might ask reflective questions that support the learner to develop personalized understandings and meanings.

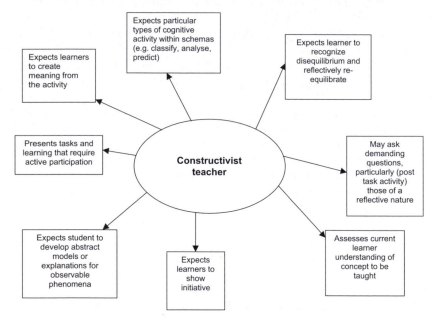

Figure 3.1 Prominent teacher behaviours and expectations implied by the constructivist learning theory

---

[1] MI – Multiple Intelligence approaches: applying Gardner's theory in the classroom to underpin the nature of the learning activities.

Driver (1995) developed a constructivist approach to teaching that first ascertains children's ideas before teaching them. As Ausubel (1968) argued: 'The most important single factor influencing learning is what the learner already knows. Ascertain this and teach him accordingly'.

Driver suggested that teachers should orchestrate the opportunity for the pupils to revisit scientific evidence and consequently restructure (or correct) their (alternate) conceptions. This approach was developed through her understandings about cognitive development and her research on pupils' conceptual understandings in science (see Figure 3.2).

Modern constructivist approaches to teaching emphasize the need for pupils to engage in activities that allow them to (re)construct their own knowledge and understanding. What is constructed depends crucially on what the learner brings to the situation as well as the nature of the learning situation provided by the teacher (Campione et al. 1995). Pupils perform appropriate (interactive) challenging, problem solving activities (but **not** necessarily of the open-endedness described in the previous chapter) and relate their findings to the previously presented explanations, concepts or ideas. They are encouraged to ask questions,

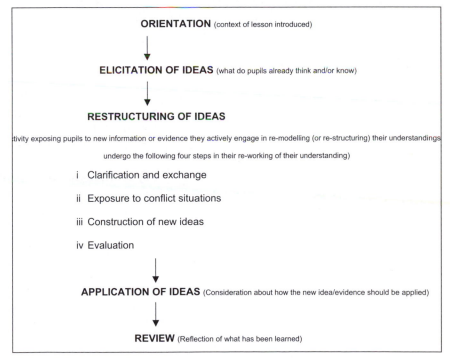

ORIENTATION (context of lesson introduced)

ELICITATION OF IDEAS (what do pupils already think and/or know)

RESTRUCTURING OF IDEAS

tivity exposing pupils to new information or evidence they actively engage in re-modelling (or re-structuring) their understandings

undergo the following four steps in their re-working of their understanding)

i   Clarification and exchange

ii Exposure to conflict situations

iii Construction of new ideas

iv Evaluation

APPLICATION OF IDEAS (Consideration about how the new idea/evidence should be applied)

REVIEW (Reflection of what has been learned)

Figure 3.2 Stages in the constructivist teaching sequence: a summary of the constructivist approach (after Driver 1985)

devise strategies and pursue thoughtful original paths to find resolutions (Brooks and Brooks 2001). Finally they are encouraged to reflect on how their final ideas contrast with their (now rejected, but earlier misconceived) understandings. The important point about this strategy is to recognize that the pupils do not begin their thinking from a blank sheet. They carry ideas to the situation gleaned from a range of prior experiences many of which originate from outside school as a part of everyday events. These ideas are often held tenaciously and can function as blocks to the learning of correct (scientific) ideas (Driver et al. 1985).

Current interpretations of constructivism are often focused on teacher activity rather than consideration of the mental processing (as suggested in Figure 3.2) of the learners. Constructivist teacher activity is usually perceived to be that which provides activity through which learners engage in reflective learning (although they may be *given* and have transmitted the conclusions that should be learned), or learners actively creating a 'product', or simply answering challenging questions, or teachers allowing students to reach their own unique solutions, or relying upon primary data sources to allow students to drive lessons, or allowing wait time after posing questions ... all ultimately to enable learners to 'come to know their world' (Brooks and Brooks 1999: 30).

Social constructivism

As with constructivism there are variations in views about social constructivism but in essence it has developed out of the work of Vygotsky. The prominent features are summarized in Table 3.1 and the interactional nature of learning between teachers and learners generalized in Figure 3.3.

It retains a central notion of thinking and understanding originating through social interactions which then inform personal constructions of meaning. The nature of the social interactions and therefore subsequent learning can be influenced by social, historical and cultural factors. Juxtaposed to Piaget's more individualistic perspective of learning, Vygotsky (1978) perceived the higher mental functions of thinking, reasoning and understanding as social in their origin. He also emphasized the importance of language in not only eliciting children's ideas but in shaping them too. He described how language was a cultural communication tool that enabled thoughts to be described. He highlighted connections between mental activity and language:

> Thought, unlike speech, does not consist of separate units. When I wish to communicate the thought that today I saw a

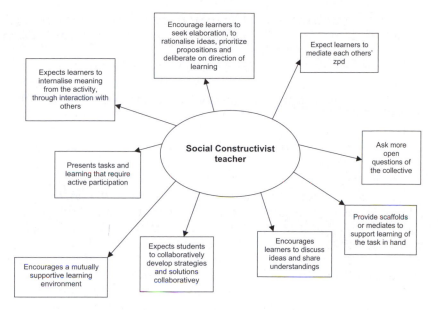

Figure 3.3 Prominent teacher behaviours and expectations implied by the social constructivist view of learning

barefoot boy in a blue shirt running down the street, I do not see every item separately: the boy, the shirt, its blue colour, his running, and the absence of shoes. I conceive of all this in one thought, but I put it into separate words. A speaker often takes several minutes to disclose one thought. In his mind the whole thought is present at once, but in speech it has to be developed successively. A thought may be compared to a cloud shedding a shower of words. Precisely because thought does not have its automatic counterpart in words, the transition from thought to word leads through meaning.

(Vygotsky 1986: 251)

Language is perceived as an instrument or tool of thought, not just providing a 'code' or system for representing the world (as Piaget perceived) but a way of transforming how children learn, think and understand. The process of children verbalizing their thinking requires development from their 'inner speech'. Supporting learners to communicate their ideas to others, in an understandable form, can be seen as an intermediate step that can promote more conscious thought, as Vygotsky explains: 'The transition from inner speech to external speech is not a simple translation from one language to another ... It is a complex dynamic process involving the transformation of the predicative, idiomatic structure of inner speech into syntactically articulated speech intelligible to others' (Vygotsky 1986: 249).

Social constructivists value and support the development of dialogic exchange because it is seen as pivotal in transforming cognitive activity into a more tangible from. Articulation to explain one's ideas involves '. . . shaping a thought first in inner speech, then in meanings of words, and finally in words' (Vygotsky 1986: 253).

Learners describing their ideas and communicating their reasoning can become an effective method to process thoughts in a conscious way, raise awareness of mental activity and subsequently create organized logic and meaning for oneself and others from these utterances. Mercer (1995) emphasizes the social nature of meaning making; he describes how different kinds of talk can illustrate whether pupils are engaged in effective social construction. In his analysis he clarifies how one pupil building positively on another's utterance is cumulative talk, but engaging critically *and* constructively with another's idea is 'exploratory'. He clarifies how different types of talk are distinctive social modes of thinking, because 'knowledge is made more publicly accountable' and 'reasoning is more visible in the talk' (Mercer 1998: 104). McGregor (2003) has illustrated how encouragement of exploratory talk can facilitate cognitive development through social interaction. Another central tenet of the social constructivists view of learning is the concept of the 'zone of proximal development' (ZPD)[2] (offering a contrasting view of cognitive or mental 'readiness' to Piaget)[3] and is described as 'the distance between a child's "actual developmental level as determined by independent problem solving" and the higher level of "potential development as determined through problem solving" under adult guidance or in collaboration with more capable peers' Vygotsky (1978: 86). Wood (1999: 17) defines this interactional process as one that can result in: 'Children's knowledge' as 'a product of the "joint construction" of understanding by the child and more expert members of his culture'.

The extent to which peers interact to collaboratively work on problems together will influence the thinking processes engaged in and the subsequent learning outcomes. As Costa (2001) indicates it is not just communication through language that is important when thinking

---

[2] The Vygoskian notion of readiness relates to the 'region of sensitivity to instruction' (Wood and Middleton 1975), or bandwidth of competence (Brown and Reeve 1987), where students are ripe for new learning.

[3] The Piagetian notion of 'readiness' defines whether a child has reached one level of cognitive competency and is ready to move to the next.

together; information perceived through the various senses is also important. Pupils can also communicate through inter*action* (McGregor 2003) through the things they *do* in response to each other's directives, suggestions or previous behaviours. A more social perspective of learning acknowledges how thinking and doing are connected, because:

> Children solve practical tasks with the help of their speech, as well as with their eyes and hands. This unity of perception, speech and action, which ultimately produces internalization of the visual field, constitutes the central subject matter for any analysis of the origin of uniquely human forms of behaviour.
>
> (Vygotsky 1978: 26)

Social constructivism connects doing, talking, thinking, inter- and intra-understanding, all within a social setting. The nature of guidance or scaffolding that teachers or peers offer in joint problem solving is assumed to develop their ZPD. The concept of scaffolding construes the ZPD as the distance between engagement and mastery of a task. It informs how to support learners in their learning or problem solving progress. Wood et al. (1976) captured the sense in which, through encouragement, focusing, reminders and suggestions, a learner can be supported in mastering a task or achieving understanding.

Light and Littleton (1999: 9) describe the building analogy of scaffolding: 'imagine building an arch with bricks it is easy to see the vital role played by the wooden *framework* used to assemble the arch. However, the role of this scaffolding is temporary, when complete the arch will hold itself up, without scaffolding it could not have been built.'

This interpretation has inspired pedagogical approaches that explicitly provide support for the initial performance of tasks to be performed later without assistance (Wood et al. 1976; Greenfield 1984; Tharp and Gallimore 1988).

Tharp and Gallimore (1988) even identify progression in the scaffolding. In the first stage the expert other directs the novice. In the second stage the learner takes over the role of 'scaffolder', often entailing 'talking oneself through' a task, remembering advice, reminders and injunctions previously given. They recognize the third stage is labelled as 'self-guidance' as the scaffolding is removed. The final fourth stage as one where there might be regression to earlier stages, when the task may be slightly different or other unknown factors may affect performance. Scaffolding in this sense is flexible and characterized by the teacher's responsiveness to the needs of the learner; as Pearson (1985) argues, it allows teachers to intervene to provide the cueing, questioning, coaching and information required to enable students to complete a task before they are able to complete it independently. Scaffolding, then, is a way teachers (or more able others) can mediate learning.

Rogoff (1990) describes how scaffolding can imply a rigid structure, but is more often perceived as the skill of asking appropriate questions to organize a child's thoughts. The adult prompts or facilitates to 'enable a child or novice to solve a problem, carry out a task or achieve a goal which would be beyond his or her unassisted efforts' Wood, et al. (1976: 90) describe a variety of strategies – for example, simplifying or reducing the task to manageable subgoals; the open or closed extent of a problem to be solved; the nature and sequence of questions posed; the detail of instructions provided for the learners to focus attention without giving away solutions. McGregor (2003) interprets scaffolding in a structural way, providing varied levels of task support in the form of differentiated worksheets that offer more or less focused guidance (see Chapter 11). A task sheet that poses a problem but has no suggestion about how to solve it offers no scaffolding. The same problem posed, but with carefully focused questions for learners to ponder, can provide supportive scaffolding to guide and direct pupils solving a problem.

Mediation

Vygotsky describes mediation in a general way as a means by which mental processing is invoked, usually between a more expert other (often a teacher) and a novice learner. Wertsch (1985) elaborates Vygotsky's ideas further to illustrate how speaking (and the use of language) is important in explicating inter and intra-mental ideas: 'He describes mediational means as a way of organising one's own or others' action, using signs such as various forms of speaking or social languages.'

Scaffolding pupils' learning is an approach to mediating thinking. Mediation can be influenced by (verbal or written) psychological tools in the form of a cue of some kind, or a series of connected questions, or a gesture toward equipment to be used, or a sign such as a nod or shake of the head, or symbols such as a diagrammatic representations of practical instructions or as Joiner et al. (2000: 49) have shown, even the nature of materials used. They illustrated how childrens' learning interactions were mediated by the tools they used. Computer simulations constrained the extent of focused discussion related to the task process. Actually manipulating physical apparatus significantly enhanced the nature of the resolution process but limited the extent of the findings. Mediation, therefore, can be viewed as the dynamic interactive process between peers or between the teacher and student(s). The interactive process may involve seesawing of both linguistic and actional exchange(s), essentially providing focus on pertinent issues (from the teacher's perspective) and exploring, clarifying, prioritizing conceptual and actional possibilities from the learners' perspectives. A more comprehensive discussion of the ways in which teachers can intervene and mediate in a dynamic way to support effective social constructivism is presented in Chapters 12 and 13.

For expert teachers to guide and support learners toward conceptual understanding(s), the teachers need to understand how learners make sense of the world. Which Duckworth (1987: 12) quite aptly describes:

> Meaning is not given to us in our encounters with the environment, but it is given by us – constructed by each of us in our own way, according to how our understanding is currently organized. As teachers we need to respect the meaning our students are giving to the events that we share. In the interests of making connections between their understanding and ours, we must adopt an insider's view: seek to understand their sense as well as help them to understand ours.

Bruner (1990: 2) described earlier constructivist views of meaning making 'to discover and to describe formally the meanings that human beings created out of their encounters with the world.' He highlighted how it focused upon 'symbolic activities human beings employed in constructing and in making sense, not only of the world, but of themselves.' He later discussed how 'folk psychology' (Bruner 1990: 35) can provide additional insight into the social and cultural effects on the processes by which, and situations in which we develop meaning.

In Piaget's and many constructivists' views the flow of construction is from one's interactions with the non-human environment toward an exchange with others. In Vygotsky's and the social constructivists' views, the flow of conceptual development is reversed, from inter- to intra-exchange.

A more socio-cultural perspective on learning

This perspective on learning focuses on the social, cultural and historical influences that shape and nurture learners' understandings, knowledge, expertise *and* skills in varied situations. Bruner (1986: 126) elucidates somewhat on the connection between social worlds (of teacher and pupil) and the ways in which learners might engage with and come to conceptual understandings. He describes an experience in a science lesson as a young boy:

I recall a teacher, her name was Miss Orcutt, who made the statement in class, 'It is a very puzzling thing not that water turns to ice at 32 degrees Fahrenheit, but that it should change from a liquid into a solid.' She then went on to give us an intuitive account of Brownian movement and of molecules, expressing a sense of wonder that matched, indeed bettered, the sense of wonder I felt at that age (around ten) about everything I turned my mind to, including at the far reach such matters as light from extinguished stars still travelling toward us though their sources had been snuffed out. In effect, she was inviting me to extend *my* world of wonder to encompass *hers*. She was not just *informing* me. She was rather, negotiating the world of wonder and possibility. Molecules, solids, liquids, movement were not facts; they were to be used in pondering and imagining. Miss Orcutt was the rarity. She was a human event, not a transmission device.

(Bruner 1986: 126)

Explaining how conceptual understanding develops, Roth (1995) refers to Greeno's (1991) use of 'environment' as a physical metaphor of an intellectual domain with resources spread throughout. Using the environmental metaphor, knowing means to know your way around, to know where the resources are (buses, maps, streets, shops, pavement) and to be able to use them appropriately. Learning in this metaphor is equivalent to moving to a new place, finding your way around and using the resources available to support you. Taking a cognitive perspective, the knower, the learning and the known are inseparable. The knower develops cognitive structures that represent an ontological 'reality' (like Newtonian laws of gravity or Watson and Crick's structure of DNA). In the environmental metaphor, more akin to the socio-cultural perspective of learning, knowing refers to the abilities to find and use concepts rather than just developing a unique personal representation of the concept(s). Socio-cultural perspectives emphasize how thinking and learning should arise through engagement in cultural practices. The learning is perceived as a gradual interactive process in which a novice engages as though in an apprenticeship. Initial participation in the apprenticeship is through legitimate peripheral engagement, which gradually advances to full participation (Lave and Wenger 1991: 94) as the novice appropriates expert practice and understanding. The process of intersubjectivity underpins development of shared mutualistic understandings more concerned with interpretation and understanding, by both participants, than with achievement of factual knowledge or skilled performance.

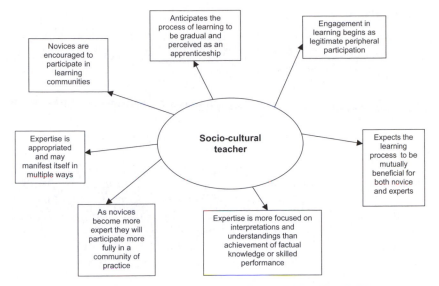

Figure 3.4 Prominent teacher behaviours and expectations implied by the socio-cultural theory of learning

Contrasting views of learning and assumptions about thinking

Contrasts in teachers' behaviours and implications for learning are illustrated in Figures 3.1, 3.2, 3.3 and 3.4.

Behaviourism

Behaviourist views of teaching and learning limit and constrain the nature of thinking possible. The approach does not purposely encourage original thinking or challenge ideas in a cognitive sense. Behaviourism encompasses the act of and engagement in thinking, as demonstrated through learning outcomes (by some action such as writing, reading, or gesticulation), but cognitive activity is implicit rather than explicit. Discussion of the thought processes or strategies devised to develop solutions is not explicated. Actions are ramifications of the thinking that is involved. The teacher is assumed to demonstrate good thinking so that learners know what to mimic and practice.

Constructivism

Knowledge, according to constructivists, is accrued within an individual (most processes are 'intermental'). Through experiences, new knowledge is acquired, which is 'checked' against existing self-knowledge. These may be triggered by disequilibrium (conflict with existing beliefs or preconceptions). This 'new' experience or information has to be accommodated and assimilated as a 'reconstructed' concept. It is only through interaction with the world-to-be-learned-about that ideas are amended. Constructivists recognize that engagement in learning requires 'doing' as well as cognitive processing, which suggests that the mind and the body are required to support the development of thinking. Essentially tasks involving practical activity appeal to the Piagetian constructivist as the reflections about the 'findings' or consequences of activities inform the learners developing cognition. The learner is perceived as key in determining and influencing the thinking done. The teacher's role is to provide challenging tasks for pupils to engage in and question learners about their inductive or deductive reasoning. The teacher is a facilitator of thinking (rather than someone creating interactive social dynamics that explicate cognitive processing) who ensures the learner reaches the appropriate cognitive culminations.

Social constructivism

Social constructivists perceive thinking as arising socially through communications with others. Intramental reflection is assumed from interactive exchange. Thinking may be supported, enhanced and extended through discussion and 'interaction' between peers and teacher and learners. Language is therefore key for more expert others to work with novices and support cognitive development within their ZPD. Cognitive development arises out of true collaboration. The teacher supports thinking by scaffolding tasks and promoting interactional mediation that focuses on explication of meanings about things. Teachers, in this paradigm, are perceived as more dynamic characters. They will be more interventionalist and ask many questions to engage and provoke learners in their social groups to learn collaboratively, more frequently asking 'What do you think?' and 'Why?' to overtly share potential socio-conflict, amongst a small learning group (or mutually supportive community) as part of the interactive learning process.

Socio-culturalism

Socio-cultural perspectives suggest that learners participate in communities of more knowledgeable others and that through guided apprenticeship they become more expert. Expertise is appropriated over time through enculturation within a community of practice. Teachers sensitive to the socio-cultural paradigm aim to support development of intersubjectivity, which arguably underpins independent collaborative learning (Ding and Flynn 2000). The purpose in supporting learners to collectively reach a resolution is not to guide them to the 'correct' explanation or elucidation but to enable them to learn together in an autonomous way and come to consider discerningly the quality of differing resolutions. Teachers guide and nurture thinking through participatory practice, which is mutually beneficial. Empathetic thinking from both novice and experienced other is engaged and enhanced through this process. Constrained socio-cultural perspectives on learning encompass learners just bringing more of their historical, cultural and life experiences to bear on the task that is to be solved. However, a more comprehensive socio-cultural approach to a task should engage learners in authentic skill development as well as cognitive growth. Progressive guidance in a thinking apprenticeship should support shared and distributed *situated cognition*.

Impact of the nature of the subject

The nature of some aspects of subject content in school, however, where objectivity is paramount (such as mathematics and science, where learners have to know Pythagoras' theorem or Newton's second law, or in history why the Second World War began; or in geography the location of natural resources and the influence on economic status of different countries); would naturally invoke a more constructivist style as the teacher has to guide students toward knowing the correct answers. This approach leading to known 'facts' that need to be transmitted or relayed tends to constrain the depth and breadth of thinking in which students could be encouraged to engage.

Subject area content or tasks where the outcomes can be more pluralist and/or subjective provide richer opportunities for a wider variety of cognitive processes to be nurtured and developed. Asking learners 'how' they might resolve a problem, or 'What strategies can you develop to ...'; or 'What do you think about ...' fits more comfortably within a social constructivist paradigm.

Teachers and educators recognizing where appropriate opportunities exist and how to nurture different kinds of thinking skills in learning activities is key to effectively orchestrating for thinking classrooms. Table 3.2 suggests potential points at which pupils are likely to hold subjective perspectives in learning tasks. These key junctures offer much potential, at which, to develop cognitive skills through social interaction (McGregor 2003) within a social constructivist paradigm. This is considered further in later chapters.

Table 3.2 A suggestion of key junctures at which to address pupils' subjectivities when engaged in learning tasks

Juncture in task	Ways of encouraging the sharing of subjective views to support more social interaction underpinning collective thinking and learning
a Preparing for the task	All participants contribute their clarification of the purpose of the activity. (What are they trying to find out?) Encourage each collaborator to reformulate the task to verify correct 'focus' or 'foci'. Participants should agree and clarify what matters and is important to focus on in the task.
b Planning the task	All participants should contribute their ideas about how they think the task should be done (and why). Collectively they should consider possible propositions, their strengths and weaknesses. All should agree (justified and plausible) how to go about the task.
c Sharing projections and prediction	All participants should share their expected outcomes (predict/project possibilities with rationale). The purpose of explicitly sharing *anticipations* of the *outcome* elucidates the connection between process and product as well as providing formative information about preconceived perspectives on the learning to be achieved.
d During in task engagement	Participants should reflect in-action to assess whether the tactics or strategy proposed is working as expected. Are any modifications needed? Do expectations 'fit' what is happening? Is negotiated reflection needed to decide whether or not to continue as originally planned (or follow an adapted tactic or method).
e Reflecting on the completed task	Participants should each share their evaluations of the task resolution. Were the tactic and methods employed successful? Would a different approach have been better? What do the findings or solution mean? What conclusions can be constructed? What has been learnt through doing the task?

Source: After McGregor (2003).

Learning theories, learning tasks and thinking

Applying constructivist principles, teachers need to recognize the cognitive skills that their students are capable of and could begin to master. As Confrey (1995) suggests, without a Piagetian-like analysis of conceptual development, how can the expert teacher select more-or-less appropriate cognitive goals or indeed perceive progression from the concrete to the abstract? The emphasis that constructivism places on action as well as linguistic exchange is key to developing thoughtful action(s) alongside conceptual understanding. Learners, engaging in unique open-ended problem solving tasks that involve pragmatic and theoretical aspects to a solution can therefore arguably develop useful, wide-ranging thinking and acting opportunities. So constructivism can serve to inform the level at which learning and thinking tasks can be posed and presented.

Social constructivism informs the approach to be taken to encourage collaborative mini-communities of learners working together to achieve a common goal through mediational means or structured scaffolding, to ensure co-constructive exchange in a social setting (indicated in Table 3.1 and Figure 3.4). The socio-cultural approach suggests how the thinking classroom should embrace the richness and diversity within small learning communities and extend applications of the problem solving process to authentic real-world situations.

Open-ended tasks are informed by the conceptual framing of an enquiry through a constructivist approach. The processes of supporting and interactively encouraging collaborating peers to resolve problems by collectively sharing propositions, rationalizing actions, prioritizing reasons, reaching consensus and reflectively evaluating outcomes, are informed by the social-constructivist view. The processes of extending reflection and engaging novice and experts to collaborate and participate in mutualistic development of expertise in authentic problem solving process(es) and outcome(s) are informed by the socio-cultural approach.

Any open-ended task or learning situation arguably encompasses the potential junctures identified in Table 3.2. However, all these steps may not be made explicit as progress is made toward resolution in a learning task. But teachers, holding this physiological framework in mind, can guide and orchestrate for collaboration, intervene and 'mediate' in the learning and ask questions to ensure 'focus' and 'intersubjectivitity' are generated and encouraged throughout the process.

Conclusion

Applying theories can help explain how we should view thinking to learn or learning to think. Educators need to heed how pupils are collectively encouraged, or not, to engage in thinking together or individualistically through learning activities. Enactment of different theories will influence pedagogic approaches that subsequently impact on how and what students think and learn. Connecting theories of learning with pedagogical practices, and the nature of implicit (or explicit) cognitive processing, is intended to help teachers realize how their perceptions of the learning process (and nature of knowledge) can influence the manner in which they plan and orchestrate for learning (and thus thinking) in their classrooms.

In behaviourist classrooms, thinking will be constrained and implied. In constructivist classrooms, particular kinds of thinking (perhaps more scientific in nature) will be facilitated, often reflectively. In social-constructivist classrooms the nature of the thinking engaged in will not be so tightly focused, but a wider range of continuously developing cognitive processes will be supported. Encouraging social interaction to metacognate and extend reflections can elucidate cognitive processing. Application of a more socio-cultural perspective embraces the development of expertise, celebrates collective collaboration and nurtures both practical and cognitive skills within authentic problem solving situations. If educational opportunities to develop thinking are narrowly conceived as purely cognitive activities for individuals to achieve then development will be limited to transmission of knowing, like behaviourism, rather than transaction and transformation (Bruner 1990; Moll 1993) of thinking and thus understanding.

Key ideas

> Different views of learning emphasize differing thought processes and outcomes to develop knowledge and understanding.

> Learning theories provide a series of perspectives that can help elucidate 'what' kind of thinking might be supported implicitly and explicitly in classrooms.

> Learning theories can provide insights into *how* teachers *can* and *do* foster thinking in their classrooms.

Perceptions of learning can implicitly and explicitly influence the pedagogy within a classroom and subsequently influence the frequency and nature of thinking and learning.

Behaviourist approaches can model good thinking for learning, but will tend to constrain the nature of thinking the pupils engage in.

Constructivist approaches to learning can facilitate development of particular kinds of thinking (for example, Piaget's schemata; Bloom's taxonomy of cognitive functions).

Social constructivist approaches can support more spontaneous development of thinking processes (as well as the thinking specifically striven for in the lesson design) through interaction in a wide range of learning situations.

Socio-cultural approaches embrace increasing participation in a community of learning to develop cognitive ability alongside other facets of expert practice.

4 The nature of thinking programmes developed within a subject context

> Meaning making is not a spectator sport. It is an engagement of the mind that transforms the mind. Knowledge is a constructive process rather than a finding ... We never really understand something until we can create a model or metaphor derived from our unique personal world. The reality we perceive, feel, see and hear is influenced by the constructive process of the brain as well as by the cues that impinge upon it. It is not the content stored in memory but the activity of constructing it that gets stored ... Humans don't *get* ideas; they *make* ideas.
>
> (Costa, *Developing Minds*)

Costa (2001: ix) argues that what our senses perceive shapes our personal understandings and mental constructions of the world. This chapter will focus on the nature of thinking programmes and how they are designed to support constructive processes. The ways in which pupils are encouraged to think and develop meaning within a subject domain are considered. The chapter will outline the aims, design, content and methodology of various programmes, including.

- the *cognitive acceleration* suite of interventions, initially conceived by Philip Adey and Michael Shayer;
- the *Thinking Through* series edited by David Leat; and
- the *Philosophy for Children* approach, originally developed by Matthew Lipman in the US, but more recently adopted and adapted by Robert Fisher within the UK.

Each of these programmes is described and considered here. However, successful implementation by subject teachers and the subsequent improvement in pupils' academic performance (discussed further in later chapters) appears to have resulted in *aspects* of these different approaches being adopted by education generally (DfES 2005) in a more infused way.

Cognitive Acceleration suite of interventions

The *Cognitive Acceleration* (CA) approach was first developed within a science subject context in the 1980s. Since the mid-1990s the approach has developed both horizontally into other subject areas (such as mathematics, technology and the performing arts) and vertically into different key stages (see Table 4.1 for summary). The programme is intriguing in that it is predicated on learning theories: the developmental psychology of Jean Piaget and the socio-cultural psychology of Lev Vygotsky (Shayer and Adey 2002: 4). Unlike in many other thinking programmes, practical activities involving manipulation of apparatus are essential for pupils to construct their understandings.

Table 4.1 Summary of published materials using the CA approach

	Science	Mathematics	Technology	Performing ARTs
KS1	*Let's Think* (2001)	*Let's Think through Maths! 5–6* (2004)		
KS2	*Let's Think through Science!* (2003)	*Let's think through Maths! 6–9* (2005)		
KS3	*Thinking Science* (2001)	*Thinking Maths* (1998)	*Cognitive Acceleration through Technology Education* (2003)	*Arts and Reasoning Thinking Skills* (2002)

Aim

The underpinning aim of the CA approach, developed by Shayer and Adey (2002: 4), is to improve students' intellectual performance by improving their cognitive processing ability. The imperative for the project development was based on earlier research (Shayer and Adey 1981) using science reasoning tasks.[1] Results from surveys, using these tasks, suggested that the low proportions of abstract thinking and more prevalent forms of concrete thinking in typical school populations from 9 to 16 years (in England and Wales) should be addressed. The Cognitive Acceleration through Science Education (CASE) project (Adey et al. 1995,

---

[1] Standardized tasks based on Piagetian notions of cognitive development. Seven levels of thinking from pre-operational, concrete and formal or abstract thinking can be assessed (see Tables 4.2 and Figure 4.1).

2001) aimed to accelerate the rate at which students, aged 11 to 14 years, develop more abstract (or higher) levels of thinking (for a specific example of descriptors of concrete and abstract thinking, see Table 4.2, from mathematics, based on Piaget's development theory). The CA intervention programme enhances pupils' information processing capability by setting cognitive challenges and encouraging the pupils to reflect and become more conscious of their own thinking.

Table 4.2 Examples of thinking levels in some strands of mathematical activity

| | More abstract → | | | | |
Reasoning	**Early concrete**	**Mature concrete**	**Concrete generalizations**	**Early formal operations**	**Mature formal operations**
Number properties	Add and subtract whole numbers; count in 2s, 5s, 10s	Place value in numbers (including decimals).	Number multiplication; negative numbers.	Generalized number; estimation in calculations.	Irrational numbers; convergence; error bounds.
Multiplicative relations	Halving and doubling; concrete '1 to many'.	Simple fractions; notions of percentages.	Percentage as fraction; equivalent fractions; concrete scaling.	Percentage, fractions and decimals as operators.	Analytical proportions; inverse proportions.
Expressions and equations	Comparison words; equal sign as equivalence.	Word expression of a number relation.	Symbolizing relations; solving linear equations.	Solving inequalities and simultaneous equations.	Algebraic manipulations and graphical methods.
Functions	1–1 mapping and its descriptions.	Two step 'function machine'.	Linear functions; mapping on Cartesian coordinates.	Tangent as ratio; non-linear graphs.	Function variables' effects of graphs; area under graph.
Probability	Always, never, sometimes	Likelihood scale.	Probability as fractions or percentage; adding to 1.	Probability as a relative frequency, P calculations.	Conditional probability, any combination.
Data representation and correlation	Concrete tally tables.	Stem and leaf; pie charts; mode and median.	Comparing averages; frequency chart, scattergram.	Box and whiskers; cumulative frequency, semi-quantitative correlation.	Describing dispersion; judging representations.

Source: After Adhami (2002).

Programme design and content

The original CASE programme was designed to facilitate a significantly higher proportion of pupils achieving complex levels of thinking (abstract or formal operations, as Piaget describes). By the end of the progressive two-year intervention (see Figure 4.1) pupils' processing ability should be beyond that which would naturalistically develop. There is interconnectivity between activities, a little like Bruner's (1966: 11) spiral curriculum, and revisiting of particular types of reasoning built in, with subsequent lessons becoming increasingly demanding intellectually. Often the lessons are in trios or quads, creating a trilogy or series of linked or sequenced activities, which can facilitate specific types of thinking becoming gradually more sophisticated. The original CA lessons were delivered once every two weeks. This was based on the notion of provoking mental processing to connect concepts over a longer period of time, rather than facilitate a raft of rapid, successive thinking lessons that required only short-term working memory.

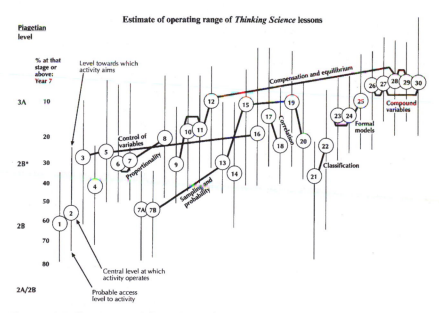

Figure 4.1 Illustration of the estimated cognitive range of *Thinking Science* lessons. From Adey et al. (1995)

General lesson structure

Adey and Shayer (1994) describe the important features of the CA approach as the 'six pillars'. The first five (concrete preparation, cognitive conflict, construction, metacognition and bridging) are important phases of a thinking lesson. The sixth pillar is the schemata or reasoning pattern, which informs the context of the lessons.

The first phase, *concrete preparation*, is the introduction and establishment of unfamiliar vocabulary and apparatus. It is perceived as the preparatory part of the lesson. *Cognitive conflict*, may arise, purposely, at various points in the lesson, and is applied directly from Piaget's view of cognitive growth developing from dissonance and through an endeavour to mentally equilibrate or accommodate new information. It is concerned with the deliberate presentation of intellectual challenges or controversial information. *Construction* is drawn from Vygotsky's (1978) concept of the ZPD, developed through social exchange. *Metacognition* is the phase that involves 'thinking about one's own thinking, becoming conscious of one's own reasoning' by reflecting and articulating 'insights' from the lessons. *Bridging* is the phase of a CA lesson where abstracting and generalizing the 'reasoning' or logical thinking applied in the lessons is related to real life contexts. These original five pillars have now been integrated to inform the general three or, four Acts (Shayer and Adey 2002) of a typical CA lesson.

Act 1 is setting up and preparing the whole class for the thinking activities. This involves the concrete preparation.

Act 2 is when the class splits into smaller groups (of two to five students) to work on the problems set. This is mainly where construction arises. The Vygotskian influences, on the development of the CA approach, extend here to consider mediation through social interaction with adults or peers. In applying the notion of proximal development, Adey and Shayer (1994) recognize that 'instruction is good only when it proceeds ahead of development, when it awakens and rouses to life those functions that are in the process of maturing or in the ZPD'. They identify 'probable value in peer collaboration', and add that

> translating it into practice, the mediating role of the teacher lies in developing the skill of first framing the tasks for the pupils in such a way to direct their attention to the problems they will meet and should discuss with each other. Then the whole class is encouraged to share the different insights and difficulties which the working groups have encountered. The ZPD is thus established collaboratively, and all pupils benefit.
>
> (Adey and Shayer 1994: 119)

The teacher support materials (Adey et al. 2001) provide guidance about mediation, but ultimately the teacher has to decide how to implement the suggestions. Further discussion of the influence of mediation on the nature and extent of thinking, through collaboration, is presented in Chapter 13.

Construction arises, within which conflict may develop, when students are working together in groups. Adey and Shayer (1994) describe how construction continues as the learner wrestles with alternate perspectives until personal equilibrium is re-established and the new information is accommodated. Yates (in Adey and Shayer 1994: 66) offers an analogy of social construction whereby pupils act as puzzle solvers, each contributing a 'piece' of information to the task solution. The teacher's role here is to support the students working and talking together.

Act 3 is whole-class reflection on the nature of solutions achieved and the thinking required to reach those resolutions. It focuses on metacognition. Reflection is informed by the Piagetian view that 'children's reflections on problems and consideration of possibilities before acting are important aspects of cognitive development' (Adey and Shayer 1994: 68). Children need scaffolded support from teachers, as well as an appropriate vocabulary to succeed in this. The processes of reflecting, using data and information to effectively connect experience and learning is an essential step from being a knowledgeable novice to becoming more expert. As Adey (1991: 30) describes: 'it is only after one has solved a problem that one can learn most effectively how one should have solved it'.

He elaborates on Vygotsky who rightly says: 'control of a function is the counterpart of one's consciousness of it', and 'if a child is going to control and direct his own thinking, he must become aware of it'.

Act 4 is optional (Shayer and Adey 2002: 5). To generalize about the thinking and connect it to other contexts; 'bridging' works best when pupils are invited to create their own suggestions. Teachers may initially model for pupils how to 'bridge' the thinking done to exemplify generalization. Pupils can be encouraged to consider a range of contexts where the schema may be used. For example, following an activity in which objects have been classified in two ways, students may see that as a useful way to organize their music collection, their clothes, or food in a cupboard (Shayer and Adey 2002: 6).

Shayer (1997) discusses the notion that both Piaget's and Vygotsky's theories are a necessary marriage for the successful implementation of this educational intervention. He describes the Piagetian contribution as the 'framing of the tasks themselves' – the 'hardware' of the lessons, and the 'conduct' of the lessons as drawn from Vygotskian approaches.

Creating an atmosphere for questioning

Setting the thinking agenda
What do you think?
Why do you think that?
How do you know?
Do you have a reason?
Can you be sure?
Is there another way?
What do you think happens next?

Developing responses
What reason do you have for saying that?
Do you agree with this?
Why do you disagree/agree?
What do you mean by that?
Is what you are saying consistent with what you first said/thought?
Are you and he/she contradicting each other?
Are there any alternatives?

Questions to encourage clarification of thought and encourage pupils to make connections and distinctions
You appear to be saying ...
Are you saying that ...?
I get the impression that ...
So as you see it ...
As I understand you ...
So from your point of view ... am I correct in assuming that you think ...?

Questions to help consolidate thoughts and construct hypotheses
Can you sum up your arguments/ideas/views?
So you think the following points are important?
Which points would you like to emphasize?
What do you think will happen as a result?
What do you predict will happen next?

Questions to focus discussion and consolidate views
In view of what you have said is this now the case?
The implications of what you have said are ...
Could your meaning/idea be taken in this way ...?
What if I interpret your ideas to mean ...?
Are you implying that ...?
Doesn't what you have said presuppose that ...?

Source: After Yates and Gouge (2002).

Figure 4.2 Question Bank (extract from ARTs project)

He adds 'Functions are first formed in the collective as relations among children and then become mental functions for the individual' (Vygotsky 1981: 85).

The nature of the thinking within the lessons

The sixth pillar of CA, the schemata, are kinds of understandings or types of thought (Rommetveit 1985: 193) described in Chapter 2. The CA approach recognizes that pupils cannot be taught these reasoning patterns (control and exclusion of variables, classification, ratio and proportionality, compensation and equilibrium, correlation, probability, formal modelling) or scientific ways of thinking about relationships between variables; they should be supported in 'constructing' their own understandings. These types of reasoning patterns are the thinking objectives for the CA lessons.

Other CA interventions

The CA approach has also been developed for 5–6-year-olds (KS1) and for 7–8-year-olds (KS2). The curriculum materials called *Thinking through Science* for KS2, should not to be confused with *Thinking Skills Through Science* (Duncan et al. 2004) in the *Thinking Through* series developed by David Leat. The activities for these pupils are not just a series of worksheets for teachers to duplicate and use in their lessons; they also contain a useful carrying case and various physical props and materials to support the thinking activities. The nature of thinking and the curricular context of these is described in Table 4.3. This table provides an overview of the range and extent of thinking and contexts of activities. For these reasons the CA approach is able to spread horizontally throughout the curriculum and vertically for KS1, KS2, KS3 and KS4.

In the programmes for 5–6-year-olds the emphasis is on development of concrete thinking within seven Piagetian schemata (seriation, classification, spatial perception, causality, theory of mind and concrete modelling). To promote social construction through discussion, conflict is purposely built into the activities. Examples include providing a picture that doesn't easily fit into a logical sequence (for example: Lost Boot, Cooking, The Cat and Snail Story) or a challenge whose solution is not obvious (for example: sorting a range of model animals into two separate groups of 'purple' and 'four-legged animals' including a purple sheep. These activities are designed to be taught more frequently (once a week) to younger children. Unlike the older KS3 pupils, who can recollect and reconnect with reasoning done in a thinking lesson two weeks previously, the 5–6-year-olds are more able to readily metacognate on weekly activities.

The KS2 programme provides activities that are more closely aligned to subject content, although there is still guidance about the Piagetian reasoning that should be included (see Table 4.3), for example: classification; causality; combinatorial thinking; relationships between variables; seriation; concrete modelling; conservation. For older students (aged 14 to 15 years: KS4) there are curricular developments for extending thinking in science. The materials (Gunter et al. forthcoming) embrace the psychology of the familiar five phases of a CA lesson, but are centred more around concepts that students are known to find difficult to understand or often develop alternative conceptions about (Driver et al. 1994, 1996). The cognitive outcomes of these lessons are based on developing, refining, modifying, connecting, evaluating or even re-structuring abstract models that explain scientific phenomena. These lessons involve some activities and demonstrations as well as active participation in collaborative discussion, debating and decision making.

Cognitive Acceleration in Mathematics Education (CAME)

This was, like CASE, initially developed for 11–13-year-olds, again based on the premise of Piagetian development that at this time adolescents are undergoing mental and physiological change, thus cognitive stimulation at this point in their development is most pertinent (Adey and Shayer 1990). The teacher support that accompanies these activities provides detailed pedagogical guidance about how to support thinking through group work and questioning (Adhami et al. 1998). The thinking objectives of the mathematics lessons are cognizant of the Piagetian reasoning patterns but focus more closely on National Curriculum attainment targets. They include number properties, multiplicative relations, expressions and equations, functions, geometric relations, shapes, orientations (in space), probability, data representation and correlation. These thinking objectives are also differentiated to illustrate the nature of progression from concrete levels in primary education to more abstract levels in secondary (see Table 4.2).

The CAME programme has also been developed for 5–6-year-olds (KS1) and 6–9-year-olds (KS2).

Table 4.3 Examples of some of the reasoning (or thinking objectives) and contexts from CA lessons

Title of programme	Reasoning patterns/type of thinking developed	Title of activity and brief outline
Lets Think! A programme for developing thinking in 5- and 6-year-olds	Listening	Clown faces. Space. Animals. All these activities emphasize and practice the social skills (of listening, speaking in turn, giving reasons) required for thinking activities in small groups in Year 1.
	Seriation	Sticks. Flowers. Marble run. Stones. Boxes. Library books. All these activities provide opportunities for children to place objects in rank order according to different variables.
	Classification	Sorting shapes. Farm animals I and II. Cars. Living? Guess what? Bricks. These activities provide a variety of opportunities for children to group and sort objects and things according to different criteria.
	Spatial perception	Crossroads I and II. Looking at shapes. Farmyard. These three-dimensional activities require children to work out deductively where objects might be or could move given particular criteria. There are purposely some large model buildings so that animals and objects in the activities cannot always be seen.
	Causality	Rolling bottles. Shadows. Transformations. These activities present evidence from which children have to construct plausible cause and effect explanations.
	Time sequence	Lost boot. Cooking. The cat and snail story. The ice cream story. These activities require children to place the story cards in a logical sequence and reason why they have done so.
	Rules of a game	In this town. Making a game. Children experience playing a game where the rules change. They also have to use their experience to create their own rules for a game.

Table 4.3 *continued*

Title of programme	Reasoning patterns/type of thinking developed	Title of activity and brief outline
Lets Think Through Science! Developing thinking with 7- and 8-year-olds	Introductory activities	Money matters. Painted doors. These activities are designed to emphasize working together as a group effectively (listening to others; considering other ideas; deciding what to do; ask questions for clarification).
	Classification	Grouping foods. Are they seeds? Classifying materials. Classification of rocks. Sorting magnetic and non-magnetic materials. These activities provide opportunities to develop understanding of variables (e.g. colour, size, shape) and their respective values (blue, red; small, large; circular, rectangular) to be used in applying criteria to classify. The pupils also develop their own categories for sorting and grouping.
	Causality	Animals and teeth. Potatoes. Shadow stick. Make a shadow puppet. The pupils explore cause-and-effect relationships in a variety of contexts.
	Combinatorial thinking	Sandwiches. This activity is designed to help pupils begin to understand the numeracy behind possible sandwich combinations that can be made from different breads, fillings and extras.
	Relationship between variables	Clothes to wear. Strength of magnets. These activities are designed to introduce the variation in nature of relationships that exists between things and their properties.
	Seriation	Classifying materials. This activity introduces pupils to a variety of variables they could use to rank or order materials.
	Concrete Modelling	Composition of soils; exploring poles. These activities provide the opportunity for pupils to build simple theoretical models that offer plausible explanations for observations they make.

Thinking Science for 11–13-year-olds	Conservation	Conservation of volume. This activity is designed to help pupils understand how the amount of something remains constant even if it changes shape or location.
	Variables (identifying/relevance/ controlling/fair test)	What varies? Two variables. What sort of relationship? The fair test. Roller ball. Interaction. These activities are focused on identifying variables, their values and the nature (proportional, inverse and null) of relationships between variables and how one variable should be manipulated and the others controlled to create a fair test.
	Ratio	Gears and ratios. These activities are to support understanding of proportional relationships between variables such as size and number etc. in the context of gears.
	Proportionality, Inverse proportionality and equilibrium	The wheelbarrow. Trunks and twigs. keeping balanced. Current, length and thickness. A variety of contexts here provides opportunities to consider direct proportional and inversely proportional relationships.
	Probability	Sampling beans. Bean growth. Spinning coins. Tea tasting. Sampling fish in a pond. Throwing dice. Understanding how median, mean and mode can provide useful information to compare populations. Collecting raw data and deriving probabilities from coins and dice throwing.
	Correlation	The behaviour of woodlice. Treatments and effects. Developing understanding about negative, positive and no correlation between variables.
	Combinations	Multiple choices. Developing an appreciation of the range of variables that can be potentially manipulated in an experiment.
	Classification	Making groups. More classifying. Applying criteria to classify and sort. Developing criteria to categorize for different purposes.
	Formal models	Explaining states of matter. Explaining solutions. Explaining chemical reactions. Developing plausible and reasoned formal models of observations made.
	Compound variables	Pressure. Floating and sinking. Divers. Recognizing how the combination of two variables combine to create a compound variable, e.g. surface area and mass create pressure.

Table 4.3 *continued*

Title of programme	Reasoning patterns/type of thinking developed	Title of activity and brief outline
Let's think through Maths! For 5- and 6-year-olds	Equilibrium	Up hill and down dale; Rebalancing. Exploring how two variables can be proportionally manipulated to balance each side the fulcrum.
	Number	Seeing numbers. Groups in a crowd. Hidden treasure. From a story to a sum. Money-go-round. Exploring notions of number in variety of contexts.
	Measurement	Measuring Shoes. Down my street. Footsteps. Develop understanding of principles about measuring and simple graphing of data collected.
	Data handling	Down my street. Sorting objects. Classifying and sorting using words and numbers.
	Shape and space	Sorting objects. My room. Sorting using two variables and applying numbers to describe spatial locations.
Thinking Maths for 11- to 13-year-olds	Number properties	Roofs. Operating on numbers. Missing digits. Sets and subsets. Accuracy and errors. Exploring properties of numbers.
	Multiplicative Relations	Tournaments. Relations. Functions. Circle relations. Developing understanding of scaling and relationships between percentages, fractions and decimals.
	Expressions and equations	Expressions and equations. Chunking and breaking up. Symbolizing relations, and solving problems algebraically.
	Functions	Two-step relations. Rectangle functions. Border and inside. Circle functions. Rates of change. Accelerating the acceleration. Straight-line graphs. Exploring relationships between variables, how they are represented as functions and presented graphically.

	Geometric functions	Triangle ratios. Graph of the rotating arm. These activities are concerned with exploring concepts linked to trigonometry.
	Shapes	Roofs. Best size desk. These activities develop understanding of a relationships between lines, shapes, symmetry etc.
	Orientations (space)	Direction and distance. This is about understanding the relations between coordinates, bearings, vectors and movement.
	Probability	Three dice. Heads or tails?. Data relations. These activities provide various mathematical ways to analyse the likelihood (or not) of things happening.
	Data representation and correlation	Length of words. Exploring the rectangle. Correlation scatters. comparing correlations. How do I handle the data? These support understanding about the nature and presentation of correlational relationships.
Arts Reasoning and Thinking Skills project reasoning	Classification	Interiors. Value and rarity. Three rooms. What is real (in the context of visual art)? Style and genre. Hell (in context of drama). Elements of music (in context of music). Applying criteria to classify attributes or objects into categories for different purposes using criteria, such as chronology, loudness, and medium.
	Frames of reference	Portraits. Part of the picture (in context of visual art). The meaning of success. Stereotyping. Hell (in the context of drama). The scene of the crime. the sounds of the city (in context of music). These activities develop relational appreciation about how elements (of music/drama/art) may be connected across time and/or space. Includes development of deductive thinking and reasoned assumptions.
	Symbolic representation	Symbols and relationships. Sense of place (in context of visual art). Colours as symbols. Hierarchy and power (in the context of drama). Sporting activities. The song remains the same. Time capsule (in context of music). These activities include the use of analogy and metaphor, gesture and mime, or signs and symbols to communicate ideas and messages.

Table 4.3 *continued*

Title of programme	Reasoning patterns/type of thinking developed	Title of activity and brief outline
	Critical reflection	Artists' voices. What is real (in context of visual art)? Mary and Jodie. Violence (in context of drama). A sense of occasion. Is this music (in context of music)? These activities provide reflective opportunities to consider artistic intention of others, justifying opinions, actions and arguments, recognizing and explaining bias.
	Intention, causality and experimentation	Viewpoints (in context of visual art). Mary and Jodie (in context of drama). The Journey (in context of music) Requires the act of making and explaining cause and effect in music, drama and art scenarios to reach desired outcomes.
	Narrative seriation	Detectives. The meaning of success. Red Riding Hood (in context of drama). These activities include sequencing, ordering stories, drama or musical pieces and even using flashbacks to develop more complex narratives.

ARTs reasoning and thinking skills programme

The arts were identified as an appropriate vehicle for cognitive acceleration for various reasons including the recognition by the Craft Council that:

> There are few areas in life where the nation's priority for education, health and employment and industry are not dependent on the development and application of creative, practical skills.
>
> (National Advisory Committee of Creative
> and Cultural Education 1999: 27)

The NFER report (Harland et al. 1995) reviewing youth participation in the arts found that a significant proportion of adolescents felt, amongst other things, that such participation gave them a sense of achievement, helped overcome shyness, and enabled them to acquire useful techniques and skills.

The intervention lessons have been devised within the context of music, the visual arts and drama. The lessons are designed for Years 7 and 8 pupils in KS3.

The philosophy is that participating students are accelerated through stages of cognitive development described by Piaget and Inhelder (Gallagher and Reid 1981) at a faster rate than with 'normal' non-interventional teaching. The 30 lessons in the programme are designed to provide intellectual challenge and while the students are involved with the task resolution the implicit (and often explicit) thinking required will contribute towards general improved cognitive capability.

The general five phases of a typical lesson are very explicit in the teacher materials. The mediational role of teachers is supported by a pedagogic description about how they should generally question and a comprehensive list of the types of questions that they should ask to evoke particular kinds of thinking is also included (see Figure 4.2).

The question bank provides a flavour of the different types of questions that are appropriate at different points in any thinking lesson. These questions alongside the described stages in the lessons provide pragmatic guidance for teachers to mediate thinking within a clear classroom framework.

Cognitive Acceleration in Technology Education (CATE)

The approach in the CATE lessons differs in a number of ways from the mathematics, science and ARTs programmes. *Cognitive Acceleration in Technology Education* is designed to be taught to the pupils once a month, over a longer period, perhaps three years, rather than two, like CASE and CAME. It places more emphasis on processing skills to solve problems, rather than focusing entirely on Piagetian reasoning patterns. The cognitive skills and strategies used are more similar to Feuerstein's Instrumental Enrichment programme (FIE) or Somerset Thinking Skills (STS). The activities in CATE are entirely cognitive, using only worksheet resources. They do not involve the element of doing some practical activity like the other CASE, CAME and performing ARTs lessons. These lessons are taught less frequently than CASE, CAME and the ARTs programme and structured a little differently to the usual CA five-phased lessons. The tasks are not designed to teach design and technology concepts or skills directly. They are, however, flexible enough to be sequenced in a coherent way to fit a delivery framework within a school. There is more Socratic type questioning of the 'what, why, how' type, both in discussion with the whole class and with individuals and small groups. The programme comprises 36 activities each of which consists of two tasks. The main task fulfils one or more key cognitive objectives and should be completed in full. The second task allows students to 'bridge' from the initial main task to ideas, strategies or prior experiences (somewhat like STS) and although it would not be necessary to complete this in its entirety, it is nevertheless an important aspect of the programme. The activities are to be administered in design and technology lessons throughout Key Stage 3 (age range 11–14 years). The lessons have been designed to increase the cognitive demand as the student moves from Year 7 through to Year 9. Each activity is accompanied by a set of teacher's guidance notes. Interestingly, like Anna Kite (2000), CATE uses the perspective of a female character throughout the activities, in an attempt to help the students more closely relate to the thinking in an everyday sense.

Thinking Through ... series

Since the inception of David Leat's very successful *Thinking Through Geography*, in 1998, a number of other books have complemented and developed the approach, to create the *Thinking Through ...* (TT) series. The series includes *Thinking Through History*, *Thinking Through Religious*

Education, Thinking Through Science, Thinking Through Primary Teaching, Thinking Through English and *More Thinking through Geography*.

Butterworth and O'Connor (2005: 1) describe the aim of the *Thinking Through* ... series as to provide 'a range of activities that are interesting and exciting to teach and that promote good dispositions for learning within the classroom'.

Aim

The aim of the lessons is to raise standards in geography. The philosophy behind the materials was to 'develop the challenge in geography' so that pupils engaged in the activities became 'better learners, think hard, ask questions, be surprised and consequently make teachers think hard, ask questions and be surprised' (Nichols and Kinniment 2001).

The programmes are designed to develop students who:

- are engaged and motivated;
- can become independent learners;
- are excited by learning;
- are willing to learn from others;
- ask questions;
- want to be challenged and can be challenging, in the positive sense of the word;
- say things that make teachers, pause and rethink something;
- leave the lessons buzzing about what has taken place and want to come back for more.

Programme design

McGuiness (1999) classifies the *Thinking Through* ... series as an 'infusion'. However, the origins were developed within a specific subject context and Leat (2001: 3) says 'they are not intended to replace but to supplement and complement other forms of good practice' to 'promote skills that are transferable'. There is no specific progression through the materials, nor indeed are any clearly classified as easier or more demanding. The teacher has autonomony about how (at levels one, two, three and four described later), which (all the activities or only a selection), where (which year group) and when (within which topic or curriculum area) to use the resources. The focus and aims of the lessons is paramount to promote good quality learning through thought provoking activities. The teacher decides whether or not *thinking* should be made explicit.

The pedagogic approach

The lessons can be developed at various levels (one to four) depending on the extent of the thinking the teacher wishes to support. The *Thinking Through* ... materials for each subject are contained within a book. There are photocopiable pages, of text, photographs and diagrams as well as much guidance for the teacher on how to conduct the lesson; many pedagogical suggestions are based on the retrospective experience of the author(s). The various lesson materials have been written to be used flexibly at any of the following levels:

1. Using and applying the teaching resources:

The lessons are exemplars of interesting and challenging ways to teach a subject and as such provide photocopiable resources. The activities should be used exactly as they are described.

2. Adaptation and development:

The strategies are flexible and adaptable and can be used with any age across all abilities. The use of the templates is described within a particular context but within the lesson materials there are opportunities to adapt the resources for upper primary or even advanced level classes.

3. Debriefing learning and metacognition:

The added dimension of reflective discussion (described as 'debriefing' in the materials) offers the opportunity for metacognition, for the students to think about the thinking they were engaged in during the lesson's activities. This is an opportunity to make explicit the implicit processes that students use to think *and* learn. Making thinking more explicit may require development of literacy to describe thinking processes and the associated skills.

4. Total infusion:

Total infusion requires the *Thinking Through* ... approach to be developed within lessons throughout the whole school. Some progress can be made towards this in secondary schools by having a whole departmental or faculty approach to teaching thinking. This has professional development implications (which are discussed in more detail in Chapter 13).

Leat in (Nichols and Kinninment 2001) argues that this approach to Teaching Thinking Through Geography (TTG) is intended to focus on the process of learning so that students can become self-diagnostic about what, where and why they need to improve their learning. Developing more explicit approaches to improve learning through debriefing, by providing immediate feedback on reasoning and responses to tasks, is also intended to enable the students to become 'critical thinkers' who are better equipped to 'take responsibility for their own learning' and become 'autonomous learners'.

Talk and group work

Talking within groups is deemed fundamental to this approach. Leat (2000: 160) recognizes that 'understanding develops through talk as ideas and interpretation are communicated and shared'. He explains that students should be working cooperatively and *in* groups rather than as individuals around a table *as* groups. He also indicates how there is much skill required to manage group work effectively and to intervene skilfully at an appropriate moment. He does in fact state 'do not interrupt groups if they are working well, even if this is tempting'.

The issue of creating a good talk environment (Carter 1991) is emphasized and various aspects of this are highlighted to indicate to teachers what should be considered as part of the pedagogical approach:

- Responding to and building upon each other's suggestions. Talk in groups should be collaborative, considering strengths and weaknesses of different ideas from different perspectives, leading to the acceptance of the better ideas and solutions (Kruger 1993).
- Developing speculative connections and interpretations, such as 'what if ...?' or 'I wonder ...' or 'maybe if ...' (D'Arcy 1989).
- More extensive student responses to questions that are posed, reducing as Sarason (1982) reports, the predominant teacher talk.
- More open questions posed by teachers.

Teachers are guided to consider Sharan (1980), Wood (1980) and Norman (1992) for further reading on the importance of small group talk.

Big Concepts

Leat (2000: 161) describes Big Concepts as 'central underpinning concepts, through which subject matter is understood'. These concepts are intended to be 'shared with the student' and used in a 'wide variety of situations'. The big concepts developed for geography are described in Table 4.4. They include providing explanations that relate cause to effects – for example 'why do the droughts occur regularly in Africa?' – or developing understanding of the inputs, outputs and workings of systems

– like a farm or ecosystem – or using classification to explore similarities and differences between places; exploring patterns or development of change over time – for instance populations, crime, ecological succession – to develop prediction and decision making through planning and thinking about the future. These concepts should be elaborated on and elucidated through the debriefing part of the lesson. In *Thinking Through History* (TTH) the Big Concepts that underpin the nature of the discipline differ somewhat. They evolved from the Schools' Council History Project (Fisher and Wilkinson 2002: 7) that emphasized evidence, empathy, cause, change and continuity to include key elements that align more closely to National Curriculum attainment targets:

Table 4.4 Summary of the Big Concepts, which inform the understanding focus of the lessons in the original TTG

Big Concept	Description of the conceptual development intended
Cause and effect	Explaining and giving reasons for something happening, e.g. explaining how changes over time affect the characteristics of a place. This is developed into recognition of *trigger* and *background* factors. Background factors are those that predispose events to happen and are more permanent, widespread and endemic, such as a long-term drought or dry season. A trigger factor is episodic, more visible, often localized, for example, the dropped match that started the bush fire.
Systems	A system has inputs, outputs, structures and processes and can reach a harmony or equilibrium when inputs are stable; for example, city, farm, factory, atmosphere, sand dunes, communities can all be represented as a system.
Classification	This is how things may be categorized, grouped or assigned depending on the characteristics of the objects being considered and the purpose of the classification, for example the North Sea could be seen as a place to fish, a recreational resource, water to cross by trawler skipper, a windsurfer and a ferry company (respectively).
Location	A more traditional example of this is industrial location, but less obvious are retailing distribution patterns, ecological succession, the geography of health, crime patterns, etc.
Planning	This is about considering whole and part, predicting the future taking account of current trends and situations, carried out individually and collectively by authorities.
Decision making	This is about making decisions from different standpoints, based on varied values and perspectives.
Inequality	This is about things that change and may be in disequilibrium, for example migration, geomorphological processes, traffic management.
Development	Quality of life for individuals and communities.

- Chronology – when did it happen?
- Range of ideas, attitudes and beliefs – what did different people think?
- Situation and diversity – what was it like?
- Change – what happened?
- Cause and effect – why did it change? What was the result?
- Continuity – how long did it last?
- Significance – what was important and long lasting?
- Interpretations – what are the differences between different accounts?
- Sources – what evidence is there?
- Communication – how convincing is this to a reader?

Thinking Through Religious Education (TTRE), *Thinking Through English* (TTE), *Thinking Skills Through Science* (TSTS) and *Thinking Through Primary Teaching* (TTPT) do not specify Big Concepts to focus on but change the cognitive emphasis to the thinking skills identified in the National Curriculum (Table 2.1).

Table 4.5 Chronology of publication of *Thinking Through* (TT) materials in different subject areas

---

Thinking Through Geography (TTG) in 1998 (reprinted 2000)
More Thinking Through Geography (MTTG) in 2001
Thinking Through Primary Teaching (TTPT) in 2001
Thinking Through History (TTH) in 2002
Thinking Through Religious Education (TTRE) in 2002
Thinking Skills Through Science (TSTS) in 2004
Thinking Through English (TTE) in 2005

Methodology

The teaching or pedagogical strategies are designed to provide 'rich learning experiences' (Fisher and Wilkinson 2002). In the original TTG they were developed to promote understanding of the big concepts. In TTG the pedagogical strategies included Odd One Out; Living Graphs; Mind Movies; Mysteries; Story Telling; Fact or Opinion; Classification and Reading Photographs (described in detail in Table 4.6). These original strategies were devised as ways of alleviating pupils' boredom in class; attempting to improve their motivation; exciting them about the subject matter; encouraging them to ask questions; and stimulating them to talk more about the lessons at home (Leat 2000: 1).

The intriguing range of strategies includes finding the odd-one-out (Which information doesn't fit the pattern?); mind movies (closing eyes and imagining life elsewhere or with a different outlook); living graphs (connecting everyday life with graphical representation of facts); mysteries (figuring out from evidence the 'solution'); story telling (like Chinese whispers with a twist); fact or opinion (How reliable is the source?); reading photographs (What does this picture imply?) As the *Thinking Through* ... approach gained momentum, materials were developed in other subject areas and also for primary teachers (see Table 4.5). The transfer of these strategies and the general approach resulted in the design of a much wider range of pedagogical strategies.

Structure of the lessons

Each lesson comprises distinct sections. To guide teachers these sections are described in chronological order. Some of these section descriptors provide information or guidance for the teacher; some directly describe potential happenings in the TT lessons. The teacher lesson materials provide descriptors of the rationale, context, preparation, launching, instructions, management of the activity, debriefing, follow-up and afterthoughts.

- The rationale introduces the pedagogic strategy and explains the mechanics of how it works (for example odd one out; mind movies).
- A descriptive context is provided that outlines for the teacher when and where this type of activity would be appropriate within the subject content (aligned with National Curriculum, literacy objectives, assessment for learning opportunities and so forth).
- The preparation required before the lesson is explained so that the teacher can ensure sufficient materials and thinking are all in place.
- The material describes how to launch the activity or tasks, to provide suggestions that help engage the students and focus their attention.
- Instructions provide pragmatic guidance about what students should be doing during the lesson.
- Advice on managing the activity guides the teacher to develop the 'thinking' and ensure that the learning also takes place. This section often involves suggestions about the types of questions to ask.
- Debriefing is perceived as the most difficult *and* most important part of the lesson. It involves the students

Table 4.6 Additional pedagogical strategies in the *Thinking Through* (TT) series

Teaching strategy	Nature of learning activities
Most likely to . . .	Students are presented with a list of options and then required to identify what they think is most likely to be representative of, or characterise a particular a situation, activity or location.
Maps/pictures from memory	Variation on Kim's game because everything that needs to be remembered is connected, transport systems in Newcastle; farming methods in Holland or the objects on the Seder Table.
Making animals	Students are given habitat or ecosystem parameters and they then have to consider the characteristics of an animal that would live in that place . . . and even design and draw this animal (that could realistically survive).
Five Ws	This is when students are placed in a situation where they have a picture – but know nothing of the background and how it came to be (e.g. aftermath of 1989 San Francisco earthquake; Northumberland farm) and have to devise and write questions (in a table) under the headings: What, Where? Who? When? Why? (The five Ws).
Taboo	Students are given (or develop their own) cards with words on (that represent important geographical concepts, e.g. within the context of water cycle; evapo-transpiration or surface run off) and a list of a few obvious descriptors that can not be used. The aim of the game is for each group to develop alternative ways to describe the word (without using the taboo terms).
Layered decision making	Students are given realistic, complex, challenging and unpredictable information to try and make sense of. During the progress of the activity the information they need to consider may be changed or updated to mirror real-world decision making, (e.g. moving house and working out the most important criteria for where decide to live; considering the location of a dam to create a reservoir). Specific focus on conflict resolution.
Concept maps	Students use cards with varied information on relating to a topic. They have to create the links and rationale for the design of the concept map. This can be developed to become very complex and consequently very demanding (e.g. comparing earthquakes).
Predicting with video	Students are asked to predict 'what happens next?' They are also expected to justify their predictions, so this can be seen as a technique to develop cause-and-effect understanding.

- explaining solutions at length;
- discussing the mental processes used, that is making explicit an understanding of the thinking (developing metacognition); and
- thinking about other contexts where this type of thinking might be useful.

  This can be important to help students consolidate knowledge or understanding of a conceptual nature ... or even help them remember information more easily. Nichols and Kinninment (2001: 72) identified the words 'describe' and 'explain' 33 times in a recent higher GCSE examination paper, indicating how important these skills are for students to succeed in social sciences.
- Follow-up describes how the thinking skills connect with the ongoing process of learning.
- Afterthoughts describe the final post-lesson reflections that a teacher might have, about how the activities could be improved for future work.

All these sections are explained in an easy, conversational way based on the author's personal experience of the activities. This is intended to inform teachers making pedagogic decisions about how best to conduct the lesson.

Thinking in other subjects

Thinking Through History (TTH)

Contains many similar approaches to TTG and MTTG, but develops a variation of living graphs, into the specific context of Lifelines (such as the rise of Hitler or development of medicine over time). It also develops Pictures From Memory, as opposed to Maps From Memory.

Thinking Through Religious Education (TTRE)

Again there are several of the original strategies from TTG in this programme. The teaching strategy that appears to develop from Lifelines (in TTH) is Fortune Lines (for example, The Life of Muhammad; The Life of Buddha) where subjective views (ecstatic, happy, OK, unhappy, miserable) at different stages in the characters lives form part of the analysis.

Reading Images is also developed from Reading Photographs; one particular activity is a series of photographs of Vaisakhi Celebrations.

The students are asked to consider initial impressions (coloured by the massive swords that the Sikhs yield) and then, as discussion is more focused, more understanding about the nature of Sikhism is developed.

Thinking Through Primary Teaching (TTPT)

Four of the previously described strategies are employed in this programme. An additional one Writing Frames provides a simple, easy-to-use writing guide. These frames could be easily adapted for young (and older, more able students). The prompts or stems provided to scaffold the thinking and writing is of general applicability. The implicit support provides guidance regarding specific genres of writing and the students writing and thinking are more organized and systematic.

Thinking Skills Through Science (TSTS)

The style of this programme is a little different from the others in the series, it purports to 'build on CASE' and 'complement CASE' and 'take teaching thinking in science further than before' (Duncan et al. 2004: 4). The exemplars do not necessarily use the developed strategies or contribute to the Big Concepts. Some of the strategies in the TTG, MTTG, TTH, TTRE, TTPT can be seen in parts of the activities. In general, however, the thinking activities appear to be more complex and are labelled usually by the content area addressed, although not always (for instance, Diagram from Memory and Three Chemical Mysteries). The format of presenting the activities to the teachers is similar. A significant development appears to be providing the resources on a CD not just on paper. These activities, like all the TT series, use paper resources (and extend to ICT in TSTS) albeit in the form of, for example, photographs, intriguing pictures, cards, graphs, time lines and writing frames, which does constrain the extent of thinking through action and doing. However, there are many opportunities for discussion and writing.

Philosophy for Children (P4C)

Matthew Lipman is generally recognized as the originator of the US programme, Philosophy for Children.

Aim

Lipman, with his co-authors, describes how the programme is designed to encourage the children to become a community of learners. Through the development of a community of enquiry within a classroom, philosophical discussions are guided to encourage thinking by interpreting, exploring ideas, proposing ideas, agreeing and disagreeing and posing questions, all to develop an 'ethical consciousness' Lipman et al. (1980).

Programme design

The programme involves reading particular novels that present ideas from a variety of sources in philosophy.

The approach in each case is fundamentally the same with the characters in the novel (or fictional text) finding themselves confronted by some kind of intellectual or philosophical challenge. The progression from a focus on language for the first few years, subsequently followed by development of formal and informal logic and then specific philosophical ideas, including, for example, ethics, epistemology, metaphysics, aesthetics and logic, is indicated in Figure 4.3. Lipman (2003) elaborates further in how to develop critical, creative and caring (maieutic) thinking within the context of philosophical tasks and even suggests that social good can arise from this approach, including a reduction of violence in society. The novels that have been written for this programme are purposely dialectical, providing models of conversational inquiry and thoughtfulness seeded with philosophical puzzles containing ambiguity, innuendo and irony. These novels have been developed to purposely extend the intellectual challenge from kindergarten (which focuses on language acquisition and reasoning in everyday conversations) to Year 12 (which comprises five contrasting novels

K-2	3-4	5-6	6	7-10	11-12
General philosophical foundations			Elementary philosophical specializations		Advanced philosophical specializations
Language acquisition	Acquisition of formal and informal logic				
					Ethics
				Lisa	Epistemology
		Harry	Tony	Suki	Metaphysics
				Mark	Aesthetics
					Logic

Source: From Lipman et al. (1980).

Figure 4.3 Progression of thinking at each grade (or year) in Philosophy for Children

within the realms of ethics, epistemology, metaphysics, aesthetics and logic).

With each novel there is a teacher's manual providing guidance on 'philosophical inquiry', which contains thinking exercises on each chapter of the novel.

The manual provides support for the classroom activities and suggests how to guide the nature of discussion that includes consideration of issues such as the function of the law, the nature of bureaucracy, the role of crime in modern society, freedom of the individual and alternative conceptions of justice. The kinds of mental acts that students are guided to engage in include: deciding, considering, wondering, remembering, explaining and understanding.

Structuring the lessons

Fisher (2000: 170) describes how to develop a community of enquiry that supports Socratic discussion. He underlines how lessons should progress in particular ways from listening to or reading part of a poem, novel or other text to creating a communal setting, sharing a stimulus, raising questions, choosing questions and facilitating discussion.

Communal setting

This involves sitting in a circle so that all can see and hear each other. The teacher is a part of this, thus creating a 'thinking circle'.

Shared stimulus

This involves having a shared stimulus, as a challenge, to think about. The starting point could be a one key question, a story or episode from a philosophical novel, a picture, photograph or diagram, close observation of an object of interest, work of art, poem, piece of music, video, reflection on experience or report of personal piece of research or work. The stimulus should be of sufficient interest to arouse curiosity and challenging to invite reflection and discussion. An example that Fisher (2000: 173) provides is a letter from a newspaper:

> Dear Teacher,
> I am victim of a concentration camp. My eyes saw what no man or woman should witness: gas chambers built by learned engineers; children poisoned by educated physicians, infants killed by trained nurses; women and babies shot and burned by high school and college graduates. So I am suspicious of education. My

request is: help your students to become human. Your effort must never produce learned monsters, skilled psychopaths, educated Eichmanns. Reading, writing and arithmetic are important only if they serve to make our children more human.

(Letter from school principal to new teachers.
The London Tablet, 10 October 1992)

Raising questions

Time should be given with an open invitation for individual, pairs or groups to raise questions about the stimulus. These questions are noted and displayed for all to see. Everyone should then have a turn at commenting on which question they would like to consider further.

Choosing a question

This can be done in various ways: through a lottery, teacher choice, individual pupil choice, list order, voting systems (one with most votes wins; second round vote if there is a tie; multi-vote of two or more votes each; transferable vote if the first choice is not a leader; progressive voting providing reason for choice).

Facilitating discussion

This can be exhausting for the teacher, but it is not necessarily they who have to lead the discussion. Pursuing reasoning behind thoughts requires persistence.

Content

An example of a novel read at Year 5 to 6 is *Harry Stottlemeier's Discovery*. This novel offers dialogue between children and children and adults. The story is set among a classroom of children who begin to understand the basics of logical reasoning when Harry, who is not paying attention in class, says that a comet is a planet because he remembers hearing that comets revolve around the sun just as planets do. The story is constructed to be a teaching model that respects the value of inquiry and reasoning, encourages the development of alternative modes of thought and imagination, and suggests how children are able to learn from one another. Each chapter (or section of text to be considered) is readable in about ten minutes and contains several 'leading ideas'. Among the leading ideas that arise in Harry Stottlemeier are:

- the process of inquiry;
- discovery and invention;
- figuring things out, inference;
- how thinking leads to understanding;
- inductive reasoning;
- styles of thinking;
- considering consequences when deciding what to do;
- what is generalization;
- contradiction;
- what is a possibility;
- causes and effects;
- explanations and descriptions.

Another novel, aimed at Years 8 to 10 describes the life of Mark, who is accused of vandalism. Other novels, also intended to be sequels to *Stottlemeier* are *Tony: Reasoning in Science* for Grades 6 and 7; *Lisa: Reasoning in Ethics* for Grades 7 to 9; *Suki: Reasoning in Language Arts*, also for Grades 7 to 9. Each text has an accompanying instructional manual.

Robert Fisher (2000) describes how to use a wide range of stories or other texts to create contexts and develop questioning to guide Socratic discussions to promote a community of enquiry.

He illustrates how the story of 'Cinderella' (Fisher 2000: 115) and other folk or fairy tales can be used to explore philosophical ideas.

Fisher (2000: 21) describes how the following sorts of questions are typical of philosophy:

- What is truth? What does it mean? Can it be proved? (*Logical thinking.*)
- What is right and wrong? How should we live? How should we treat others? (*Ethical thinking.*)
- What is knowledge? How do I know? Can I ever be certain? (*Epistemological thinking.*)
- What is a person? What is time? Is there a God? (*Metaphysical thinking.*)
- What is beauty? What is a work of art? How should we judge a work of art? (*Aesthetic thinking.*)

He has also illustrated how to use this philosophical approach to develop thinking through consideration of poems (Fisher 1997).

Conclusion

Each of the three approaches described in this chapter offers very different perspectives and programmes to support thinking within a subject context. Comparisons of their aims, programme design, content and methodologies highlight how implementing thinking programmes in subject areas require quite different pedagogical approaches. The aims of CA are to accelerate the cognitive development of children through challenging mental stimulation. The TT series aims to motivate and engage pupils in good quality learning experiences that may or may not involve explication of the thinking involved. P4C aims to stimulate children and arouse curiosity and develop thoughtful Socratic questioning techniques.

Structurally, the programmes are also very different. For example, CA offers a sophisticated framework that is progressive and scaffolds high aspirations in a cognitive sense. The interventions are regular and can support gradual cognitive development. The lessons have a very clear structure, which includes presenting cognitive conflict. The TT series provides some very intriguing pedagogic approaches that can excite and entice students to think and learn, but it does not suggest or orchestrate for regular thinking experiences. The different parts of a thinking lesson are clearly identified and described. Philosophy for Children also provides very structured lessons with a clear framework for regular opportunities to develop thinking.

The CA approach has shown that it can be applied across a range of subjects, from visual art, drama and music to technology, science and maths. The TT strategies are also flexible and adaptable enough to be utilised across a range of subjects from geography, history and religious education to English and science. Philosophy for Children can also be integrated into any subject content by selecting a purposeful, but comprehensive range of books (or connected literature) to be studied in a philosophical way. Each approach has also been developed for both primary and secondary education. All the schemes highlight the importance of structuring and presenting activities in particular ways, questioning students to ascertain their ideas and reflecting on the ways they progressed through tasks, processed information or reached a solution, and on how teachers can influence the extent to which students understand the thinking they engaged in.

Key ideas

To support good quality thinking, programmes need to include:
- clear cognitive aims
- regular progressive interventions

To support good quality thinking, lessons need to include:
- motivating activities that are purposeful, both in thinking and learning outcomes
- authentic (and appropriate in subject content) and challenging tasks (that may include controversial ideas) to arouse interest and focus attention
- time and opportunities for pupils to work collaboratively on tasks
- varied nature of tasks that appeal to wide range of learners
- structured components that support progressive development of thinking

To support good quality thinking in subject lessons, teachers need to:
- understand the thinking, reasoning or cognitive skills to be achieved
- understand that both cognitive processes and learning outcomes are linked and that students need support in making the connections explicit
- place more emphasis on *the* students describing and explaining *their* ideas
- mediate the thinking processes by supporting collaboration and using questions:
  - to stimulate thinking
  - to encourage pupils to describe ideas and suggestions
  - to encourage students to discuss and deliberate over alternate viewpoints
  - to evaluate progress and success
  - to promote reflection of the thinking pupils engage in
  - to promote bridging or transfer of the thinking processes to other contexts (including everyday situations)
- scaffold thinking and not 'give away' answers or solutions too quickly or easily

5   The nature of general thinking skills programmes

No object or principle is so strange, peculiar or remote that it may not be dwelt upon till its meaning becomes familiar – taken in on sight without reflection. We may come to see, perceive, recognise, grasp, seize, lay hold of principles, laws, abstract truths – i.e.: to understand their meaning in very immediate fashion. Our intellectual progress consists, as has been said, in a rhythm of direct understanding – technically called *ap*prehension – with indirect, mediated understanding – technically called *com*prehension.

(Dewey, *How We Think*)

In this statement Dewey (1910: 120) is drawing attention to how reflection on and consideration of new information, through mediation, supports intellectual progress and ultimately comprehension of this new information. In this chapter, the ways in which cognitive and social skills that pupils use, often unconsciously, in the process of learning, are deliberately emphasized. These programmes aim, in different ways to, make more explicit the thinking processes and skills needed for learning.

The aims and design of some of the more prominent programmes that centre on developing specific kinds of cognitive skills are outlined. The programmes considered include Feuerstein's Instrumental Enrichment Programme; Blagg's Somerset Thinking Skills; de Bono's CoRT materials; Lake and Needham's Top Ten Thinking Tactics and Dawes et al.'s Thinking Together. Each of these will be described to highlight similarities and differences. The comparison is intended to inform educators who must match 'needs requirements' with thinking and learning outcomes.

Feuerstein's Instrumental Enrichment Programme

In the 1970s, Feuerstein was concerned with helping retarded children to improve their performance in school. He developed an Instrumental Enrichment programme (FIE), a series of *instruments*, involving tasks that directly focused on the development of particular cognitive processes. To implement use of the instruments effectively, a different style of teaching was required: the Mediated Learning Experience (MLE). This pedagogical approach has been used by several different countries, from Israel where it originated, to France and more recently the UK and US.

Aims

The general aim of the Feuerstein's Instrumental Enrichment (FIE) is to develop particular kinds of cognitive functions, which Feuerstein identified as deficient (see Table 5.1). The intention was to improve individuals' social adaptability to ultimately contribute toward real-life (as opposed to scholastic) problem solving skills. Feuerstein believed that behaviours and skills were modifiable through mediated experience. The programme was designed to provide a structured succession of mediated cognitive experiences (Feuerstein et al. 1980). Emphasis is placed on development of mental process skills rather than knowing or understanding curricular facts or concepts. Feuerstein identifies how specific kinds of thinking skills (detailed in Table 5.1) should be focused upon and developed through a variety of *instruments* or carefully designed activities that draw attention to, develop practice in and offer more extensive use of particular cognitive abilities (or functions as he refers to them).

Feuerstein describes the programme as a 'mediated learning experience' because it is through teacher intervention and mediation that the children are guided to make sense of the world around them. Teacher mediation encourages the students to apply the principles they learn in the thinking programme to deal with increasingly complex problems and situations they may find in real life.

Programme design

The various instruments are designed to develop particular cognitive skills. A series of tasks, collated as a unit, provides the substance of each instrument. The instruments are selected to match the specific needs of the pupil under treatment. They are comprised of rather abstract, content-free tasks that can be successfully used with a wide range of learners, including young people from culturally deprived backgrounds, or with learning disabilities, or gifted underachievers or even adult learners in continuous education. The pencil-and-paper instruments are designed to provide opportunities for students to develop strategies and working habits that they can apply to problem solving situations. They are encouraged to generalize rules and principles, which can then be transferred to a wide range of contexts. In order to create insight and reflective or metacognitive thinking teachers need to mediate transferring

Table 5.1 Description of the thinking skills which the FIE programme specifically focuses upon

Thinking skill	Deficient performance	Improved performance
1 The ability to find relationships between objects and events.	Does not understand relationships or order; often relies on luck or happenstance; solves problems by trial and error.	Search for and deduce relationships; confidence in drawing accurate conclusions.
2 The ability to organize data into categories.	Cannot make meaning of otherwise separate phenomena.	Can project relationships among broader, complex concepts.
3 The ability to compare and contrast.	Does not look for relationships; episodic grasp of reality.	Can organize and integrate bits of information into meaningful system.
4 The ability to perceive data and events accurately.	Unable to separate self from surroundings; can't differentiate between inner and outer sources or reference.	Can form internal frame of reference needed to structure life experiences.
5 The ability to differentiate (divide a whole into its parts) and integrate (joining parts into a whole).	Does not see interrelationships, differences, distinctions; can't see the whole from its parts.	Uses cognitive strategies for differentiation and integration.
6 The ability to resist an impulsive approach to tasks.	Can't wait for instructions; does not think of next steps; talks before thinking.	Stops to think before acting; explores alternatives; assesses consequences.
7 The ability to remain motivated to complete difficult tasks.	Gets bored quickly; loses interest in task; rarely completes assignments.	Exhibits intrinsic motivation to complete; joy in work.
8 The ability to perceive and understand principles and formulae expressed in numerical patterns.	Does not perceive pattern of order, thus makes connections by accident or stereotypes.	Can draw accurate conclusions from events or data.
9 The ability to recognize spontaneously problems and project cause and effect relationships.	Does not see problems as they develop; does not seek or connect causes with effects.	Sees problem situations and takes initiative to solve; understands cause and effect.
10 The ability to use language with precision to encode and decode instructions.	Does not use precise words; can't follow complex instructions; can't interpret implicit instructions.	Seeks clarification of instructions; understands implicit instructions.

or bridging the newly acquired strategies to real-life circumstances. Each task usually requires about an hour of teaching time. They are intended to be used three to five times a week over a two- or three-year period.

Content

The programme consists of 14 instruments (examples of which are outlined in Table 5.2). Each instrument is designed to develop particular kinds of cognitive functions, ranging from identifying which pieces fit the blanks in complex geometric patterns, to depicting logical relationships between people as mathematical functions, to observation and analysis of pictures deliberately incorrect (in a structural or perspective sense). Practice in developing and using these cognitive abilities provides the content of the programme. Within each instrument there are several opportunities to practise using a particular cognitive function (with similar exercises, usually becoming more complex). The task sheets are culture-free and do not require linguistic or reading skills for learners to be able to use them to achieve.

Methodology

Central to the approach is teacher mediation, scaffolding and focusing pupils to think carefully about how to solve the problems posed. Important to FIE is extension beyond the context of the task and generalizing about 'where else' the cognitive strategy could be applied.

A teacher (or even parent) can mediate learning. The person who does this is someone who:

> Mediates the world to the child by transforming the stimuli-selecting stimuli; scheduling them; framing and locating them in time and space; grouping certain stimuli or segregating others; providing certain stimuli with specific meanings as compared with others; providing opportunities for recurrent appearances; bringing together objects and events that are separate and discrete in terms of temporal and spatial dimensions; revoking evens and reinforcing the appearance of some stimuli; rejecting or deferring the appearance of others; and through this, providing the ... modalities of selecting, focusing, grouping objects and events. What is even more important, the mediating individual enables the child to extend his activities over dimensions of reality that are not in his immediate reach either temporally or spatially.
>
> (Feuerstein et al. 1979: 365)

Table 5.2 Outline of some of the instruments used in (FIE) to develop cognitive functions

Instrument	Description of a typical task	Cognitive functions developed
Organization of dots	For given geometric shapes to be reoriented and transformed within frames of differently arranged dots.	• Definition of the problem • Selection of dots that are relevant to the figure that is sought • Planning behaviour. • Hypothetical thinking and use of logical evidence. • Spontaneous comparison of projected figure to the model. • Summative behaviour
Orientation of space I	A frame with a dot and an arrow in it are given. Subsequent frames contain either the dot or the arrow; the student has to reason where the missing arrow or dot could go.	• Definition of problem when no instructions are given or when tasks vary from frame to frame. • Hypothetical thinking: 'if … then.' • Use of logic to solve tasks for which the information is not directly provided. • Comparison as a strategy for checking one's work. • Internalization of the relationship between the elements of the system of reference.
Comparisons	Given different abstract geometric shapes (of varied orientations, shading and size) similarities have to be identified.	• Ability to keep in mind a great number of parameters during the process of elaboration. • Making a plan that will take into account the complexity of the tasks. • Use of hypothetical thinking and hypothesis testing to evaluate the alternative response. • Selection of relevant cues as reference points.
Analytic perception	Given a wide variety of abstract shapes, the student has to choose which combination fits together like a jigsaw to complete a specified outcome.	• Spontaneous comparison to model. • Establishment of relationship between parts, and between the parts and the model. • Categorization of parts according to their shapes and colors. • Visual transport of parts to the model.
Categorization	Students have to categorize objects into a schematic classification system.	• Comparative behaviour to ascertain similarities and differences. • Selection of relevant attributes. • Summative behaviour. • Projection of relationships. • Determination of cognitive categories.
Numerical progressions	Students have to deduce relationships between numbers, given a schematic view and some inserts.	• Use of relevant tacit cues like index (the place of a number in the progression). • Projection of relationships between the elements of the progression.

→ Increasing complexity

Family relations	Information about family members are given in three forms: list, schematic diagram and logic gates. From varied pieces of information students have to work out who's who.	• Definition of problem in order to determine what one is being asked to do. Using only information that is relevant. • Comparison between elements and relationships to determine similarities and differences. • Enlarging the mental field by bearing in mind a number of discrete elements and the relationships among them. • Hypothetical thinking and the use of logical evidence to justify one's conclusions. • Overcoming an episodic grasp of reality by seeking the links and bonds that unite separate entities.
Temporal relations	Factual information, related to time, is given in riddle (textual) format. Students have to work out how when different events occurred.	• Comparison of the temporal characteristics of events. • Use of relevant cues. • Formulation of hypotheses.
Illustrations	Pictures with 'incorrect' aspects to them are presented. Students have to work out what the problem is?	• Definition of the inferred problem. • Use of relevant cues as a basis for inference. • Use of comparative behaviour. • Use of summative behaviour. • Hypothetical thinking and use of logical evidence to support conclusions. • Establishment of relationships between the individuals, objects and events shown in the illustrations.
Instructions	Students are given written descriptions and pictorial representations. They have to work out which correspond and which do not.	• Definition of the problem. • Comparison of completed drawing with verbal instructions. • Use of relevant cues to clarify ambiguities. • Hypothetical thinking and use of logical evidence to support hypotheses.
Syllogisms	Given information, students have to apply logic to infer relations between things.	• Appropriate definition of problem. • Spontaneous comparative behaviour between attributes of a set and those of set members. • Selection of relevant data for elaboration. • Overcoming episodic grasp of reality by establishing relationships. • Broadening of mental field to simultaneously elaborate information from several sources. • Elaboration of cognitive categories on the basis of conceptual criteria. • Use of summative behaviour. • Hypothetical thinking and search for logical evidence.

Increasing complexity →

The mediator, then, plays an essential role in manipulating the presentation of the stimuli in such a way that the child relates to the problem or task and can engage with it in a purposeful and meaningful way. Mediation, its nature and role in thinking are discussed further in Chapters 12 and 13.

Somerset Thinking Skills (STS)

Nigel Blagg developed the theoretical framework of Somerset Thinking Skills course from FIE, but it was also influenced by information processing analyses of intelligence, problem solving approaches and various curriculum projects that emphasized the importance of group work and social aspects of learning (Blagg 1991: 128).

Aim

The course targets students aged 10 to 16 years old. The general aims of this course are to improve the level of competence and confidence with which pupils solve problems. They are encouraged to develop the skills to become proactive learners within any problem solving situation. Participation in the programme supports transformation from a passive recipient of information to an active searcher and generator of ideas, thereby enhancing self-esteem.

Programme design

A series of visually stimulating materials provides the springboard for the lessons (like FIE). The materials are arranged in modules around themes. Whereas the FIE emphasizes reduction of impulsivity and overcoming 'deficient functions' the STS programme concerns itself with wider issues of learning style and cognitive strategies as well as the cognitive resources underlying these areas. The modules are designed to be progressive and used in an ordered sequence as listed below (apart from the final one, organizing and memorizing, which can be used flexibly).

There is a range of open and closed tasks. Many do not have a 'correct' answer, although there are some tasks designed with very specific solutions in mind. Many tasks deliberately make use of ambiguity to provide the opportunities for students to develop justifications for their views and in so doing prompt more debate and discussion.

Content

The sequence of the seven modules that constitute the Somerset Thinking Skills course are:

1   Foundations in problem solving.
2   Analyzing and synthesizing.
3   Comparative thinking.
4   Positions in time and space.
5   Understanding analogies.
6   Patterns in time and space.
7   Organizing and memorizing.

Foundations in problem solving

This module offers a wide range of visual stimuli, including contexts (such as the living room, a child's bedroom, around the world, and on an island) to engage students in thinking about a wide variety of problems. There is a suggested list of questions that students are encouraged to consider at different stages of the problem solving process:

1 Understanding the problem

- Look carefully:
    - Have I notice all the details?
    - What does the problem remind me of?
    - What do other people think?

- Decide the problem's purpose:
    - What is this problem all about?
    - What do I need to do?
    - Why do I need to do this?

2 Planning what to do

- Think back:
    - What have I done before that might help here?

- Think ahead:
    - What might cause difficulties?
    - How can I avoid these?

- Think how:
  - What way can I tackle the problem?
  - How best can I work with others?

3 Doing and reviewing

- Doing the task:
  - Is everybody working as best they can?
  - Are things going according to plan?

- Look back:
  - Did my plan work?
  - How well did we work together?
  - What skills did I use?

- Look ahead:
  - Where else could I use these skills?
  - What would I do differently next time?
  - What rules have I learned?
  - How could I improve my skills?

Analyzing and synthesizing

This module builds on the foundations module. It provides more opportunities to apply the vocabulary developed around problem solving. The tasks are designed to consider a range of cognitive skills including: connecting whole-part relationships, sequencing, ordering, searching, describing, classifying, interpreting, synthesizing, deciphering, logically deducing, summarizing, brainstorming. All of these cognitive activities are applied to a range of tasks, often presented in a pictorial or symbolic way. Examples of tasks include connecting different scenarios in various rooms of a house; deducing what happened in a burglary; figuring out how to redesign a garden patio; recreating regular patterns on a quilt; refining a car production flow chart and analyzing instructions for correct detail.

Comparative thinking

This focuses on the distinction between describing and comparing and promotes consideration of the purpose of categorizing. Craftsmans' tools for example are provided for the learner to think about the ways in which they are different and similar *visually* and then how they may be *used* in different ways. Typical choices a pupil might face, for example, purchasing a bicycle, are used as a focus for comparative thinking. Students are encouraged to consider issues such as what characteristics are important, or which factors are most valuable in the purchase. In other tasks, pupils are challenged to think about the use of classification and comparative thinking in a range of contexts including a zoo, a shoe shop and the kitchen.

Positions in time and space

This module heightens awareness about the temporal and spatial considerations that might be important for solving problems, for example ordering and sequencing actions or events in the context of a party or an accident scene or recognizing hazards and their implications on streets or roads.

Understanding analogies

This module connects directly with comparative thinking. The intention is to show how analogy, metaphor and simile can all be reduced to a sequence of comparisons. The role of analogy, metaphor and simile is considered in everyday communication through activities focused on cartoons, wall charts, pictorial representations, symbols, signal systems, television and media influences and coded conversations.

Patterns in time and space

This module extends the thinking about positions in time and space by exploring possible three-dimensional patterns. Many of these thinking activities are posed as puzzles. There are also tasks set within a birthday-party context, out at the restaurant, developing a biography of an unknown person through analysis of evidence and even considering the best and worst travel routes via various modes of transport.

Organizing and memorizing

This module revisits many of the ideas developed previously. The tasks are designed to emphasize flexible, strategic thinking. Many different activities are presented that illustrate important points about how to enhance memory skills. They are fun for pupils to engage in and reflect upon.

Types of tasks

Within each module there are three different types of tasks:

- stimulus activities;
- artificial tasks;
- naturalistic tasks.

Stimulus tasks initiate the module and are deliberately open to establish the nature or context of the activities within the module. Pupils are offered many opportunities in this kind of activity to share ideas and develop justifiable reasoning.

Artificial tasks are similar in purpose to the FIE tasks, designed to expose, develop and offer practice in particular cognitive functions, for example, recognizing patterns, seeing connections.

Naturalistic tasks simulate real-life situations and provide the opportunity for the pupils to apply the cognitive functions they have previously developed.

Methodology

Teaching is through mediation, the MLE as applied in FIE. Blagg et al. (2003) describe it as an art, because it is a dynamic, interactive process arising between teacher and pupils. It has to be personalized (for instance through questions, gesture, or notation) to support development from the particular understanding currently held toward achieving the next cognitive step.

Top Ten Thinking Tactics (TTTT)

Lake and Needham developed this programme as a simple and easy-to-use structured programme, for 8–12-year-olds. The intervention is aimed at junior children, pre-secondary school. Lake and Needham (1995) argue that no more than ten basic thinking strategies (or tactics) should be developed with these older primary children. The programme designers assumed that primary teachers would not have sufficient time in their curriculum to deliver a comprehensive thinking skills programme that introduced a wide range of functions, skills and strategies. With only ten tactic names to remember Lake and Needham suggested that the brevity and alliteration would enable children to recall the strategies readily and incorporate them into their active vocabulary. They propose that 'neither a diet of pure instruction nor a regime of leaving them to find everything out for themselves, but an ethos of guided intervention by adults' is required. The philosophy is that children are actively engaged in applying thinking tactics. Eleven activities (including one that revises all the strategies) have been developed so that with the purpose of learning elucidated for them, they can see where their learning is leading and thus feel more confident. Lake and Needham (1995) described how the strategies should be regularly practised and claim that to achieve true value the thinking has to be transferred from the programme sessions and beyond.

Aim

To use thinking tactics to help students become more effective learners. Mediation is emphasized. Mediation frames, focuses and filters stimulation from the outside world to the child, but also ensures that the learner develops a sense of readiness and willingness to respond to external stimuli. The mediational focus is to encourage learners to *use* and *develop* their intelligence. The emphasis on pedagogy suggests that if the MLE is inadequate cognitive processing and subsequent development may be impaired.

Programme design

The 11 activities are perceived in quite a flexible way, rather than as prescribed lessons. This is because many of the materials do not fit what might be thought of as something to be 'taught' and some of the activities may take longer than a single lesson. The materials are intended to be used to aid National Curriculum requirements and should occupy no more than one hour a week.

The support material for the teacher provides an overview of the programme, its aims and purpose. For each activity there is a narrative that highlights which thinking strategy should be emphasized and a description about how the activity should proceed. The teachers are also provided with guidance on the aims of mediation and even what to expect regarding students responses. They are given suggestions about the sequence and nature of questions that could be asked and discussions that should be encouraged. It is suggested that the students be encouraged to use and practise the tactic names and that the teachers should indicate where, and sometimes how, the thinking could be transferred to other situations (usually within another school context). Lake and Needham (1995: ii) suggest using STS, as it follows on and appropriately extends the TTTT programme in a similar way but considers more complex problems, challenges and situations. The students are provided with a summary guidance sheet that describes the approach to thinking throughout the programme simply and with alliterations.

The ten tactics in which pupils are regularly encouraged to engage include pinpointing the problem, systematic search, planning, correct communication, check and change, comparing and contrasting, getting the point, using several sources, self-awareness and setting my own targets. It deliberately reduces the scope of cognitive capabilities focused upon compared to the range of 45 mental resources identified by FIE and described in STS.

There is a hierarchy to the thinking demands. The first five are described as basic to virtually all successful problem solving in the classroom. They are simple to learn and can be applied straightforwardly (even mechanistically, the authors declare!) involving no higher order thinking.

1 Pinpointing the problem – this is the development of awareness of the need to clarify what the problem is and what the task entails before proceeding. This thinking will obviate the loss of value for those children who tend to rush blindly into solving a task before thinking it through and deriving little learning from the experience.

2 Systematic search – this involves encouraging the children to go beyond simple scanning of material to searching with a purpose, inwardly reflecting, modifying and rejecting hypotheses while continuing to look at the data.

3 Planning – rehearsing a way forward before attempting a solution. This involves paying selective attention to relevant information.

4 Check and change – constantly checking on your work, being prepared to change direction and to try new ideas if your chosen solution is clearly not working.

5 Correct communication – making your instructions and wishes as clear as possible, so that others can gauge precisely what you are thinking.

The later tactics involve higher order thinking and become increasingly important as pupils work more autonomously (Lake and Needham 1995: iii).

6 Comparing and contrasting – automatically looking for similarities and differences, categorizing, making connections, seeing finer points of difference.

7 Getting the point – sifting through the initial and often confusing information, for relevant and irrelevant material.
8 Using several sources – thinking about more than one piece of information at a time. Combining inputs to make sense of the whole.
9 Self-awareness – becoming aware of own particular ways of learning (styles), recognizing strengths and weaknesses.
10 Setting your own targets – understanding what your purpose is, whilst also recognizing the goals that others have for you. Having your own ideas and wishes about what you hope to achieve.

Content

Activities centred on time and space underpin much of the approach, because as Feuerstein highlights spatial and temporal cognitive abilities are crucial for adequate mental performance (Lake and Needham 1995: iv). The content and context of the activities includes sequencing (ordering everyday and historical events); recognizing relational positions (from diagrams identifying what is 'in front of' or 'behind' other objects in the same picture); describing cause and effect (developing propositions from a selection of pictures); using simple coordinates to communicate movements and time travel (describing things happening).

The activities have a narrative-type quality built into many of them. The importance of telling a story, provides the opportunity for emotion and feelings to be included in the thinking activities, as well as grabbing the imagination of the children.

Methodology

The activities usually comprise two linked tasks. Task one sheets are used to introduce a particular thinking tactic. A second task sheet provides additional practice in a different context (usually) and finally reflecting to transfer the thinking processes completes the lesson.

Mediation is key to the pedagogy. The importance of not telling a child answers is emphatically described. The teacher's guide explains that mediation involves questioning, waiting, prompting and modelling.

De Bono's CoRT programme

Although de Bono is well known for his work on lateral thinking (often used in the world of corporate business) he designed this programme in the 1960s to teach thinking skills in schools. He believes that thinking is a skill that can be improved by training and practice and has devised the CoRT materials to do exactly that.

Aims

The *Cognitive Research Trust* (CoRT) programme is aimed at younger high schools students or older primary children. The aim is to introduce them to thinking 'tools' and then improve the use of these skills through repeated practice. De Bono perceives 'intelligence' as the power of a car. The performance of the car, however, is not determined only by its power, but the skill with which it is driven. His aim through the CoRT and other lateral thinking approaches is to teach students how to develop their thinking skills through regular practice of different types of thinking. He perceives intelligence as a potential and thinking as an operating skill and suggests that if you have a less powerful car then you need to develop much better driving skills to make up for the lack of power in the car.

Programme design

The CoRT programme is designed to equip students with various 'tools' or techniques that can scaffold or support application of different thinking skills. De Bono draws the analogy with carpenters who need the plane, saw and drill to do their job. Each tool is used in a different way for a different purpose. The skilled carpenter knows when to use them to achieve the desired outcome(s). The CoRT programme provides teachers with a guide that includes descriptions of the 'tools' to be taught, a model lesson sequence, how to teach thinking, problems for the students to work on to practise the use of these techniques and test materials.

Content

There are 60 lessons in the CoRT programme. The materials are grouped into six clusters: CoRT 1, 2, 3, 4, 5 and 6; each of which contains ten lessons (each can last between 35 minutes to an hour, depending on timetable constraints). The themes of the thinking skills involved in the six CoRT programmes include breadth, organization, interaction,

Table 5.3   The themes for the CoRT lessons

CoRT lesson	Theme
CoRT 1: Breadth	To broaden perception so that in any thinking situation the pupils see beyond the obvious, immediate and egocentric.
CoRT 2: Organization	Basic thinking operations and their organization for use, i.e: when to use 'recognize', 'analyze', 'compare', 'select', 'find other ways', 'start', 'organize', 'focus', 'consolidate' and 'conclude'.
CoRT 3: Interaction	Intended to be interactive, constructive argument. Not about critically finding fault. Emphasis on winning an argument to bring about an aim. Includes: examining both sides (EBS); the type, value and structure of evidence; agreement, disagreement, irrelevance (ADI); being right and being wrong; outcomes.
CoRT 4: Creativity	To develop effective new ideas and engender fun. Commonly referred to as 'lateral' thinking by de Bono.
CoRT 5: Information and feeling	These lessons are concerned with practical information, eliciting it and assessing it. Includes information, questions, clues, contradiction, guessing, belief, ready-mades, emotions, values , simplification and clarification.
CoRT 6: Action	The purpose of thinking is to end up with some 'action'. The thinking in this series of lessons deliberately contrasts with that of a contemplative nature.

Source: After de Bono (1973).

creativity, information and feeling and action. Table 5.3 provides more detail descriptions of the skills developed and the ways in which the CoRT materials support this.

To provide some insight into the nature of one of these themes, CoRT 1 is described further. The materials are easy to read and understand.

The different circumstances that de Bono presents to apply the thinking tools or techniques illustrate how easily students could adapt these ways of thinking to virtually any situation at all.

Methodology

These materials are designed to be 'simple, practical, clear, focused and serious' (de Bono 2000). As such they do not require teachers to be trained in their use (unlike most other thinking programmes). The basic format of the lessons enables them to be used over a range of ages (from 6 years to adult) and abilities (IQs: 75 to 140). The lessons are such that various local and/or national issues (context or content) can be integrated into them.

The model lesson sequence:

1 Introduce and describe the thinking 'tool' and explain simply what it does.
2 The teacher models the use of the 'tool'. He/she openly explicates application of the tool for a specified task (given in teacher guide). Individual student responses should be sought.
3 The students work in groups of four, five or six. They are given several specific practice items that reiterate how to use the 'tool' in different problem situations. The teacher is given some example suggestions in the guide that the students are challenged to work out.
4 Once the students have practised using the tool and made suggestions and the teacher has guided them to the target points, the process involved in using the tool is explicated.
5 The principles of using the tool are then described by the teacher.
6 Students are then given projects to work on using the tool.
7 Feedback is gathered from groups regarding their use of the thinking tool for their projects.

The lessons are designed to be used over a single period of about 35 minutes. The students are provided with notes that offer support to explain the tool and the projects they should think about.

Student feedback (or outcomes) can take several forms:

1 In-turn group output: through its spokesperson each group in turn gives its output or adds one more point to the master list.
2 Designated group output: one group is designated to give its output through a spokesperson and then individuals in other groups can comment on this or add to it.
3 Individual within group: here the thinking takes place in groups but the teacher asks named individuals to report on the thinking of their group. The teacher may also respond to ideas from individuals.
4 Individual output: this refers to lessons done on an individual basis.
5 Written output: this can be from groups or individuals and can take the form of notes written in answer to a question. The essay-type output is restricted to individuals and is more suitable for a test situation.

Table 5.4 Outline of CoRT 1

CoRT 1 lessons breadth theme	General description of thinking skill	Example of student projects
Plus, Minus, Interesting (**PMI**) (*What do I think of an idea?*)	Students have to think about ideas and decide: 1 What positive (**plus**) aspects there are 2 What negative (**minus**) aspects there are 3 What intriguing (**interesting**) ideas there are	Idea: all seats should be taken out of buses. **P**: more people can get into each bus; it would be easier to get in and out of bus; buses would be cheaper to make and repair; **M**: passengers would fall over if bus stopped suddenly; old people and disabled people would not be able to use the buses. **I**: Could lead to two types of buses, one with and one without seats; the same bus could do more work.
Consider all Factors (**CAF**) (*Exploration of a situation before developing an idea*)	This is to focus students attention to any factors that can influence a situation, but are not necessarily the most obvious or important	Idea: some years ago in a big city there was a law that all new buildings had to have large parking lots in the basement so that people working in the building would have somewhere to park. After a while this law was changed because it was found to be a mistake. Why? (*They had forgotten to consider the factor that providing parking lots would encourage everyone to drive to work in their cars and so the traffic congestion on the road becomes worse than ever.*)
RULES	This provides the opportunity to practice both PMI and CAF on a proposed rule or rules.	Idea: a group of people sail to an island to start a new life. They abolish money, property and all the old rules. They soon find that nobody wants to do the hard work needed to grow food and build houses. Do a CAF on this situation and then invent some rules.
Consequence and sequence (**C & S**)	C & S is concerned with the action that one or others intends to take. The intention is to extend thinking beyond the immediate into the future. CAF is thinking about a situation at that moment, C & S is about thinking ahead.	Idea: a new electronic robot is invented to replace all human labour in factories. The invention is announced. Do a C & S on this.

CoRT 1 lessons breadth theme	General description of thinking skill	Example of student projects
Aims, Goals, Objectives (**AGO**)	This is concerned with introducing and emphasizing purpose. It is a device intended to focus student attention on intention behind actions.	What are your objectives when you turn on the TV? You are the commander of a spacecraft approaching earth from another planet. What different objectives might you have? Do three alternate AGOs.
Planning	This is intended to bring together objectives (AGO), consequences (C & S), the factors involved (CAF) and the treatment of ideas (PMI).	A general plans his battle. A boy plans his holiday. A family plans a picnic. A girl plans her career when she leaves school.
First Important Priorities (**FIP**)	This is intended to allow students practice in making judgements and prioritising things. This is done after a PMI, CAF, AGO or C & S.	If you were organizing a party what would your priorities be? A 19-year-old boy wants to spend a year traveling around Africa. He asks his parents for some money. What should their priorities be in deciding whether to help him or not?
Alternatives, Possibilities, Choices (**APC**)	This is intended to explore all possibilities, alternatives or choices that can change a situation beyond the obvious.	The brightest girl in the class starts making mistakes in her work on purpose. What possible explanations are there? Fewer people want to be scientists. What possible reasons are there for this and what possible actions can be taken?
Decisions	This brings the opportunity to bring FIP and APC together. In making decisions all factors need to be considered (CAF); be clear about aims and objectives (AGO), assess priorities (FIP), look at consequences (C & S) and discover alternate courses (APC). A PMI can be done on the decision once made.	A politician has strong personal views about capital punishment. She is against such punishment. But she knows that the majority of her voters are in favour of capital punishment. When she has to give her opinion in the senate on the matter, what should she say? A friend of yours has quarrelled with the leader of the gang you hang out with. This friend has dropped out of the gang and wants you to drop out too. You have to decide whether to stay with the gang or not. How do you decide?
Other People's Views (**OPV**)	This is a deliberate effort to focus on other people's views about situations.	Do an OPV on a someone who has just realized they are on the wrong airplane going to the wrong city. A boy refuses to obey his teacher in class. The teacher reports him to the principal who suspends him. The boy's parents object. What are the viewpoints of the boy, his parents, the teacher, the principal and his classmates?

The teacher can operate a master list of points or ideas on the blackboard. Alternatively, the teacher can ask the students to make a master list of all the ideas put forward and can then pick on individual students to read out their lists. After each practice item, a certain amount of discussion may be allowed but this should be kept brief. With the more able students, certain parts of a lesson or even a whole lesson may be given over to individual essay-type outputs but this should be in addition to the lesson, not instead of it.

While students work on projects there should be open discussion. The teacher can question any student or accept comments from any student. The purpose of the discussion is exploratory and there is no need to go through the questions one by one. They are only meant as suggestions. They are intended for use when there is difficulty in getting a discussion going. The teacher need not pretend to have all the answers, and can throw a question back to the class for discussion. The purpose of this discussion is to explore the particular process of thinking on which the lesson is based.

Thinking Together

Dawes et al.'s *Thinking Together* (2000) aimed at KS2, is a series of curriculum activities is based on Mercer's work (1995, 2000; Mercer et al. 1999) focusing on the use of talk to promote thinking.

Aims

A programme of activities designed to improve children's critical and constructive reasoning. Each activity has a cluster of specific aims that contribute toward developing individual appreciation of appropriate ground rules and behaviours that contribute toward more effective group work in thinking skills lessons. The aims of the first five lessons are:

1. *Talk about talk*. Raise awareness about how children talk. Introduce vocabulary (for example: chatter, screech, grumble, whisper, scream, persuade) that describes ways of talking, to enable pupils to practice using them.
2. *Talking in groups*. Start children working together in talk groups. Establish group cohesion. Help children take turns in talking.
3. *Deciding on ground rules*. Raise children's awareness of group talk. To introduce relevant vocabulary (for example: opinion, agreement, reason, critical, assertion).

4 *Using the ground rules*. Allow groups to practice their use of ground rules for talk in a structured context. To develop an under-standing of personal morality.

5 *Reasoning with the ground rules*. To apply all the ground rules for talk to reasoning problems. To ask relevant questions.

Programme design

The 16 activities are designed to be delivered as a series of separate but sequential lessons. The first five lessons provide opportunities for the participating children to experience and reflect upon how it is best to speak to each other when working together on collaborative problems designed to make them think. The later 11 lessons require the children to use their newly developed communication skills to 'reason together' or think out-loud (Mercer 2000).

The main features of a lesson are:

- Aims – which should be made explicit at the start.
- Introduction – this involves explaining the aims and giving instructions for the group work.
- Group work – this is where the children work collaboratively on tasks in their groups.
- Plenary – this is where the lesson aims are re-stated with subsequent discussion about whether the children feel they have achieved them.
- Follow-up work – this is the opportunity for further practice or reinforcement.

Content

The first five lessons are centred on talking and thinking, making it explicit when working with others in groups. The subsequent activities they engage in build on the basic collaborative skills developed and focus on:

- *Persuasion* – developing vocabulary related to this, writing a persuasive letter and finally developing a short role-play that 'persuades' someone to change their mind.
- *Kate's choice* – a friend has stolen something for a laudable reason; the children have to think about the choices they have as Kate or the friend.
- *Who pays?* – a local shop has problems making money because so many school kids steal the sweets and cans of drink; the children

have to consider different viewpoints and discuss the morals and consequences of shoplifting.

- *Water voles* – the plight of water voles throughout a year is considered. The children take on different roles (farmer, animal activist, fox, heron and so forth) in the game to explore factors that affect the voles' survival.
- *Town plan* – this is to encourage children to engage in joint decision making within a planning and environmental context.
- *A fair test* – the children jointly investigate solubility of different materials in the kitchen. They have to hypothesize and plan an investigation that is fair.
- *Non-fiction* – this task involves the children reading to make sense of and deepen their understanding of a scientific concept. They have to apply ground rules for talking when analysing text.
- *Looking into poems* – this task is designed to encourage the children to develop justifications for reasons. They have to read three poems and discuss their understandings and appreciation of each and reach some group agreement about them.
- *Staying friends* – this activity connects with citizenship. The children have to apply the ground rules to discuss the social and moral issues surrounding bullying of friends.
- *Strategy* – this activity involves two groups of pairs working together to solve a mathematical problem. They develop their understanding of a grid system by using coordinates within a computer program to 'find' Hurkle. Their group work involves developing search patterns and making decisions about where Hurkle might be.
- *Making a meaning web* – this task involves using electronic means of communicating with children from other groups, classes or schools. They have to develop a meaning web about the topic they are studying by communicating with each other.

Methodology

This is broadly social constructivist in nature, drawing from Vygotskian ideas about the ways children learn together. It is suggested that the pupils work in 'talk groups' on their tasks. This approach really emphasizes how talking is important to engage in social exchange that encourages more shared and explicit thinking.

The teachers are given guidance about how to use observations of the talking to make some formative assessment of the child's thinking. The questions teachers are guided to consider include 'Does the child initiate conversation?' 'Does the child listen carefully?' 'Can the child describe experiences?' 'Does the child ask questions?' 'Does the child give reasons?' 'Does the child generate alternate viewpoints?' 'Does the child ask others for their views?'

Conclusion

Programmes and materials purporting to develop thinking ability can differ significantly in the ways that they achieve this. The longevity of the programme, the regularity of interventions, the nature of the cognitive skills activated and enhanced, the context within which the thinking is done and the pedagogy required to support it varies significantly. The aims of each of these programmes are very different. The FIE identifies cognitive processes that are often lacking in young people and provides very specific and focused materials to improve these abilities. The focus and mediation required to enhance these is shared to some extent by the STS and the TTTT. The STS however, integrates these skills and aligns them to achieve problem solving capability. The TTTT simplifies and modifies them to provide younger children with strategies to use. De Bono's CoRT materials also strive to enhance cognitive capability, but the approach is much more discussionary and textually driven, unlike FIE which is mostly abstract and often free of language syntax. The context of the CoRT materials provides a wide range of opportunities to consider thinking in everyday life. *Thinking together* emphasizes how the nature of talking can provide insight into the cognitive processes entered into through task engagement. What is often missing in these programmes is clear guidance for teachers to help students see *where* and *how* to use the best tools or techniques explicitly in everyday life situations (now and in future) and which tools or techniques are best in which learning situations and why. If the teacher is thoughtful enough to support application, bridging and transfer, some of these cognitive techniques can be used and integrated in almost any aspect of school life, the curriculum and life outside school.

Key ideas

Key components of general thinking skills programmes include:
- specificity in the nature of cognitive skills to be developed
- explicit introduction to a wide range of cognitive skills
- often sustained intervention (for a year or more)
- introduction to, or activation of, a particular skill(s) followed by range of opportunities to practise the skill
- often structural progression through the programme, with tasks becoming more complex and challenging

The types of tasks developed in the programmes include:
- wide ranging contexts for skill development, from abstract to textual and pictorial to purely conversational
- very varied, little conformity, although some commonalities between FIE, STS and TTTT
- open nature of potential solutions to tasks
- activities perceived flexibly (not necessarily within lesson constraints)
- transfer (or bridging) of thinking processes to other contexts, often everyday life

There is obvious requirement for teacher mediation through:
- questioning
- thinking (wait) time
- giving cues and clues, not answers
- modelling good thinking
- supporting small groups working collaboratively together

Varied forms of outcomes used to make judgements about thinking, include:
- pupils spokesperson for group ideas
- all individuals expected to 'produce' task outcome
- group (poster) presentations
- completed individual worksheet

... the emphasis (curricular or cognitive) will be determined by teachers' understandings of thinking outcomes.

6   The nature of infused thinking

> ... we do not have much of an idea of what a thought *is*, either as 'state of mind' or as a process. Indeed 'thought' as it is usually discussed may be little more than a way of talking and conversing about something we cannot observe. It is a way of talking that functions to give 'thought' some form that is more visible, more audible, more referable, and more negotiable.
>
> (Bruner, *The Culture of Education*)

Thinking while learning is something we should be doing regularly. However, the cognitive processes through which learning arises are not directly visible or audible, as Bruner (1996: 108) points out. Endeavouring to help students become more aware and knowledgeable about their thinking during learning can explicate and make more obvious links between cognitive activity and learning outcomes. Attending to and imaginatively highlighting these processes during content laden learning has led to some educators and psychologists to develop an *infused* approach to teaching thinking.

What is infusion?

Swartz et al. (1998: 528) describe how 'infusion' is the approach that teachers use when blending explicit instruction about thinking skills and processes with content instruction. It involves pedagogic approaches that enhance students' thinking *and* comprehension of the subject matter. Nisbet (1990) claimed that 'programmes that taught component skills', such as the FIE did not guarantee the transfer of thinking skills, and that these skills were perceived as 'add-on' or fragmentary. He argued that thinking should be infused in learning so that it is not separated from its context. Arguably, it is more likely to be incorporated into current practice, and transfer is more likely if thinking is embedded in all teaching and learning in a 'thinking curriculum'. McGuinness (1999) describes it as a 'middle way, which attempts to capture a situated view on learning while at the same time keeping general cognitive development in mind.' She elaborates by suggesting that the 'thinking curriculum' is where teaching thinking is infused across all areas of the curriculum. To develop the infusion approach she explains that 'contexts' within curricular subjects 'have to be identified where the thinking skills and topic understanding are explicitly and spontaneously pursued'. Perkins (1995) also recognizes how thoughtfulness infused into the teaching of subject matter can result in deep conceptual under-standing. Fleetham (2003: 28) acknowledges how infusing thinking is about 'steeping, pervading or instilling' thinking into classrooms. He describes the difference between infusion into a specific subject where thinking skills are used to enhance what is already taught, and infusion across all classroom activity where thinking percolates through all aspects of teaching and learning. In his view, a variety of pedagogical strategies (which he refers to as tools) can be used by any teacher to infuse thinking in their teaching.

Swartz and Parks (1994) describe how varied teaching approaches can be applied in infusion lessons to emphasize different outcomes, such as 'teaching thinking skills and processes', 'fostering collaborative thinking' or support 'learning of content'. They also highlight how methods that promote thoughtful learning will vary from discipline to discipline. Swartz (2001: 266) recognizes how the challenge of 'infused thinking requires refocusing of teaching objectives, standards and themes to encompass a thinking-oriented curriculum'. He argues, however, that teaching higher order thinking should not be technically difficult as the kinds of thinking skills it involves are comparing and contrasting, predicting, finding causes, locating reliable sources of information and deciding on what things to do, which are what we would do almost everyday of our lives. He goes on to explain how it is possible to engage in these thinking skills, operating at a rather superficial level, for example, when just listing a few ways something is different or similar when comparing and contrasting, or allowing guessing as a prediction without reason. However, bringing insight to these mental activities requires more careful and skilful thought. Infusion lessons provide the time and opportunity to help students improve from less skilled thinking to more skilful ways of thinking, not only about the content they are learning, but also about incorporating it appropriately into the conduct of their lives.

Programmes and approaches adopting infusion

Several of these are described in this chapter. First, Swartz and Park's work on how a particular approach aims to promote types of critical and creative thinking (see Figures 1.2 and 6.1) in a range of subject areas, which can eventually extend right across the subjects and throughout

Thinking skill:	Curricular subjects/content areas				
	Language arts	Mathematics	Social studies	Science/Health	Art/Music/Physical Education
Comparing/contrasting					
Classifying					
Parts/whole					
Sequencing					
Uncovering assumptions					
Reliable sources/accurate observations					
Reasons/conclusions					
Causal explanation					
Prediction					
Reasoning by analogy					
GenerallasationConditional reasoning					
Generating possibilities					
Generating metaphors					
Decision making					
Problem solving					

Source: After Swartz and Parks (1994).

Figure 6.1 Framework for a curriculum organizer to integrate content objectives by thinking skill or process

the year groups. The second project described, in this chapter, is McGuinness's Activating Children's Thinking (ACTs I) and Sustaining Children's Thinking (ACTs II), designed for KS2 children. It too is more of an approach rather than a prescribed programme. Third, some elements of de Bono's approaches that can (and are) being used in an infused fashion are also described. His 'thinking hats' and 'action shoes' (1976), that could be usefully and purposely integrated at almost any age or within any subject, are outlined. Fisher's (1997) ideas about infusing thinking into games is also mentioned.

Infusing critical and creative thinking into content instruction

This approach was developed by Swartz and Parks (1994) to help students become better thinkers.

Aim

The aim of infusion in the critical and creative thinking approach is to improve student thinking *and* enhance content learning. Through this approach thinking skills required to achieve subject learning are identified and highlighted. The nature of *skilful* thinking is emphasized to resolve learning tasks. Working and thinking together in a social way is also encouraged. Prompting thoughtful content learning with varied instructional methods include guided reading, asking higher order questions, writing frames for reflection, scaffolded essay writing, cognitive mapping and Socratic dialogue.

Approach design

Teachers use opportunities where both the skill and the subject matter can be taught in a complementary manner. An example of a curriculum organizer intended to guide teachers to map out thinking opportunities within a range of contexts, including mathematics, science and social science, is given in Figure 6.1. Swartz and Parks also provide a wide array of graphic organizers (referred to later as thinking diagrams by McGuiness et al. 2003) to guide and direct the nature of the thinking required for learning tasks. A wide range of graphic organizers have been developed to support each of the various thinking skills listed in Figure 1.2. An example of two graphic organizers are provided here (see Figures 6.2 and 6.3) to illustrate their general format. For the full range of these organizers, designed to guide and articulate a comprehensive list of thinking skills, see Swartz et al. (2000).

The sequence or progression of thinking skill development is not prescribed for the teachers in this approach. They are encouraged to incorporate thinking into the curriculum as they proceed through a scheme of work or unit of study. Teachers are guided to scan the curriculum and identify where *a few powerful examples* of using a thinking skill or process could be developed. Designing the lessons to

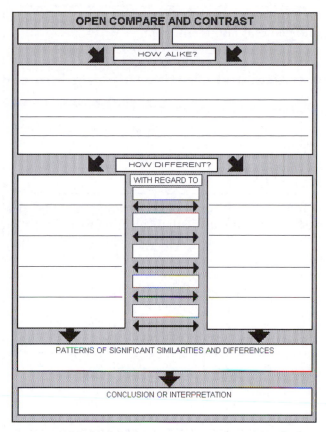

Source: From Swartz and Parks (1994).

Figure 6.2 Open compare and contrast graphic organizer

clearly and effectively demonstrate the thinking *and* teach significant curriculum objectives is strongly encouraged. The 'best fit' approach is recommended to highlight dramatic opportunities and add interest to lessons. Once several lessons have been developed a systematic review across the curriculum is suggested so that a more comprehensive coverage of the thinking skills is possible (as indicated in Figure 6.1).

Swartz et al. argue that the relevance of the thinking then becomes more apparent. There is a larger pool of tasks and contexts for teachers to share good practice, more opportunities for the thinking to even be evaluated or assessed. Eventual vertical (throughout years), as well as horizontal (throughout subject areas) integration can be developed, all of which should contribute to a lasting curriculum reform (Swartz et al. 2000: 556).

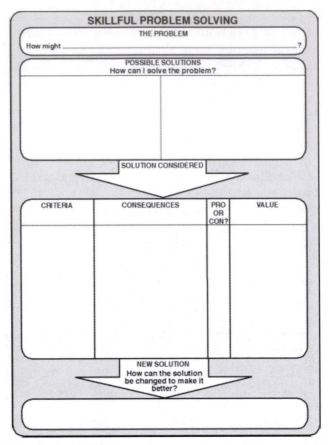

Source: From Swartz et al. (1994).

Figure 6.3 Problem solving

Organization of infusion lessons

These lessons are conducted using a four-step strategy. First, the teacher introduces the students to the thinking skill or process by demonstrating its importance. Second, the students are guided with explicit prompts (using the graphic organizers) to engage in the thinking as they learn about the content in a specific subject area. This part of the lesson provides the opportunity for the students to carry out the thinking to learn in an orderly sequential manner through the scaffolded support of the graphic organizers. Third, the teacher asks the students reflective questions. The intention is that once the activity is completed, the student is distanced from *what* they were thinking about to consider *how* they were thinking. Lastly the teachers provide additional opportunities for students to engage in similar thinking again, but with an opportunity to be more independent (Swartz et al. 2000: 9).

Content

An example lesson focuses on thinking about the accuracy of observation and reliability of sources of information. The lesson begins with a teacher-staged scuffle in the corridor outside the classroom. The student witnesses then provide accounts of what happened. The teacher then compares the conflicting accounts about what happened. In the light of these accounts the battle of Lexington, in 1775, at the start of the Revolutionary War, is then considered. As students attempt to determine which of the twentieth-century historians, and then which of the eyewitnesses, gave the most accurate account of the battle, they reflect on why one historical account may be more accurate than another. The thinking in this history class is scaffolded using the graphic organizer for problem solving (Figure 6.3). Swartz et al. (1998), however, indicate that not all lessons lend themselves to infused thinking. They say 'selecting good contexts for infusion lessons is crucial in designing effective instruction' (Swartz et al. 1998: 553). They elaborate by describing how the key to choosing appropriate contexts is finding examples that 'offer rich development of the thinking process and rich instruction of the content objective'. Some examples, illustrating how lessons can be elaborated to support thinking are detailed in Table 6.1.

As can be seen from the examples described above, 'infusion lessons are crafted to bring into content instruction an explicit emphasis on skilful thinking so that students can improve the way they think. Classroom time is spent on the thinking skill, or process, as well as on content'. (Swartz and Parks 1994).

Methodology

Using the graphic organizers (or 'thinking maps', as they are referred to in McGuiness et al.'s ACTs) are a key element to the infusion approach, as they focus and clarify the thinking steps to reach a solution of some kind. There are also complementary lists of questions that guide what is appropriate for the teachers to ask. The guiding questions that support them involve compare-and-contrast thinking, which would be used by the teacher if the class were studying the lives of Douglas and Lincoln (outlined in Table 6.1) for example:

Table 6.1 Some examples of 'rich' opportunities for students to develop their thinking within subject content

Learning task (in subject context)	Elaboration of the learning task to support explicit thinking	Thinking skill developed (taken from Table 1.2)
Literacy lesson about the lives of Abraham Lincoln and Fredrick Douglass.	Composing a list about how their lives were similar. Describing how their lives were different through focused analysis. Connecting observations through describing patterns of significant similarities or differences. Development of a conclusion about their lives.	Compare and contrast.
Primary-level lesson to develop listening skills and vocabulary development based around exploration of the story of 'Henny Penny'.[1]	Discussion around the question. Should the other animals trust Henny Penny? How can we determine if Henny Penny is reliably informed? Reflection, once all the animals are led into the Fox's den, of the purpose of considering reliability of information and the potential impact, in life, if information given is believed uncritically.	Reliability of sources of information.
Reading comprehension of the story 'Sarah, Plain and Tall' by Patricia Maclachlan (1985).	After reading about Sarah's background considering when what they could do and with what consequences in the main character's position when she has to decide whether to stay with the family she has joined in Oklahoma from her home in Maine (2000 miles away) in the later part of the 19th century.	Decision making.

Note: [1] Jacobs, J. *English Folk and Fairy Tales*. Available at: http://www.authorama.com/english-fairy-tales-47.html
Source: Analysis of Swartz (2001: 268–9).

- How are they similar?
- How are they different?
- What similarities and differences seem significant?
- What categories or patterns do you see in the significant similarities and differences?
- What interpretation or conclusion is suggested by the significant similarities and differences?

These scaffolds could provide the support for students to respond in a systematic, organized and detailed way to studying the lives of two very different men or any characters in historical or present-day contexts. The scaffolds could also be used to compare and contrast any objects, places or happenings in almost any subject area.

It is intended that students work together when using their graphic organizers, so that they can discuss and exchange ideas. Teachers are expected to facilitate reflection on the thinking engaged in by encouraging group interaction and facilitating class discussion that metacognates on how different students reached their conclusions and where else they might apply the thinking technique. Teachers are also expected to model good thinking and generally foster thoughtful student behaviours. Students are encouraged to question each other in different ways. They should question for clarification (if they don't quite understand others' ideas); question to extend an idea (and in so doing develop elaboration of suggestions) and question to challenge (to check out the robustness of an idea). In summary an infusion lesson is organized in the following way:

- introduction;
- thinking actively;
- thinking about thinking;
- applying your thinking.

They should achieve subject understanding as well as explicating the thinking involved.

Activating Children's Thinking (ACTs I) and Sustaining Children's Thinking (ACTs II)

McGuinness et al. (2003) describe infusion as that which 'introduces into one thing a second thing which gives it extra life, vigour and a new significance' – something that introduces an invigorating approach into content instruction. Beside this additional invigoration, which can lead to deeper understanding, they claim that the benefits of this approach are that:

- thinking skills are directly matched with appropriate content in the curriculum;
- classroom time is used optimally;
- teaching for thoughtfulness is directly supported across the curriculum;
- transfer of learning can be more easily promoted in other areas of the curriculum and reinforced at later stages.

From the initial Activating Children's Thinking Skills (ACTs I) McGuiness et al. have developed Sustaining Children's Thinking Skills (ACTs II).

Aims of the ACTs programme

They describe how their project is based on five aims or principles: for students to learn meaningfully; to infuse thinking across the curriculum; to allow time for discussion of thinking to make it more explicit; to acquire specific skills and strategies to become a good thinker and promote the development of a 'thinking curriculum' in a 'thinking classroom'.

The cognitive aims of the ACTs programme are developed from Swartz and Parks' (1994) thinking skills taxonomy. The specific cognitive processes emphasized include:

- Compare and contrast (how are things similar or different?)
- Parts/whole relationships (how do parts of something make up its whole?)
- Sequencing (ordering or ranking information.)
- Uncovering assumptions (what does that mean?)
- Reliability of sources (where is this information from? Is it trustworthy?)
- Reasons/conclusions (why is something so?)
- Causal explanation (how does one thing affect another?)
- Prediction (involves hypothesizing: given X, what next?)
- Reasoning by analogy (paralleling ideas within different contexts).
- Generalization (developing a framework, model or suggestion that connects multiple pieces of information together).
- Conditional reasoning (if this, then that must be so).
- Generating possibilities (creating new ideas).
- Creating metaphors (devising a unique analogy).
- Decision making (weighing up pros and cons to inform a view or decision).
- Problem solving (includes thinking up different possibilities to reaching a solution).

Opportunities for potential development of each of these kinds of skills can be identified within subjects and then mapped out across the curriculum (as Figure 6.1 suggests). The lessons are then redesigned to inaugurate the thinking. McGuinness et al. (2003) indicate how this approach enables pupils to go beyond merely absorbing information and provides the opportunity to effortfully search and uncover meaning or impose and analyse structure. The aim is to develop thinking where it opportunely supports the learning engaged in and subject matter to be thought about. As Swartz and Parks (1994), highlight identification of appropriate potential opportunities for developing a range of different types of thinking in the curriculum is central to the approach. The TT series, described in an earlier chapter, fits the infused approach (McGuinness 2005), with thinking enhancing and supporting subject content understanding.

Design of the programme

This is for the teacher, and/or department and/or whole school to decide. Development of a conceptual map can aid planning and clarification about which skills should be emphasized where and when. The intention is that all the skills identified should be activated and practiced across the curriculum. How often each skill should be practiced and whether all skills should be developed within a month, semester, year or several years is unclear.

Organization of the lessons

McGuiness et al. (2003) describe the important components of an infused thinking lesson (see Figure 6.4). There are four clearly defined stages that highlight the focus as the lessons progress.

Initiation of infusion lessons includes explication of the purpose of the learning, which includes introducing the subject concepts to be studied and the way that a particular thinking skill will support this. The second phase is where the children actively work together in small groups on challenging tasks. They are encouraged to discuss ideas and question each other. Thinking diagrams (developed from Swartz and Parks' graphic organizers) are used to direct their cognitive activity. The third phase after the task is completed centres on reflection. The children are guided to share their thoughts about the thinking they have engaged in as well as evaluating the ways they approached the tasks. The final phase is about applying their thinking, considering where else they might use the thinking – maybe in school (described as near transfer) or at home in everyday life (described as far transfer). Thinking actively constitutes the majority of the lesson.

Content

All the thinking lessons are developed within a curricular context. Pupils are guided through lessons within history, geography, science, English, physical education, mathematics, personal and social education or art, with the type of thinking to be developed in mind, for example *comparing and contrasting* objects/events; *making predictions* about the

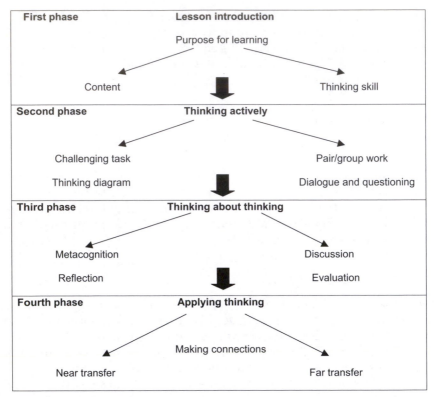

Source: From McGuinness et al. (2003).

Figure 6.4 Structure of an infusion lesson

outcome of investigations; *examining alternative courses of action* for literary characters. Opportune thinking can naturally support the subject learning. Sequencing, for example, is very appropriate when considering historical events or time-lines of industrial, social, cultural or any other development. Within science, sequence and timing are pivotal in life cycles and stages of growth. Physical education, which focuses on dance, can provide the opportunity to consider choreographical order of beginning, middle and end of routines. Mathematics naturally offers the potential to explore and predict patterns and sequences within a range of numbers, integers, fractions and so forth.

Table 6.2 provides some descriptions of the thinking engaged in various subject contexts.

McGuiness et al. describe how there are six types of thinking that the infusion lessons seek to develop. Within each of these types of thinking, specific cognitive processes are promoted. The six types of thinking are:

Table 6.2 Descriptions of some ACTs activities that develop particular types of thinking

Thinking skill	Subjects		
	English	**Physical education**	**Science**
Whole/parts relationship	Parts of a sentence. Students are encouraged to consider components of a sentence, including adjectives, apostrophes, full stops, capital letters, verbs, nouns, pronouns etc. They then focus on a particular part of the sentence that might be missing and explain what would happen if it were missing and then define the function of the missing part.	A football match. Pupils are asked to think about the important parts of a football match. They should identify parts as goalkeeper, lines, ball, defender, net, coach, referee. They then think about what would happen if a particular part was missing and how it would affect the match and then clarify what they believe the function or job of that part is.	Parts of a plant. Pupils are introduced to the parts of a plant. They have to consider what would happen to the plant if a particular part were missing.
Comparing and contrasting	Pupils are expected to compare two different poems about winter, 'Jack Frost' by Gabriel Setoun and 'Jack Frost in the Garden' by John P. Smeeton. They are to consider the similarities and differences in language, vocabulary, styles, mood, events, location, time, etc.		Investigating similarities and differences in two materials or two objects. Pupils compare and contrast a range of properties, for example melting and boiling points.
	History	**Personal and social education**	
Decision making	The Irish famine. Watch the video *Days of Hunger* up to point where the daughter dies. The pupils have to develop possible ideas for things the family could do and then decide which would be best and why.	Bullying. This lesson would be introduced by reading the book 'I feel bullied'. Mixed groups of students are given the making choices thinking diagram. They have to consider all the different ways that Michael (character in the book) could deal with bullying and then consider one way he would deal with it and think about the consequences of that particular way.	

Table 6.2 continued

Thinking skill	Subjects
Problem solving	**History** (cont.) Attacking a round tower. The context of this activity is the Vikings in Ireland. The construction of a round tower had been previously taught. The pupils had to consider difficulties encountered by Monks and Vikings attacking/defending their round towers. The pupils first focus on defining the problem, then generating solutions and finally selecting the best possible solution on the basis of consequences.

1   Searching for meaning and understanding.
2   Thinking critically.
3   Developing flexible and creative thinking.
4   Problem solving.
5   Decision making.
6   Metacognition.

Searching for meaning and understanding

This type of thinking focuses on uncovering patterns in information, analyzing and classifying objects and clarifying ideas. The types of cognitive processing involved include sequencing, ordering, ranking; sorting, grouping, classifying; analyzing parts and wholes; recognizing similarities and differences; finding patterns and relationships; comparing and contrasting.

Thinking critically

This type of thinking is about scrutinizing and adopting a sceptical stance to assess reasonableness of ideas and examine possible links between cause and effect. The kinds of cognitive processes activated are: making predictions and formulating hypotheses; making conclusions, explaining conclusions, not making inaccurate assumptions; distinguishing fact from opinion; determining bias, reliability or evidence; being concerned about accuracy and connecting cause and effect.

Developing flexible and creative thinking

This type of thinking involves generating ideas, looking for alternatives, building and combining ideas, acknowledging that questions can have more than one answer and being able to take multiple perspectives.

Problem solving and decision making

These are often combined, and are seen as more complex because they build on other kinds of thinking (for example generating possibilities, classifying information, relating reasons and conclusions). They involve the cognitive processes of identification, clarification, generation of solutions, predicting consequences, deciding on course of action, evaluation of effectiveness of solutions, prediction and so forth.

Metacognition

McGuinness et al. (2003) describe this as crucial for enhancing thinking skills. It involves the reflection and evaluation of the thinking used (by themselves and others) in the learning tasks.

Methodology

McGuinness emphasizes how ACTs is a 'methodology' to enhance thinking skills. Initially developed for upper primary schools in Northern Ireland, this approach has been successfully adopted and adapted for KS3 and A-level classes (McGuinness 2000). This methodology requires a different approach to those lessons where content understanding is paramount and transmission of factual information is key.

Six thinking hats

Edward de Bono uses a variety of different methods that he describes as 'tools' to 'teach thinking directly'. He has developed the CoRT thinking programme (1976), which was discussed briefly in Chapter 5, and other 'tools' that can be used in a more 'infused' way. An example of an 'infused' tool that could be used to support development of conceptual understanding of subject matter and involve specific kinds of thinking is the six hats approach. This approach helps children recognize how to use thinking techniques in a organized way, and offers both critical and creative opportunities for thinking, which are not constrained by curricular outcomes.

Aims

This technique is designed to enable the learners to think in different ways rather than engaging in several different types of thinking simultaneously. Learners wear different thinking hats (metaphorically rather than literally). Teachers often say 'put your thinking cap on'. For example, the red hat symbolizes emotion and feelings (this can be related to getting 'hot under the collar' or 'steaming hot', often referred to when describing emotive thoughts). The green hat represents new ideas (green is often a colour associated with new growth of plant shoots). De Bono's intention is to reduce confusion and bias in the way people may perceive or review a problem, by using a method to separate out aspects of thinking about something. He utilizes the hat idea because it is an item of clothing you don't keep on all the time, you can quickly change it to another colour and it conveys the sense of 'role-play' whilst 'wearing' it. Table 6.3 summarizes the nature of thinking that the children should adopt when wearing that coloured hat.

Approach(es)

This can be simply to provide a problem or issue and ask the class to put on a coloured hat and apply that thinking. The method can be developed to become more or less complex through single or paired hats, a combination of hats or all six hats used similarly by all class participants, small groups, or even thinking individualistically on personal projects.

Often, in developing the use of the thinking hats, de Bono advocates learning to use them, initially, in pairs – for example, white and red hat thinking. White hat thinking is neutral and focuses on facts. What is known about this situation or problem and what would it be useful to

Table 6.3 De Bono's (1976) six thinking hats: a technique that develops particular kinds of thinking

Coloured hat	Direction of thinking	Focus question(s)
White hat	Focus on the facts, figures and information available.	What information do we have? What do we need to know? What information do we need to get? What questions do we need to ask?
Red hat	Description of emotions, feelings, hunches and intuition without giving reasons.	What do I feel about this matter right now?
Black hat	Focus on what could go wrong. Identifying faults or weaknesses. Applying caution.	Does this fit the facts? Will it work? Is it safe? Can it be done?
Yellow hat	Focus on identifying the value or advantages in something. Focus on the benefits and savings there might be.	Why should it be done? What are the benefits? Why it is a good thing to do?
Green hat	Focus on exploration of new and alternate proposals, suggestions, and ideas.	What can we do here? Are there some different ideas/alternate things we can do?
Blue hat	Focus is on thinking about thinking.	What are we here for? What are we thinking about? What is the end goal?

know? The information and data regarding a situation are viewed dispassionately. Red hat thinking is all about what do you feel. No rationalization required. In fact de Bono states that red-hat thinking should not be justified as that would 'destroy the whole purpose' (1976: 83) of using the hat. Like Goleman (1995) and Lake and Needham (1995) he acknowledges that emotions can influence the nature and course of thinking. Another pair, black and yellow, support thinking about the negative aspect and then the positive aspects of a particular idea or suggestion. The blue hat is metacognitive, so could be used after any other (permutation of) hat thinking. In developing thinking through the use of this technique, de Bono provides thinking exercises, including:

- Can computers do red-hat thinking?
- Which of the following are white-hat thinking and which are red-hat thinking?
  - Pollution is a growing problem
  - I feel pollution is now the world's number one problem
  - We are not doing enough to control pollution
  - Pollution is everyone's business
  - Polls show that people do care about pollution
  - I do not know what I can do about pollution
- Some-one suggests to you that you should take up one of three hobbies: gardening, carpentry, disco dancing. Do some white-hat thinking on each. Then follow this with red-hat thinking.
- For a young person thinking about choosing a career, what aspects would include white-hat thinking and what aspects would red-hat thinking cover?

The most sophisticated use is to eventually utilize all six kinds of thinking together. However, if all kinds of thinking are used, normally one kind of thinking is applied at a time, in a sequential way. As with all the infused thinking approaches, the teacher makes the pedagogic choices about where, what and how to integrate thinking into the content-laden curriculum. It is useful for teachers considering using de Bono's 'hats' to think of them as techniques and define them as pedagogical strategies (like those in Leat's *Thinking Through* ... series) to support development of different kinds of thinking. Blue-hat thinking is reflective or metacognative. Red-hat thinking is emotional, where students might be encouraged to develop maieutic thinking (Lipman 2003: 127) or emotional sensitivity as Daniel Goleman (1995) describes it. White-hat thinking is where students consider all that is positive about an idea and black-hat thinking is when students are encouraged to think about the disadvantages of an idea. Green-hat thinking often encourages more creative ideas and black-hat is often more critical in nature. Green- and black-hat thinking can directly support development of creative and critical thinking respectively. Consider the proposal that all cars should be yellow. Black-hat thinking would include notions about loss of individuality in the colour of your car, losing your car in the supermarket car park or even difficulties for crime scene witnesses in describing notable characteristics of a car. Green-hat thinking could include development of novel ideas like customization developing in the form of 'shades' of yellow and other artwork or the shape of a car becoming more diverse and pronounced to make them visibly different.

Flexible content

As can be seen from the above examples, any colour hat or type of thinking can be applied to life, school and/or subject learning. The content is not restricted but teachers need experience in how to recognize the opportunities to develop these kinds of thinking.

Six action shoes

This is very similar to the six hats but instead of just *thinking* about the issues, problems or situations the shoes simulate thinking about possible courses of action and their consequences. Imagining putting on shoes, implies that action can be taken by 'walking the talk' rather than just thinking about things. Navy formal shoes, for example, highlight 'routine tasks' or ways of working. When wearing them, metaphorically, thinking about how steps in the routines of school, learning or life can be changed to improve or address the situation or problem faced can be stimulated. Grey trainers symbolize actively researching something and making observations. Brown brogues are associated with entrepreneurial activity. Orange gumboots represent action; pink slippers a humanistic perspective and purple riding boots symbolize authority. Wearing each of these in turn, like the hats, can stimulate creative thinking in particular directions about consequences of actions. A more sophisticated approach could be wearing two different shoes at the same time. In an educational sense careful consideration about where it is appropriate to use these is called for. Reflecting on courses of action taken by historical, literary or political characters can invoke creative and critical thinking. For example, how would the Second World War have developed if Churchill wore pink slippers? In Shakespeare's *Romeo and Juliet*, would there have been a different outcome if Romeo wore grey trainers for longer?

Developing infused thinking through the use of games

Fisher illustrates how to develop different cognitive strategies (both critical and creative) through the use of games (Fisher 1997). This approach can be fun and develop a very comprehensive set of thinking skills (Fisher 1997: 4). These embrace most of those already described in the ACTs approach. Fisher highlights how this approach can offer variety in learning activities and can provide very motivating introduction or plenaries for lessons or topics of learning. There is obvious opportunity, depending on the style of game, to create opportunities for both critical and creative thinking. To focus the thinking the kinds of skilful questions suggested include:

- *Thinking about the game*:
  - Is the game easy or difficult? Why?
  - What other games do you know like this? How are they similar? Different?
  - What kind of game is it? Can you categorize it?
  - Do you know the rules? Do they make sense?
- *Thinking in the game*:
  - What do you need to do to win, or achieve your target in the game?
  - What strategy do you need to use to win?
  - What will stop you winning?
- *Thinking through the game*:
  - Were you successful? Why or why not?
  - What strategy did you use? Was it a good strategy?

Fisher advocates the *community of enquiry* approach (just as in P4C) because in a community setting all the students can see and hear each other; they have a turn in playing; they have time to think about the questions; they have the opportunity to raise questions and time is made to discuss and review participation in the game.

Conclusion

Kirkwood (2001a) supports the development of infusing thinking into content instruction because it should have 'the added benefit of enhancing children's understanding of syllabus topics (and thus raising their attainment), while simultaneously providing many natural opportunities for a range of skills to be learnt and practices in varied contexts'. As McGuiness et al. (2003: 12) emphasize, content instruction can become invigorated and can lead learners to deeper understanding. Kirkwood further argues that children require sustained support in developing their application of thinking skills, so that they value it and become more independent in reaching judgements. Progression and sustainability are still issues for those developing curricular frameworks to support infused thinking in schools.

Infusing thinking requires teachers to be familiar with the types of thinking *and* the nature of cognitive skills that it is appropriate to develop in learning. Planning sustained and progressive development of thinking skills also requires empathy with and understanding of a different kind of pedagogy that promotes more open exchange and appreciation that there is 'no one right answer' in thinking. Teaching that explicates the sharing of thinking strategies is significantly different from the teaching required to 'transmit' information and factual details.

In summary, teachers need to be thoughtful in the way that they design their curriculum programs so that thinking skills are comprehensively developed. They should also organize their lessons to emphasize appropriately the cognitive processes and nature of thinking required alongside the content objectives. Finally, they should develop a different set of teaching skills that draw out from learners their mental processing to reach solutions.

Retaining the infusion of thinking within content teaching can constrain the nature and extent of the thinking involved. Applying tools like de Bono's thinking hats and action shoes techniques can offer additional stimulation to create ideas and offer more opportunities to think outside the context of the curriculum and generally 'think outside the box'.

Key ideas

> It is possible to develop content understanding and emphasize the thinking strategies and cognitive skills required to achieve learning.

> Teachers need to understand *what* constitutes (in a conceptual and cognitive sense) an effective and useful *infusion* lesson.

> Teachers need to plan for comprehensive and progressive development of types of thinking and their associated cognitive skills.

A wide range of techniques can be used to explicate thinking in lessons.

Teachers need to develop understanding and practice in a mediational pedagogy that supports development of thinking.

A comprehensive breadth of graphic organizers provides general scaffolded support to *direct* thinking in particular types of learning situations.

Teachers require different pedagogical approaches to transmit content objectives *and* draw out cognitive processing.

The emphasis on thinking (processes and/or outcomes) will be influenced by teachers desired learning outcomes.

Further exploration is required to investigate the tensions between pedagogy concerned with ensuring conceptual understanding and that, which elucidates cognitive processing.

7 Effectiveness of thinking programmes

> The aims of illuminatory evaluation are to study the innovatory programme: how it operates; how it is influenced by the various school situations in which it is applied; what those directly concerned regard as its advantages and disadvantages; and how students' intellectual tasks and academic experiences are most affected. It aims to discover and document what it is like to be participating in the scheme, whether as teacher or pupil; and in addition, to discern and discuss the innovation's most significant features, recurring concomitants and critical processes. In short, it seeks to address and to illuminate a complex array of questions.
>
> (Palett and Hamilton 1977: 10)

As Palett and Hamilton (1977: 10) indicate, there are many influencing factors that can impact upon the success of an innovative programme introduced into a school. Factors including school culture, management support, teacher, pupil and parent expectations, resourcing levels, timetable constraints, differing interpretations about implementation can all affect *how* a programme works and *what* level of impact it will have. Assessing the impact on thinking is even more challenging because judgements have to be made about what constitutes *better* or *more skilful* thinking. As McGuinness (2005: 107) describes, we wish students to 'go beyond the mere recall of factual information to develop a deeper understanding of topics, to be more critical about evidence, to solve problems and think flexibly, to make reasoned judgements and decisions rather than jumping to conclusions.'

This chapter considers the evidence for this kind of success through the implementation of thinking programmes in schools. For some there is copious evidence of particular kinds of impact, for others there are scant indications of success. The impact of thinking programmes has often been measured through IQ, intelligence or standardized tests of some kind. The implicit nature, quality and extent of thinking, however, is difficult to assess accurately in a direct, testable way. Varying evidence, often of a quantifiable nature, is presented by experts, authors, researchers and developers to illustrate success or otherwise of different programmes and approaches and their associated or inferred impact on students performance. Judgements about improved performance ranges from increased use of particular words such as 'but' or 'because' in discussing problems (Mercer et al. 1999) or (better) adaptiveness to work demands (Feuerstein et al. 1981) or (even better) tactical manoeuvres in basketball (Bell 2005). Teachers, researchers and policy makers need to be aware of the substantiated or unsubstantiated claims of the various approaches and, even more importantly, become cognizant of the research still needed to measure improvements in thoughtful learning.

This chapter provides a somewhat chronological and descriptive overview of reviews assessing the impact of thinking skills. More detailed findings about specific programmes and approaches are considered later to try and ascertain indications for teachers wishing to know 'what works?' (Hattie et al. 1996; Marzano et al. 2001) 'to what extent?' (Slavin 2004) and 'why?'

Nickerson's four components for teaching thinking

Nickerson (1981), in an early review, focused around the question 'Can thinking skills be taught?' He highlighted four components of teaching programmes that enhanced thinking skills: abilities, methods, knowledge and attitudes. By 'abilities' he meant how students should exercise their minds (not practising computational type operations, now readily carried out by computers) and he argued that teachers should concentrate more on having students think and not worry so much about *what* they learn. The second component was to use systematic methods or strategies, consciously and appropriately – for example, developing step-by-step thinking to support problem solving or using mnemonics to memorize ideas, etc. His third component was knowledge. He described how we underestimate the amount of knowledge needed to become a skilled performer in something, such as music or art. He argued that chess players, artists, scientists, writers and so forth require years of accumulated knowledge before they are able to perform skilfully and that, characteristically, we use our 'thinking abilities less than optimally' (Nickerson 1981: 24). Nickerson's fourth component centres on attitudes; he describes how evidence indicated that students who were genuinely interested in what they were learning were more likely to learn effectively than those who were not. Positive attitudes that could foster improved intellectual performance included, a strong belief in learning, a lively sense of curiosity, a sense of pride in one's work and respect for opinions differing from one's own.

Nisbet's evaluation

Some years later, Nisbet (1990) reviewed the research literature on evaluation of thinking programmes. He described how 'infusion' and 'philosophy for children' were current and developing perspectives of the ways in which thinking should be developed. He also highlighted how the use of computers heralded the onset of a new approach, requiring a conscious application of thinking strategies. He detailed how methods that could make thinking explicit and enable the process to be understood more clearly included: modelling (by the teacher, of ways problems could be solved); cooperative learning (having students reason to each other); discussion, argumentation and Socratic questioning. He claimed, however, that all these methods to explicate thinking were underpinned by metacogniton. He described the aim of metacognition as giving pupils practice in monitoring their thinking, making the strategies explicit and then internalizing them so they become part of their habitual mode of thinking.

McGuinness's review

Some years after Nisbet's evaluation, McGuinness (1999) was commissioned by the DfEE[1] to review thinking skills programmes in the UK. Her review was intended to 'identify current approaches to developing children's thinking and to evaluate their effectiveness' and consider the 'general direction of current and future research and how it might translate into classroom practice' (McGuinness 1999: 1). She identified the emerging core concepts in a framework for developing thinking skills. She indicated that, although the theoretical emphasis can vary, the general framework included: the need to make thinking skills explicit within a curriculum; teaching through a form of coaching; taking a metacognitive perspective; collaborative learning (including computer-mediated learning); creating dispositions and habits of good thinking; generalizing the (content) framework to (include) curricular thinking; and to develop thinking classrooms and thinking schools. She emphasized, however, that considerable evaluation still needed to be done to link the critical features of the framework to learning outcomes in different contexts. She categorized and reviewed three types of 'interventional' programmes: those intended to develop general think-

---

[1] DfEE is the government Department of Education and Employment, as was in 1999. It is now the Department for Education and Skills (DfES).

ing skills (such as FIE); those that target subject specific learning, such as science (CASE, CAME) and those that can be infused across the curriculum (ACTs). McGuiness (1999) also argued that a successful prototype for developing curricular materials possesses strong theoretical underpinnings; well designed and contextualized materials, explicit pedagogy; teaching support and programme evaluation. She rightly emphasizes that curricular materials alone are not sufficient. In her review of the evidence, she suggests the extent to which the various existing programmes affect pupils' thinking:

> CASE ... succeeded in raising pupils' grades in GCSE public examinations (on average 1 grade) two to three years after the programme had been completed. Philosophy for Children has an impact across a wide variety of cognitive and social development measures. On the other hand, Blagg's evaluation of instrumental enrichment showed no direct learning gains but did impact positively on attitudes and behaviour.
>
> (McGuiness 1999: 29)

Other general findings

As Cotton (1991), McGuinness (1999), Kite (2000) and Wilson (2000) all note, the increasing interest in thinking skills and the incorporation of related work into teaching programmes has led to many more calls for reviews of, and analysis of, the evidence.

Cotton (1991) summarized findings from 56 research studies and reviews that indicated how nearly all programmes and practices investigated found positive gains. In her review, most of the studies were carried out in the US. They indicated how a focus on thinking resulted in development and improvements of 'high-order thinking skills' (including analysis, synthesis, evaluation, predicting, making inferences, self-questioning and other metacognitive functions) formulating hypothesizes, drawing conclusions, elaborating, solving problems, making decisions, identifying assumptions, determining bias, recognizing logical inconsistencies and others. The range of subjects within which improved achievement was noted in content-based work were mathematics, general science, chemistry, art, social studies and geography. Other notable impacts of thinking programmes included improved performance on IQ, SAT and thinking skills tests, length of time spent on task and level of participation in learning.

Generally those that looked at achievement over time found that thinking-skills instruction accelerated the learning gains of participants, and those of an experimental or quasi-experimental nature showed that students developed skills that outperformed those in control groups. Gains in creative and critical thinking, metacognition and inquiry training were noted where instruction specifically focused on these skills. Asking higher order questions and lengthening wait time were also shown to foster thinking skill development and increase student participation.

Wilson (2000) highlighted how there are many examples of good practice in classrooms. There is much enthusiasm for teaching thinking but there is a lack of clear guidance about *how* teachers should deal with the increasing pressures of the curriculum to successfully change their teaching focus to create a climate of enquiry.

Higgins et al. (2004) applied a more sophisticated meta-analysis approach to explore the impact of thinking skills programmes. They identified 191 studies and used a narrative synthesis method (synthesizing from the literature whether the researchers had successfully provided evidence that they had achieved the goals of their studies) to evaluate the effectiveness of thinking-skills interventions on pupils. This involved a literal review of the aims and outcomes of the studies on thinking programmes. They attempted to interpret findings sufficiently to make 'fuzzy generalizations' (Bassey 1999). They referred to this as a 'best estimate of trustworthiness' (BET). Their intention was to explore the empirical evidence available to support the teaching of thinking in schools in order to test the conclusions of the positive but largely descriptive reviews previously undertaken (McGuinness 1999; Wilson 2000).

They applied a working definition of a thinking-skills programme for the purposes of their review that stated:

> thinking skills interventions are approaches or programmes which identify for learners translatable, mental processes and/or which require learners to plan, describe and evaluate their thinking and learning. These can therefore be characterised as approaches or programmes which:
> - require learners to articulate and evaluate specific learning approaches; and/or
> - identify specific cognitive and related affective or cognitive processes that are amenable to instruction.
>
> (Higgins et al. 2004: 1)

The programmes that are commonly used in schools, and that Higgins et al. (2004) sought evidence about, included Instrumental Enrichment (Feuerstein et al. 1980), Philosophy for Children (Lipman et al. 1980), Cognitive Acceleration through Science Education (Adey et al. 2001) and Somerset Thinking Skills (Blagg et al. 2003). In their synthesis of the evaluative evidence of the impact of the different programmes they gave credence to the various verifiable and validating measures taken to illustrate success (Higgins et al. 2004: 37). They examined evaluative studies from peer-reviewed academic journals and conference papers and noted appropriate aspects of the study design, namely whether pre-tests and post-tests were carried out, whether there was a control group, whether teachers and students completed reflective questionnaires and so forth, within the research study. Studies containing both quantitative and qualitative data were selected for consideration but it was noted that the quality of reporting for qualitative findings was often rather opaque. The findings from this narrative synthesis indicated that programmes such as CASE (Adey and Shayer 2002), Metacognitive Strategies (DeCorte 1999), Instrumental Enrichment (Feuerstein 1989), the use of talk to develop reasoning (Mercer et al. 1999) all had a positive impact on cognitive abilities. However, the differential nature of the impact of these approaches did not enable clear comparative generalizations to be made about *how* the programmes affect student performance. Higgins et al. (2005) subsequently developed a more rigorous, quantifiable approach to ascertaining the effects of interventions, which aimed to highlight the aspects of the programmes that could offer most potential in the classroom. They focused more closely on the studies that included standardized tests (such as Raven's matrices or other tests devised by the researchers involved), curricular performance (in tests or school examinations) of the pupils and those that clearly showed how experimental groups performed significantly better than control groups. The qualitative nature of many studies is indicated through the rigorous selection of only 29 of the original 191 relevant publications initially identified. Their review approach highlighted how

> ... quantitative synthesis indicates that thinking skills programmes and approaches are effective in improving the performance on tests of cognitive measures (such as Raven's matrices) with an overall effect size of 0.62. (This effect would move a class ranked at 50th place in a league table of similar classes to 26th or a percentile gain of 24 points). However, these approaches also have a considerable impact on curricular outcomes with the same effect size of 0.62. The overall effect size (including cognitive, curricular and affective measures) was 0.74.
>
> (Higgins et al. 2005: 3)

Higgins et al. (2005) also compared effects of general instructional strategies with those that specifically focus on the cognitive. They found that reported gains from other educational interventions appear not to produce such impressive effects. Hattie et al. (1996) evaluated a wide range of learning skills interventions and found a mean effect size of 0.4. Marzano et al. (2001) averaged an effect size of 0.65 for interventions across the knowledge, cognitive, metacognitive and self-system domains. Effect sizes are statistically calculated through comparisons of the standard deviation of a control and experimental population. The effect size can be translated to a percentile gain. For further details see Marzano et al. 2001: 6–7 and 159–60.) The range of strategies used (Marzano et al. 2001: 7) included identifying similarities and differences; summarizing and note taking; reinforcing effort and providing recognition; homework and practice; nonlinguistic representations; cooperative learning; setting objectives and providing feedback; generating and testing hypotheses; questions, cues and advance organizers. Metacognitive interventions (Marzano et al. 2001; Higgins et al. 2005) were recognized to effect the greatest impact (see Table 7.1).

Taggart et al. (2005) focused on the research evidence that suggests how pedagogical approaches could be used to develop generic thinking skills in young children. Their findings suggest that developing general thinking through good teaching or 'best practice' was characterized by episodes of 'sustained shared thinking', interactions where two or more individuals worked together in an intellectual way to solve a problem, clarify a concept, evaluate activities or extend a narrative' (Siraj-Blatchford and Sylva 2004). Characteristic practice, in institutions judged to be excellent, involved high incidence of teacher intervention to develop child-initiated activities deliberately to deepen the children's thinking about what they were doing. Taggart et al. (2005) also noted how independent working together on problems to be solved; roleplay or other projects in an engaging and stimulating classroom situation offered the pupils the opportunity to make their own choices and decisions. When guided to reflect the nursery children were capable of reviewing their work and developing further ideas. Jacobs (2004) indicated that young children could extend their metacognition thinking into a writing form, even in Years 1 and 2. Providing

Table 7.1 Analysis of effect sizes for different programme interventions

Programme	Effect size	Confidence interval	Number of studies
Instrumental Enrichment	0.58	0.28, 0.88	7
Cognitive Acceleration	0.61	0.25, 0.96	4
Metacognitive strategies	0.96	0.76, 1.16	5

Source: After Higgins et al. (2005: 31).

appropriate writing frames, enhanced their presentation of arguments in an 'intellectual' and 'sophisticated way' (Riley and Reedy 2005). Other examples of good practice existed in drama (Mallet 2004), mathematics (Lowrie 2002), design and technology (Pitri 2001) and information technology (Kumpulainen et al. 2004). Even in primary classrooms it appears that pupils can develop reasoned arguments based on evidence or information of some kind, plan simple steps to do things, illustrate metacognition through discussion and reflective writing, suggest and develop ideas from or for investigations. These skills contribute to problem solving capabilities and creativity that pupils can apply in a variety of settings (Craft 2003). These learning environments augment imaginative propositions and/or approaches, provide some organization and/or structure to the tasks in hand and provide opportunities for the youngsters to consider alternative strategies, improvements or adjustments that could be applied to their projects or ideas. Teachers, it appears, were able to develop these general thinking opportunities successfully within a wide variety of curricular contexts.

More specific evidence

Effectiveness of FIE

Rand et al. (1979) and Feuerstein et al. (1981) report on evaluations of FIE used with two groups of low functioning, low-status Israeli adolescents, 12 to 15 years of age. These (128) students were described as disadvantaged, socially backward and culturally different as members of minority groups. One group lived in a residential facility; the other attended a day care centre for after school social and educational activities. The FIE materials were designed to meet the needs of the individuals cognitive deficits. The FIE involved 400 pencil-and-paper cognitive exercises, took between 200 and 300 hours to complete and continued over a period of two years. The students were tested using an aptitude test (Thurlstone Primary Mental Abilities Test), achievement (academic) test and two non-intellectual tests. Both groups showed gains on non-intellectual test, and, in particular, tests designed to measure interpersonal conduct, self-sufficiency and adaptiveness to work demands. The investigators also reported that subsequent tests performed when students were later inducted into the military service (two years after completion of the programme) showed that the gains of the experimental group had persisted over those in the control group. It also appeared that those with lower initial tests scores made larger gains over those with higher starting scores at the beginning of the intervention.

Feuerstein et al. proposed that realization of *structural* change, enabled through the mediated learning experience, should show a cumulative gain in cognitive performance over time compared to those not structurally changed. (Structural change, here, is taken to indicate how individuals have adapted their mental approach(es) to solving problems.) Testing the experimental group before the intervention, a year into the programme, immediately on finishing the programme and two years later showed a linear progression (Feuerstein et al. 1981).

> The advantages demonstrated by the Instrumental Enrichment program may in part be due to its content being unrelated to that of the school subjects since it forces both teacher and student to concentrate on problem solving strategies without being distracted by the curriculum material at hand and the need to commit so much of it to memory.
>
> (Feuerstein et al. 1981: 761)

Arbitman-Smith et al. (1984) discuss how immediate changes are most likely to affect the general area of intellectual functioning and that improvements in academic performance are secondary. They also emphasize how cognitive changes that provide learners with new problem solving capabilities are not measured adequately by standardized intelligence tests. They highlight, too, how training students purely in cognitive processing cannot provide the knowledge that is required to solve in a particular subject area such as chemistry or economics. As such, scholastic tests measuring academic prowess do not indicate how problem solving capabilities have developed because these tests are not content free. They concluded that the format of the tests may prevent students from showing what they know and mask processing gains.

Blagg's (1991) evaluation of the effects of FIE had the objective of improving the educational opportunities for 14–16-year-old low-achieving adolescents in four public schools in a town in Somerset. He reported on the use of standardized attainment tests, various ability assessments (including linguistic, verbal reasoning, speed of processing, visual memory and other cognitive measures that collectively contributed to an IQ assessment), student and teacher interviews before and after intervention. He also intended to assess the students' perceived enjoyment, relevance and extent of participation in the programme, and he attempted to investigate changes in self-esteem. Overall, teachers indicated that *some* students became more active contributors in class, more self-disciplined, more able to describe approaches to solving problems, more able to recognize relationships between ideas and principles spontaneously in different curricular areas. Teachers who were interviewed about the training they received to be able to teach the FIE programme said (Blagg 1991: 93):

> I have been teaching for 30 years. This was the first time I had been provoked into thinking about how pupils think ...

> Its changed my view on thinking – made me more aware of the mental landscape.

> Now I always ask what they [pupils] have learned from the lesson ... I should have always asked that before but didn't.'

They also noted that they became more informal and less transmissive. Teachers noted that there were, however, difficulties in managing small-group work and class discussions:

> I used to pride myself on my ability to promote and manage lively class discussions. In retrospect, these were often no more than heated exchanges of prejudiced positions. Pupils didn't listen to the different points of view or even consider coming to some shared agreement.
>
> (Blagg 1991: 120)

Blagg summarized how Feuerstein had produced pioneering work by identifying the cognitive map, recognizing deficient functions and then suggesting how a mediated learning experience can be extremely powerful in beginning to develop pupils' cognitive capabilities. He noted however, the lack of flexibility and adaptability of the materials for students with different levels of ability.

CoRT evidence

The CoRT programme and development of lateral thinking (de Bono (1976: 217–29) reports several experiments that show how CoRT students, compared with control groups, can generate many more relevant ideas. One example question given to students was 'Should children be allowed to leave school as soon as they have learned how to read and write?' The CoRT students generated about twice as many points that reflected a greater range of concerns than control groups. Edwards and Baldauf (1983) reported on an instructional experiment that involved the rotation of classes in an Australian boys school. The 72 boys (approximately 15 years old) were involved in 20 50-minute sessions, with four science subjects, during a five-week instruction block. Different groups of boys received the science and CoRT teaching at different times over one school year. The findings indicated that both the *quality* and *novelty* of ideas generated by the boys was significantly increased. Interestingly Nickerson et al. (1985) carried out a subsequent analysis and found that the boys scoring better in the CoRT tests also scored better in the science tests, but did *not* necessarily perform better in the IQ tests! It appeared that the lateral thinking CoRT materials did support development of some aspect of performance in science, but not IQ.

The CoRT materials are designed to develop both 'alternative' view points, encouraging learners to be much less egocentric. In so doing they consider how other people might feel or behave toward ideas or actions and develop lateral thinking – innovative perspectives or propositions about everyday situations. The CoRT materials have been used for many years in several countries with a range of abilities and ages of students:

> In Venezuela every school child is required to spend two hours a week on thinking throughout their education. In Malaysia, Senior Science Schools have been teaching thinking explicitly for ten years. In Singapore, Australia, New Zealand, Canada, Mexico and the USA the CoRT programme is used in many school districts.
>
> (De Bono 2000: 14)

The nature of the lateral thinking stimulated by this approach can help develop pupils' mental attitudes and principles that are favourable towards lifelong learning, as well as the ability to adapt to circumstances that will shift and change rapidly in the twenty-first century.

Cognitive acceleration evidence

CASE

The earliest, original CASE intervention (Shayer and Adey 2002: 9) where experimental groups were compared with 'control' subjects took place between 1984 and 1987. A pretest was administered before the programme was implemented; a posttest was used at the completion of the teaching and again some time later to assess long-term impact on the pupils' performance. This first evaluation (reported in Adey and Shayer 1994) showed that, as predicted, there were improvements made in the general processing capacity of participating students. Adey and Shayer (1994) describe how the impact of the cognitive acceleration programme, an intervention designed to be taught to 11–13-year-olds in science, produced long-term (three years after the intervention) far-transfer effects (beyond just science performance). Even though the context of the thinking programme was science, significant gains were seen in mathematics and English examinations. Effect sizes were in the range from 0.3 to 1.0 standard deviations, which translates to between half and one GCSE grade above the predicted performance (Shayer 1999a). This first study was small scale, with only about 130 students in each of the experimental and control groups. Further reports of effects and scope were also reported in Adey and Shayer (1990) and Shayer and Adey (1992). From 1991 onward, Adey and Shayer offered CASE professional development and were able to collect data of the impact from successive cohorts. Shayer (1999b) reports on the effects of CASE on over 2000 pupils. Evidence illustrates the extent and nature of long-term, far-transfer effects after pupils have been involved in the Thinking Science programme (the curriculum materials of the CASE project) for Years 7 and 8. The data indicate that CASE schools scored consistently higher grades at GCSE (three years after the Thinking Science programme was taught) than control schools with the same level intake. Adey and Shayer (2002: 11) describe this 'as evidence that the effect of CASE intervention on pupils' thinking is quite general, and their general intellectual development has been enhanced'. CASE has been implemented internationally in Finland, Australia, Germany, Holland, Korea and America (Adey 2004). Resnick (in Brittan 2004) acknowledges that CASE is widely taught in Europe and is successful because it fosters intelligent habits and 'treats kids as smart every day.'

Adey and Shayer (1994) conclude that:

> CASE can have long-term, replicable effects on young adolescents' academic achievement. Although the results do not present us with a perfectly clear-cut picture of what works, when it works, and how it works, they do provide a real indication of possibilities.
>
> (Adey and Shayer 1994: 112)

CAME

The Cognitive Acceleration in Mathematics project, similar to CASE, but with a slightly different emphasis, is designed to support pupils 'understanding' of big ideas or conceptual strands (Adhami et al. 1998) within the mathematics National Curriculum. There is no deliberate intention in this approach to make 'far-transfer' gains through 'bridging' from the reasoning patterns in the activities. The programme focus is on developing conceptual understanding within the mathematics curriculum. The emphasis, however, remains on the thinking processes, rather than mathematical knowledge. Adey and Shayer (2002: 12) present findings that indicate added value for pupils engaged in the Thinking Math programme extends beyond the subject into science and English. Comparisons between the control schools and the CAME schools was statistically significant in mathematics, science and English.

CATE

The Cognitive Acceleration in Technology Education project was reported on by Hamaker et al. (1998). They compared nine experimental classes and eight control classes (just over 200 students in total). Their results indicated some improvements in pupils' performance in other subjects but the data did not show significant, consistent gains in mathematics, science and English. Interviews with teachers indicated that they felt they had augmented their teaching repertoire; developed strategies to enhance peer–peer constructive talk and helped students develop better problem solving skills through the associated training programme.

ARTs

Wilks and Yates (2002) reviewed progress of implementation of the ARTs project in four Wigan schools. No assessments or measures of impact are yet available but pupils were reported to be enthusiastic when they knew they had a 'thinking' lesson, and teachers enjoyed using the materials, even if they did not always focus appropriately on the 'reasoning' objectives and metacognition.

Philosophy for Children (P4C)

Initial evaluation of P4C by Lipman, compared 20 fifth-grade students who were taught the programme for 40 minutes, twice a week for nine weeks, with a control group receiving social science instruction instead. The students were given five tests before and after the nine-week course. In one test there were no significant differences but the tests for 'inferences', 'opposites', 'analogies' and 'similarities' all indicated significant gains by the P4C group (Lipman 1976). The effects of P4C have also been studied by a number of researchers. Sternberg and Bhana (1996) highlighted concerns over the lack of control groups in evaluation studies that they reviewed. They questioned the overall descriptions of methods used. Student populations, class selection and subject dropout, for example, were often not addressed and statistical analysis was often lacking detail. They noted that the programme did appear to be more motivating than most thinking programmes and there were widespread gains in verbal tests of critical thinking abilities. They also suggested that P4C was 'highly teacher sensitive' and required 'extensive teacher training'. Fisher (2000) describes how there are difficulties in evaluating P4C because of its wide-ranging goals and the absence of appropriate evaluative instruments. P4C has been used especially for learning-disabled and emotionally handicapped people. An experimental and control group were compared in a small study. The results (Simon 1979) indicated that the experimental group gained significantly in critical thinking and inference. Lipman et al. (1980) report on other evaluative studies of P4C and indicated that outcomes can be influenced by teacher emphasis. Reading and reasoning can be improved by teachers who stress reading or reasoning. Another study, undertaken by the Educational Testing Service of Princeton, over two years, investigated effects of P4C on 200 students compared with another 200 controls. The teachers were trained for two hours per week for a year. The experimental groups were taught for about two hours per week. The students were in Grades 5 to 8 in two schools in New Jersey, in the US. The test results indicated that P4C was effective in improving the intellectual performance of the students, particularly reading, mathematics and various aspects of both creative and formal reasoning.

Trickey and Topping (2004) carried out a more recent review of evaluative studies of P4C. They reviewed only studies that included pre–post measurement of experimental and control or comparison groups, which Slavin (2004) would describe as characteristics of a well-designed experiment providing 'well-founded information'. The meta-review subsequently included only ten studies, deemed to 'establish casual relationships as free as possible from contamination by confounding variables' (Slavin 2004: 370).

The ten projects that Trickey and Topping reported on that provided experimentally controlled evidence included studies by Lipman et al. (1980) (authors of *Philosophy for Children*); Williams (1993), Dyfed County Council (1994), Sasserville (1994), Fields (1995), Doherr (2000) and the Institute for the Advancement of Philosophy for Children (2002). This review indicated that, even though many studies compared and contrasted experimental and control groups, the measures used ranged from reading scores, established self-esteem tests, word-recognition tests; reasoning tests; intelligence tests; and teacher observations. Population sizes involved in the research studies ranged from 20 to 400 pupils. Positive outcomes included listening and talking skills, confidence levels, verbal and non-verbal reasoning; higher scores in the intelligence, reading and word tests used; appreciation of another's viewpoint; reduction in angry behaviour and more supportive group interactions.

Thinking Together

This approach 'depicts children's emergent understandings as the product of the collective thinking made available to children through observation, joint activity and communication' (Mercer 2000: 133). Wegerif et al. (2005) have shown how this pedagogical approach, set within a variety of curricular contexts can result in the development of children's talk about thinking. Mercer et al. (1999) showed that the pupils exhibited better scores on tests for non-verbal reasoning scores (through the use of Raven's Progressive Matrices) and in understanding of curriculum subjects compared with those in 'control' classes. Wegerif et al. (2005) analysed the use of key words in contextual talk (KWIC) developed by Wegerif and Mercer (1997) between students. They scrutinized verbal exchange for utterances including '... because ...', 'I agree' and 'I think ...' Their findings suggest that teaching students to work together and engage in dialogue of a particular nature using the Thinking Together approach can improve the quality of learning interactions. Wegerif (2002) extends suggestions about facilitating thinking between peers by using computers. His evidence suggests that teaching thinking using software can provide a 'tutor', 'mind-tools' and support for learning conversations. He elaborates, though, that success crucially depends upon *how* the technology is used. *Much* depends on the role of the teacher (Wegerif 2002: 3). McGregor suggests how the teacher interprets and implements any programme (see Figure 7.1) and enacts a thoughtful pedagogy (see Figure 7.2) can significantly influence successful development of pupils' thinking.

Conclusion

Interpretations and communications about success of thinking programmes can sometimes, as Nickerson (1988) suggests, be 'unsubstantiated claims, one-sided assessments, and excessive promotionalism'. He reflects that authors developing and assessing their own programmes need 'more self-criticism', especially as it is somewhat 'paradoxical that some developers of programs to teach critical thinking have had less than severely critical attitudes towards their own work'. Claxton (1999) reiterates that many 'entrepreneurs' make 'grand claims for proprietary methods that are not substantiated by objective evaluation', describing how many of the published evaluations have been based on short trials with small numbers and using measures of limited validity. Arguably positive effects of some of these 'novel' thinking approaches could be due to the 'Hawthorne effect', simply because they offer the learners such a

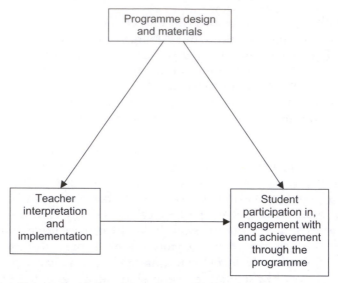

Notes: The efficacy of a thinking programme can be influenced by a number of factors:
1   The design and presentation of the materials themselves and their 'fit' with the normal school policies and practices.
2   The teacher and his/her interpretation of the materials can hugely influence the way the thinking lessons are conducted. There may be pedagogic tensions because the programme is not similar to or easily incorporated into the teacher's usual approach. The teacher may not receive appropriate training and support to interpret the materials with the originators intent (further elucidation in Figure 7.2).
3   The involvement and participation of the students, coloured by their perceived value of the thinking programme, will influence the nature and extent of their achievement.

Figure 7.1 Connecting influences on thinking skills programmes in schools.

contrasting experience to the usual lessons and learning (predominantly transmission or learning-by-rote). The impact of studying effects of a thinking programme that focuses more attention on the students, provides unusual and more engaging activities, may not be sustained once the initial, intensive instruction for novice teachers and students ceases (Nickerson et al. 1985). Nickerson et al. (1985: 316) list the plethora of IQ, intelligence, mental abilities, verbal and non-verbal reasoning, achievement tests and various other puzzles and assessments that have been (and in some cases are still today) used to assess the impact of various thinking programmes. As indicated in Figures 7.1 and 7.2 there are many factors, however, that influence implementation of a thinking programme that have not been assessed, measured or even acknowledged in some studies.

1 Understanding philosophy of the programme or approach.
   - Is the process more important? ... or is the content more important?
   - How far should students understand the philosophy – there are different aims to 'content'-driven lessons.
2 Be familiar with and understand how the materials work (in a practical management and organizational sense).
   - Should there be demonstration; modeling; discussion or reflective collaboration of important or key points?
   - Should everyone have a copy of all materials or only one per group?
   - Should the materials be used selectively, differentiated or as is?
3 Recognize what pedagogical approach(es) is/are appropriate.
   - Which aspects of a lesson should be explained (or given)?
   - In which aspects/parts of lesson should constructivist/social constructivist or sociocultural emphasis come into play?
   - When should I ask questions? What kinds of questions? When should I give the right answers? ... or shouldn't I?
   - How big a group should it be? How should I orchestrate for the most effective discussion?
   - Should I apply particular ground rules/behavioural expectations?
   - How much freedom and time should they have in discussions?
   - When is best to reflect? (Only at the end ... or part way through?)
   - Should I provide visual/auditory and kinesthetic representation of the introduction/tasks and plenary?
   - Will my students talk to each other and disagree without malice?
   - Will my students understand 'sharing ideas', allowing each other time to explain what they think and why? Will they be mutually supportive? Do they know how to be collaborative?
4 Consider how it may need modification and differentiation for particular students.
   - Will my students understand the terms/words used?
   - Will my students see how it helps them with ... x and y?
   - How will my students connect the ideas to 'life' or other problem solving situations?
   - Supporting and applying the correct thinking processes.
   - Will the way I do it mean they have 'analyzed' 'compared' and 'contrasted'; 'synthesized' 'sequenced' correctly?

- Will it matter if I have 30 different ideas and outcomes for the same task?
- How will I assess their thinking capability?
5 Reflect on the success of the lesson/programme (both thinking and learning)
  - What needs improving next time?
  - How will I improve it next time?
  - Is what I am doing good enough to make a difference?
  - Who can help me develop better thinking in my lessons?

Figure 7.2 Examples of teacher concerns and potential influences on the implementation and success of a thinking lesson/programme

Many schools have engaged in brain-based theories of learning. Accelerative learning is also called 'accelerated learning' (not to be confused with interventional *Cognitive Acceleration*), 'whole-brain learning', 'brain-compatible learning' and perhaps more holistically perceived as ways of provoking the neuro-anatomical brain and engaging the mind to learn through multi-modal strategies that use both hemispheres of the cerebral cortex. The emphasis is on reducing stress so that the learner feels relaxed, sufficiently for the blood to nourish all parts of the brain and physiologically enable the body and mind to learn most effectively. It is usually understood to be a battery of techniques (Noble and Poynting 1998) designed to create a relaxed but motivational learning environment, in which students' individual learning styles and different parts of the brain are catered for through an array of strategies involving stimulation of the senses, memory aides, changes of activity, positive affirmations, and so forth. These techniques are often sold as 'based on research' (Smith 1998: 28; Smith and Call 2000: 26–7). However, Bruer (1997) suggests that there are overgeneralizations (and misconceptions) about what we know about the brain and how that can inform educational practices. Bruer cautions about the development of brain-based education. He describes how it consists of a mixture of rather basic but quite dated results from cognitive science and experimental psychology mixed in with really bad brain science. He describes how the synaptic development of children up to the age of 10 is more rapid than at any other time. Early childhood experiences fine-tune the brain's neural connections, those that are unused wither and those that are used repeatedly are maintained. Thus by providing rich, stimulating environments at this time, children can develop more dendritic connections. It appears that lack of stimuli may result in potential loss of learning opportunities. Bruer suggests that we should remain sceptical about brain-based educational practice, and look more carefully at what behavioural science can convey about teaching, learning and cognitive development.

There is much evidence that a focus on thinking can improve students academic performance, but the varied nature of evidence does not enable easy analysis of 'what' exactly influences improvements in thinking and learning performance. The 'what' could be the varied stimuli, received through the programme, its design, the nature of the thinking tasks, the progression from simple to more complex activities, and the regularized intervention. It could also be the change in teacher emphasis, developing more sophisticated methods of questioning, developing more cognitive challenge, modifying expectations of students' cognitive engagement, refining learning objectives to include the procedural aspects of thinking as well as the conceptual understanding achieved, changing the social interactivity between students, valuing dialogue more, recognizing success through a wider range of media, encouraging more bridging from specific contexts to everyday life ... and transferring their valued pedagogic shifts to other 'non-thinking' lessons too.

A wider acceptance of educational research that provides rich qualitative evidence supporting quantitative findings could provide valuable insights into *what* works and *how*. Systematic reviews tend to use established or intelligible tests of some kind, which immediately assess some cognitive skills and not others. Reviewers also tend to assess carefully the structure of the programme(s) and not always, *how* it is implemented by practitioners in their schools and classrooms. The outstanding issues of curricular design, the nature of pedagogy, the culture of classrooms, teachers' beliefs about learning as well as the nature and impact of their professional development all require further clarity, investigation and connection with thoughtful learning. However, what is more obvious are the common aspects of successful thoughtful pedagogies that include more open approaches to the development and reflection of and about thinking processes. Interactive classrooms that value talking about thinking; offer challenges or tasks that involve collaborative participation; involve questioning, predicting, rationalizing, recognizing alternative perspectives and certainly being metacognitive (McGuinness 2005) are all features of classrooms where thinking is actively and successfully pursued.

Slavin (2004) highlights how studies exploring *what* and *how* require careful design to provide evaluative evidence that is reliable and well founded to enable practitioners and policy makers to make informed, discerning decisions. Thoughtful experimental design is desirable so that justifiable evidence can be generalized and presented for educators to make informed decisions about curricular and pedagogical issues. As Bassey (1999) claims, we need more fuzzy generalizations from case studies of a more qualitative and illuminatory nature. Studies of the impact of the nature of pedagogy on thinking are emerging (Dawes et al. 2000; McGregor and Gunter 2001a, 2006; Leat and Higgin 2002; Adey 2004; McGuinness 2005), but more insights are needed to further illuminate *how* and *why* some programmes appear to be more effective than others.

Key ideas

There is substantial evidence that teaching programmes that focus on thinking, can improve pupils' academic performance, cognitive processing and problem solving abilities.

A wide range of measures including IQ tests, reasoning tasks, noting particular words, gauging change in social behaviours and even assessing the novelty of ideas are currently made to assess improvements in thinking.

Further work is needed to more accurately measure development of thinking.

It is not curricular materials alone that influence improvements in pupils thinking.

It is not clear exactly which aspects of teachers' pedagogy, approaches or beliefs most strongly influence the development of pupil's thinking.

Metacognitive approaches appear to be very influential.

Aspects of mediational pedagogy likely to affect pupils thinking are:
- the nature, sequence and frequency of questions posed
- creating time for thinking opportunities
- recognizing value of collaborative processes (including sharing perspectives and rationalizing propositions to each other)
- providing challenging tasks and challenging pupils' ideas and suggestions
- encouraging reflection of the thinking processes and learning outcomes
- supporting transfer and connectivity of thinking outcomes and processes to other contexts

8 Development of creative thinking

Leonardo da Vinci was wrong. But he was *insightfully* wrong. He came to a mistaken idea about flight, but the pattern of thinking behind the idea was exemplary.

(D. Perkins, *The Eureka Effect*)

Even brilliant thinkers can generate ideas that are incorrect. Students in classrooms are often concerned about sharing their inner thoughts or novel ideas because they may be deemed *wrong* by others. However, like da Vinci (Perkins 2000: 3), they may also proffer ingenious solutions to problems. When challenged to think creatively they may feel anxious because, as Roth (1995) highlights, each individual has his or her own way of interpreting anything, so producing new or innovative ideas can involve something of a risk. Creative thinkers, such as da Vinci, are able to generate unique visual interpretations (in a variety of forms) of the world around them, invent machines and even write original prose. Creative thinking can therefore manifest itself in many forms. Various perspectives and definitions of thinking creatively will be considered in this chapter. Creative thinking will then be compared and contrasted with critical thinking. The various ways in which creative thinking is supported and nurtured through various thinking programmes and pedagogical approaches will also be considered.

Defining creative thinking

Creative thinking is defined in many ways (see Figure 8.1). It is essentially perceived by Swartz et al. (1998) as the generation of possibilities. They describe creative thinking as 'the active use of our creative imaginations'. They suggest that we generate ideas as a result of our past experience, which furnishes the raw material of creative thought, and our ability to take apart and creatively combine ingredients from past experience. They highlight how we often do not consider other ways of looking at things; we tend to establish habits or routinized ways of doing things. For example, when packing the shopping you

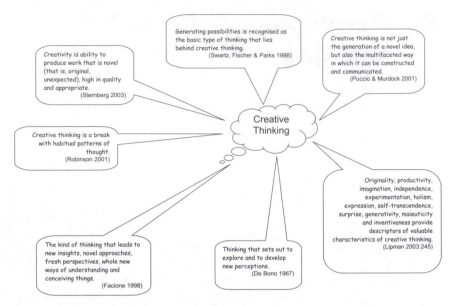

Figure 8.1 Definitions of creative thinking

might pack the heaviest things at the bottom of the carrier, lightest at the top. Therefore, at the checkout you put the heaviest things, such as jars, tins and bottles on to the counter first. Bread and other light, fragile goods are always last to be placed for packing. When students come into a new class at the beginning of term, they usually sit in the same place each time for the subsequent classes – but often they are not told where to sit, they just do it. It appears that once we have a 'method that works', we don't expend extra time or energy considering alternatives, unless a problem arises. For example, if a package of cheddar cheese is broken open by the adjacent tin in the shopping bag, or if students sat together are disruptive. Then it seems appropriate and obvious to reflect on what is happening and consider alternate approaches or ideas. Creativity, then, involves divergent thinking (as indicated in Figure 8.2a) the ability to come up with new, original ideas, which by its nature will be unusual. It could be described as the antipathy of critical thinking, which involves scrutiny of given information, data or evidence of some kind (indicated in Figure 8.2b).

Originality of creative thinking

Original ideas can be so on a number of different levels. Ideas can be original to the person involved; original within the learning community

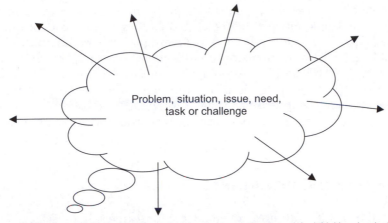

a   Divergent thinking which is creative (each arrow indicating original thinking developing from the problem, situation, issue, need, task or challenge).

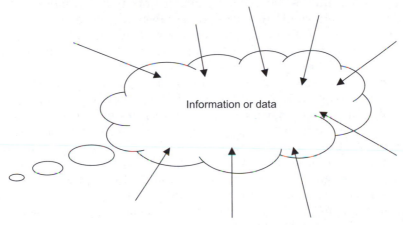

b   Convergent thinking, which is more critical in nature (each arrow represents an aspect of critically scrutinizing given information in some way).

Figure 8.2 The contrasting nature of creative and critical thinking

(group or classroom or school); or original within a country or the world as a whole (Robinson 2001). Creativity is the ability to see things in a new way, to see problems that no one else may even realize exist, and even develop new, unique, and effective solutions to these problems. As Lipman, emphasizes, it may illustrate many characteristics (2003: 245). It should be original, but not purposeless or inappropriate (Sternberg 2003). The originality may offer a 'fresh' or even astonishing idea and it should be productive, resulting in valuable outcome(s). It should involve imagination that explores realms of possibilities. It should celebrate those who think independently and do not necessarily conform to others' views. It should involve searching and experimentation. It should be holistic, recognizing connections between part-whole and means-end relationships. It should be expressive in the way ideas are conveyed. It can be maieutic in nature, illustrating creative caring for others. It can be inventive, that is original, and offer potentially promising ideas, but it may not necessarily be practicable or immediately valuable.

Creativity and intelligence

Fisher (2000: 138) indicates how we become creative when we are able to look at things from a new perspective. He relays how Einstein believed the key to learning was flexible thinking and that 'To raise new questions, new problems, to regard old problems from a new angle requires creative imagination, and makes real advances'. Robinson (2001: 111) describes creativity as a function of intelligence, drawing on different capabilities. He suggests that creativity is not only found in great men or women, whose visionary ideas have historically shaped the world we currently live in and that the 'creatives' in a company department who keep irregular hours, don't wear ties, and arrive at work late because they've been struggling with an idea appear to be set apart from the rest of us by their extraordinary gifts. He elucidates how the word 'creativity' itself, mistakenly, suggests some sort of separate faculty like memory or sight. Creativity is also not confined to special activities such as, painting a picture, composing a poem, choreographing a dance or sculpting a figure. These activities require diligence and persistence as well as creativity. Scientists, technologists, business people, educators, in fact anyone can be creative in the things that they do. The innovation of new techniques, new products, new selling strategies, new approaches to preparing for examinations are all ways these people can be creative. Somewhat unlike critical thinking, however, new ideas and innovative approaches often take time to develop. They may need nurturing or cogitating upon. They may even need critical review to assess their viability. How a creative suggestion is refined, modified or improved requires critical appraisal, this suggests the close association between creativity and critical thinking, described by Alec Fisher (2001) as critico-creative (considered again later).

Robinson (2001: 115) emphasizes how creativity also involves *doing* something, for example within mathematics, engineering, music, business, whatever, so creativity requires a context. He elaborates how creativity can be rooted in imaginative thought, in envisaging new possibilities. In schools, development of imagination in a productive and creative way should be focused upon. Nurturing and eliciting the internal private imaginings to explicit, appropriate and applicable ideas for and within learning should be key for teachers. Students should not be hesitant and feel reluctant to proffer diverse, alternate propositions or products.

> Creative thinking is a break with habitual patterns of thought. Creative insights often occur by making unusual connections, seeing analogies between ideas that have not previously been related. All of our existing ideas have creative possibilities. Creative insights occur when they are combined in unexpected ways or applied to questions or issues with which they are not normally associated
>
> (Robinson 2001: 135).

Koestler (1975) describes this as a process of bi-association, bringing ideas from different areas that are not normally connected. This notion informs how de Bono's random word technique and Buzan's creative character-istics (described later) can be used effectively to stimulate creative thinking. De Bono (1993) describes how we need creative thinking to improve life, design things, solve problems, create change and improve systems, but it is a skill that has been somewhat obviated because, as Robinson and others point out, it has been perceived as a given gift or talent that one either has or does not have, so nothing can be done to change it. Arguably, memorizing and learning by rote, systematic and organized factual information for the academic purpose of examination success has previously constrained the development and value of creative thinking. Creative thinking can also be described as lateral thinking, which can be generated randomly but can also be learned using various techniques (Buzan 2000; de Bono 2000). De Bono developed the notion of lateral thinking in 1967 (de Bono 1993: 186). He describes it as 'thinking that sets out to explore and develop new perceptions.' He proposes that lateral thinking can be provoked and learned with various tools or techniques (like CAF, OPV or random word). He argues that jokes and humour are excellent models of lateral thinking, with the punch lines often using alternative perceptions of familiar situations.

Facione (1998) describes creative or innovative thinking as the kind of thinking that leads to new insights, novel approaches, fresh perspectives, whole new ways of understanding and conceiving things. The products of creative thought include the obvious things like poetry, music, dance, dramatic literature, inventions and technical innovations. But there are some not-so-obvious examples as well, such as ways of developing a question that expand the horizons of possible solutions, or ways of conceiving of relationships that challenge presuppositions and lead another to see the world in imaginative and different ways. These are certainly the kinds of creative thoughts we *can* and should support in schools.

Modes of communication or presentation

Robinson's ideas about developing creativity and placing a thinker within a medium are supported by Puccio and Murdoch (2001), who describe how creativity is communicated through a multifaceted approach. They describe how nurturing creativity requires awareness and understanding of the relationship between novel, past and current knowledge. Teachers have used multiple-intelligence (MI) approaches to inform 'modes of presentation' and to allow students to present their ideas through music (song, rap, melody, rhythm or rhyme), drama (mime, skit), prose (poem, play, verse), art (poster, illustration, photograph) etc. This can provide an authentic 'context' or tools by which the creative ideas are more powerfully stimulated and communicated.

Critical and creative thinking

Critical thinking is evaluative or reflective consideration about the validity, nature or substance of an idea or proposition – critically assessing a newspaper article, or judging the execution of a play, or deciding which is the best design option for a technology project. It is the type of thinking needed to scrutinize, analyse and criticize. It may involve the application and comparison of fixed or developed criteria that enables 'standardized' assessment of some kind. Standard intelligence tests measure this kind of convergent thinking.

Creative thinking is the generation or suggestion of a unique or alternative perspective, the production of an innovative design or a new approach to a problem or artistic challenge. Making judgements about students' creative thinking requires inclusion of criteria that acknowledges individuality, as Lipman (2003: 243) describes. This means that teachers need to think more laterally, to reshape conventional use of traditional criteria used to assess students' cognitive development if creativity is to be more widely acknowledged and celebrated in schools.

By its very nature, critical thinking is concerned with critiquing something already in existence and creativity is concerned with generating something new, not previously available to critique.

Ontologically and epistemologically speaking, critical thinking could be perceived as more objective in its nature and outcomes and creative thinking as more subjective in its character and products.

Constructivist perspectives of learning recognize that objectivity within the thinking process is key. More sociocultural emphasis within the classroom recognizes a more pluralistic nature of coming to understand through acknowledgement of learners' subjectivities. Teachers adopting a particular pedagogical approach or model described in Chapter 2 may intuitively facilitate or support more-or-less subjective or objective creative or critical kinds of thinking (respectively).

Creativity and problem solving

In problem solving situations learners may seesaw between critical and creative thinking, going back and forth in the generation of ideas, critical reflection of suggestions and subsequent refinement, modification or regeneration of further innovations until a suitable solution is reached. A group of students in a drama lesson resolving how to design, produce and enact a playlet or skit to illustrate 'anger' or 'sadness', will consider between them various body poses, actions or gestures that convey these emotions. They may consider previous experiences of a family or peer-peer situation, or scenes from movies or plays or classroom encounters that inform ways in which they could communicate emotion. Participation in this kind of process involves, critical reflection of examples of 'anger' or 'sadness' *and* creative transformation about how to convey these emotions in a way that others will understand. To elucidate when the two types of thinking are used requires metacognitive processing. Metacognition, or reflection of the thinking processes and outcomes, can render the creative or critical aspects more explicit. Teachers recognizing the difference in nature between these two processes are better informed to guide and steer learners to reflect in particular ways and more effectively support thinking and problem solving.

Supporting creativity

Problems with defining creativity often lay with particular associations within the arts, in the complex nature of creative activity itself, and the variety of theories that have been developed to explain it. Some people doubt that creativity can be taught at all (National Advisory Committee on Creative and Cultural Education 1998). It is sometimes thought that only rarely are people creative and that creativity involves unusual talents. There are some who think that notable and outstanding creativity is not developed through educational support, and may even gain strength from educational failure. There is also a somewhat elite conception of creativity that focuses attention on achievements that have been of historic originality, pushing back the frontiers of human knowledge and understanding, for example, da Vinci, Galilei, Newton, Van Gogh. Their achievements constitute the highest levels of creativity. It is possible, however, that any student in school has creative capability that can and should be encouraged (National Advisory Committee on Creative and Cultural Education 1999). Perkins and Tishman (1993) investigated the nature of critical and creative thinking and found that passions, attitudes, values, and habits of mind all play key roles. They defined a thinking disposition as a tendency toward a particular pattern of intellectual behaviour. For example, good thinkers have the tendency to identify and investigate problems, to probe assumptions, to seek reasons, and to be reflective. However, further research revealed that often learners possess these abilities, but are not disposed to use them. In order to encourage learners to think creatively and engage in task resolution they need to perceive open-mindedness and recognize the situation from more than one perspective to feel inclined to invest the energy in doing so. Inviting students to engage in worthwhile, authentic, open-ended tasks to solve, provides the opportunities to overcome these potential barriers. Puccio and Murdock (2001) elaborate on how creative thinking is closely associated with the process of creativity. They suggest that it relates to the steps and cognitive skills associated with a person's progression from a problem or need for a creative solution to produce an outcome. Torrance's (1974) definition of creative thinking connects with this:

> A process of becoming sensitive to problems, deficiencies, gaps in knowledge, missing elements, and so on; identifying the difficulty; searching for solutions, making guesses, or formulating hypotheses about the deficiencies; testing and retesting these hypotheses and possibly modifying and retesting them; and finally communicating the results.
>
> (Torrance 1974: 8)

This definition outlines the stages people may go through as they engage in creative problem solving. Puccio and Murdock (2001) also identify how creative thinking and problem solving are essential in the workplace. Employers value the ability, of employees at all levels, to solve problems creatively for the success of their organizations. The problem solving process illustrates how critical and creative thinking are inextricably connected when engaged in resolving issues or finding solutions to problems. The purpose in attempting to define creative and critical thinking is to enable educators to recognize the kinds of thinking they could support in a planned way so that students in school have the opportunity to become more skilful in problem solving.

Thinking programmes, pedagogic strategies, tools and tactics to develop creative thinking

Within each thinking-skills programme there are opportunities for the development of creative thinking. Opportunities can be built-into the structure or nature of activities, the design of the lessons or the pedagogic strategies. Table 8.1 summarizes some of the *obvious generalizable* opportunities. In earlier chapters more specific activities are described where these opportunities can be pursued. Development of creative ideas or suggestions is not always explicitly orchestrated in the thinking pro-grammes; the suggestions made in Table 8.1 may be curtailed if the teacher does not perceive *and* value the opportunity (as implied in Chapter 7).

Cognitive acceleration (CA) approach

The CA approach offers opportunities for creative thinking whenever pupils are asked to predict 'what do you think will happen?' or hypothesise and explain, not only what, but why they think a particular course of events are likely. Within the CA approach the pillar of *construction* provides an ideal opportunity to have pupils construct and define what their expectations of something are.

Another pillar, bridging, can also offer differentiated opportunities (by outcome) for pupils to develop their creative thinking. Making personalized connections from the thinking done in the programme lessons, to other curricular areas, as well as activities engaged in at home, on the sporting field or in any other aspect of their leisure time requires creative thinking.

Activating Children's Thinking (ACT)

Infused thinking approaches purposely invite pupils to generate possibi-lities and look for alternate perspectives in learning tasks. There is wide recognition, too, that problems posed are likely to have various possible solutions, proffering resolution and strategy developing openings.

Creative thinking is stimulated by answering questions like; 'what would it be like if . . .' Swartz et al. (1998) illustrate how brainstorming and posing a series of questions can help generate creative possibilities skilfully:

Table 8.1 Obvious potential for creative thinking to be developed in some of the programmes reviewed in earlier chapters

Programme	Nature of creative thinking potential
CA suite of programmes (described in more detail in Chapter 4)	CASE: Developing any predictions or hypotheses about 'what will happen next?' In Act II, of the lessons, pupils are often invited to project what they think is going to happen. Facilitating pupils creating their own bridges or transferring the thinking done to alternative contexts. CAME: Pupils are often invited to share their different methods of solving problems. Creativity in working out solutions in different but logical ways is noteworthy. CATE: Approaching problems in varied ways and designing a range of different solutions is celebrated. ARTs: Generating criteria by which to classify music and art; experimenting with artistic expression through performance in drama, creating a work of art and composing a musical piece; using symbols to create and communicate imagery, perspective and other ideas.
ACTs (described in more detail in Chapter 6)	Generating ideas and possibilities. Looking for alternate perspectives in learning tasks. Acknowledging that a question or problem may have more than one solution. Building and combining suggestions to form more complex imaginative ideas. Planning learning and generating possible strategies before engaging on task.
Thinking Together (described in more detail in Chapter 5)	Looking for generation of new ideas. Considering alternative viewpoints. Thinking of useful information to share. Development of exploratory talk.
Thinking Through ... series for geography, history, RE, English, science. (described in more detail in Chapter 4)	Using mysteries and mind movies. Reading photographs, pictures and maps. Taboo, 5Ws, Odd One out. Story telling.

FIE; STS; TTTT (described in more detail in Chapter 5)	Encouraging the students to develop connections from the thinking activities to everyday life and naturalistic problem solving.
De Bono's six thinking hats/action shoes/OPV/CAF/Po/Random word, etc	Applying green hat thinking. Generating consequences of wearing any shoes, or combination there of, in problem situations. Thinking of alternative viewpoints.
P4C ... stories, texts and games for thinking (described in more detail in Chapter 5)	Creating varied narratives for characters in stories. Explaining why particular scenarios map out. Interpreting meanings in a philosophical way.

1   What is the task for which you are considering possibilities?
2   What possibilities can you think of?
3   What are some other types of possibilities?
4   What original or unusual possibilities can you generate by combining possibilities already listed?
5   What information would you need in order to decide which of these possibilities is best for the task?

All opportunities that offer a range of differentiated outcomes or suggestions can potentially support creativity. Chen and Siegler (2000) extend Siegler's earlier ideas (1996), in Figure 8.3, about how thinking strategies may develop and evolve. Typically the students might focus on one solution, and after considering its strengths and weakness, build on the positive aspects to recreate another possibility. Thus new solutions can arise out of the discarded ones.

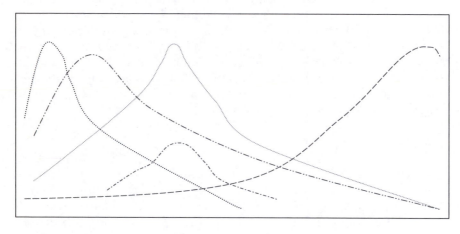

Prominent strategy in problem-solving process:	
Strategy 1	....
Strategy 2	— . — . — . —
Strategy 3	....
Strategy 4	— . — . — . — .
Strategy 5	— — — —

Note: Each different line represents the emerging prominence of five different suggestions and its longevity.

Source: After Chen and Siegler (2000).

Figure 8.3 How strategies develop in problem solving

Application of the infused approach may, however, constrain some creativity, as teachers have to hold in mind the dual role of the lessons, to also 'deliver' conceptual and factual understanding while encouraging thinking.

Thinking Together

The tasks within this programme use poems, stories, games and social dilemmas, all of which can offer rich opportunities for much creativity. The open nature of many tasks, with no specified outcomes and the suggestions of open style questions all support the development of creative thinking.

Thinking Through series ...

Describes creative thinking skills as those that enable students to generate and extend ideas, suggest hypothesis, apply imagination and to look for alternative, imaginative outcomes. The pedagogic strategies that can support this include: 5Ws; Odd One Out; Mystery; Taboo; Living Graphs; Story telling; Pictures, photographs and maps from Memory; Mind Movies (all described in Chapter 4).

These are all pedagogic approaches applied to learning activities where there are opportunities for students to creatively extend and apply ideas to the content material provided.

STS/FIE/TTTT

These programmes are designed to improve particular types of cognitive processing and in that sense the outcomes are objective. However, the opportunities to solve problems naturalistically and transfer thinking to everyday life requires more creative thinking. This is important because, as Lambert (2000) illustrates, the nature of problems and their associated solutions differ at school and in real-life. In each of these situations key questions can be used to focus on the nature of creative thinking, incubation time is needed, often discussion with others is crucial and finally reflection can stimulate rich and diverse ideas. Real-life situations can provide, it seems, many more opportunities for students to employ creative thinking to potentially develop unique solutions to 'real' problems (Lambert 2000).

Objectivity, subjectivity and thinking creatively

Figure 8.4 *suggests* how the nature of subject matter and its intrinsic objectivity or subjectivity can influence the predominant type of thinking engaged in. For example, CASE, set within the context of science, has specific cognitive objectives to be achieved; CAME is designed to support understanding of mathematical objectives, although creative, thoughtful alternate strategies to achieve a resolution are celebrated.

These subjects intrinsically require more objectivity and therefore support predominantly more critical thinking. The *Thinking Through ...* series is objective in that the subject content has to be accurately considered, but the strategies by which students become familiar with curriculum material is very creative. The horizontal bars (in Figure 8.4) suggest the relative proportions of critical and creative thinking

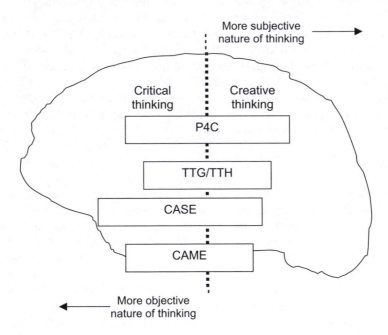

Note: Educators need to be aware of the influence of the nature of the subject to be learned to pedagogically intervene and develop opportunities for creative *and* critical thinking.

Figure 8.4 How the proportion of critical and creative thinking in different thinking programmes may differ

employed in the different approaches. It will extend further into creative for English (TTE) because the outcomes of the learning activities are more subjective, which can potentially support more creative thinking. The purposeful and often scientific nature of the novels that P4C appraises can provide a balance of both creative and critical thinking in the programme.

Buzan and creative thinking

Tony Buzan provides a plethora of ideas to develop your creativity (Buzan 2000). One idea that could be generalized and applied to a range of objects, depending on the subject and the nature of the learning task, is what he describes as '10 creativity characteristics'. He uses a paper-clip exercise to demonstrate how it works. McGregor and Gunter (2001a, 2006) have used the approach in professional development activities to elucidate creative thinking. When asked for ideas about how a paper clip could be used, the average person would probably think of 'about 24 uses when given as long as they need' (Buzan 2000: 23). This list would probably include a clip for small clothes on a clothes line, a nose clip, a Christmas-tree object hanger and a way of exploring magnetic strength of magnetic metals. Given scaffolded suggestions about how to view the problem very differently, informed by '10 characteristics of behaviour that identify exceptionally creative individuals' (Buzan 2000: 23), students and teachers can be supported to develop a much more diverse list of ideas in a shorter space of time. Consideration about how to develop new ideas from old ideas; use colour; use different shapes; magnify reality; view things from alternate perspectives; respond emotionally or even express a connection with energy – are tactics that can encourage creativity. Buzan describes this technique as a way of giving your brain a workout. Educationally this kind of approach can be used to support the development of a range of creative activities including creative writing (thinking about a character or developing a narrative in a story/play or skit), thinking of a new or innovative technology project, developing a decorative theme for an art production or even producing a leaflet/poster for a sales promotion.

Von Oech (1986) also suggested that to develop creativity in a pragmatic way (Sternberg 2003) learners could be encouraged to adopt another's view when engaged in problem solving. Adopting the role of explorer, artist, judge, or warrior, for example, can serve to overcome mental blocks and provide the stimulation to foster creative productivity.

De Bono's lateral thinking techniques

Alternatives, possibilities and choices (APC)

This technique emphasizes viewing situations from different perspectives, considering alternative courses of action and solutions to problems, generating alternative explanations of how something happened and creating alternative designs to fulfil project briefs.

Provocation (Po)

This approach is designed to provoke consideration of new plausible and useful alternate ideas through a variety of techniques. The first technique is to think about stupid or silly ideas that might initially seem totally unreasonable, such as using radio beams to shoot down aeroplanes. This idea has since been developed because radar is now used to 'detect' the whereabouts of aeroplanes. Other techniques include:

- *Reversal-type provocation*. Thinking about what is normally done and then considering the reverse to generate new possibilities – for example, thinking about gardeners no longer regularly cutting the grass during the summer or store owners paying customers.
- *Escape-type provocation*. Thinking about something usually taken for granted and then considering what would happen without it – for example, a house with no windows or tennis on a court with no service line.

These techniques can potentially support development of very creative ideas, but teachers have to be thoughtful themselves to use them effectively. They often need to model good ideas for learners to be 'spurred' into creative action.

Random word technique

De Bono describes this as a lateral-thinking technique, used by people who need to create new ideas. It is a way in which new ideas can be stimulated. A list of random words (which are seemingly unconnected to the task at hand) can be used and applied to stimulate subsequent ideas. Students may be involved in a new design and technology project. They may have to think about a new range of stationary, furniture, clothing or electrical gadgets. When working on a design project, random words that have to be connected in some way can trigger creativity. For example, horse, egg or tree could stimulate ideas about equine-shaped or hair-coloured stationary; or egg-shaped furniture or naturally textured clothing. The technique may initially seem impossible, but working collaboratively in small groups, the range of ideas produced can be amazing!

Six hats and action shoes

The six hats and action shoes have been described previously in Chapter 6. Green thinking is essentially the creative hat, although many ideas are often developed through sequential adoption of a variety of hats (and shoes).

Philosophy for Children

This approach regularly asks pupils for alternative viewpoints, especially in relation to responses or possible reactions or perspectives of a variety of characters in stories. Fisher (2000) extends this approach creatively into thinking about games, how to strategically play them and how to devise them too. Both these kinds of exercises, stimulated through Fisher's imaginative questioning style, can be very productive.

Supporting teachers understanding of creative thinking

Teachers often find it difficult to understand the difference in nature between creative and critical thinking. An interactive participatory activity that McGregor and Gunter (2001a, 2006) have devised to illustrate this is described in Figure 8.5: the paper origami exercise. When given the paper shape to consider with no prompts and little time to cogitate, a few ideas are presented. With more time and further social interaction to devise, adapt and adopt others' ideas, suggestions become much more diverse and increase at least twofold. Teachers can also compare this activity with 'finding the photograph' (Figure 9.2), an exercise that requires more critical thinking. Teachers *contrasting* their *thinking experiences*, working on both the origami and photograph exercise, come to realize the difference in nature between creative and critical thinking respectively. A summary of their collective observations is presented in Table 8.2.

This exercise can be used to illustrate the nature of creative thinking. It works best with small groups (a trio) of collaborators with diverse experience and backgrounds.

Steps:

1   Each group is given a triangle of paper (roughly half size of A4 sheet):

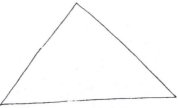

2   They are shown how to fold the bottom long edge over by about 2 mm twice:

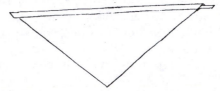

3   They are then shown how to hold the two tips and carefully insert one into the other so that the shape is then joined at the longest edge:

4   The teachers are then told to leave the paper object on the desk in front of them and share ideas about what it could be.

The kinds of responses that teachers give include:
- Bishop's mitre;
- napkin holder;
- cuff protector;
- collar;
- pencil holder.

5   These ideas are then shared amongst the whole group (written onto a flipchart).
6   The teachers are asked to then reflect and think about the possible uses that this shape might have.
7   Again discussion in small groups and then collective sharing on a flipchart includes the following suggestions:
    - an apron;
    - a sleeve protector;
    - a sweet scoop;
    - a garden trowel;
    - part of a Christmas cracker;
    - modern sculpture;
    - chair/table leg scuff protector;
    - arm band;
    - design for eraser at end of pencil;
    - brush (artist or hairdresser's) holder;
    - candle holder;
    - vase design;
    - worn as bandana;
    - headscarf;
    - skirt design.
8   The teachers are then shown how when the paper shape is released from an elevated position it glides through the air like an aerofoil. An aerofoil (or airfoil) is a part of an aircraft's or other vehicle's surface that acts on the air to provide lift or control, e.g. an aileron, wing, or propeller.
9   The teachers are then guided to reflection on the nature and process of the thinking that they have just experienced. The main points that are derived from the discussion:
    - No one worked out the 'correct' answer!
    - Doesn't matter about correct answer when developing thinking skills, as long as there are reasons behind the suggestions.
    - Creative thinking is more open than critical thinking.
    - Creative thinking can produce several correct or plausible answers.
    - To encourage creative thinking teachers should ask open questions.
    - Judgemental responses to suggestions should not be given immediately if a wide range of propositions is sought.

Figure 8.5 Paper origami exercise

Table 8.2 Comparison of the nature of thinking creatively and critically through contrasting tasks

Creative thinking (e.g. origami task)	Critical thinking (e.g. finding photograph task)
More open task	Less open task
Many possible, plausible outcomes	Often only one correct outcome
Requires open questions to encourage it	Requires more focused questions to encourage scrutiny and appraisal of something
Requires imagination	Requires reflection on matter to be considered or critiqued
Often requires longer 'incubation' or cogitating time	Can be more readily engaged in or almost immediately applied to a situation
More contemplative in nature	More reactive in nature
Often slower/longer to nurture	Can arise more rapidly
Originality predominant	Preconceptions critiqued, considered or scrutinized

Claxton (1999: 163) identified four stages in the creativity process:

1 Preparation
2 Incubation
3 Illumination
4 Verification

These processes are to some extent illustrated in the origami exercise. In preparation, teachers (or learners) are introduced to the task, they prepare the paper shape and fold it ready for the thinking challenge and know what is expected. They then need time to think about possibilities and incubate their ideas. Illumination or insight arises as they explain their ideas about the possibilities of the paper shape. Their ideas are verified when others also share their similar and juxtaposed propositions.

As Professor Lewis Minkin quoted in *All Our Futures* (1999: 30) describes 'Creative play – seeking to see the world afresh – is at times a fight against the fascination which familiar associations and directions of thought exert on us. Young people need to be encouraged to understand the importance of this kind of *play*'. Playing with possibilities is key to creative problem solving.

Generalized pedagogic approaches or tactics to develop creativity

Pedagogic tactics to support thinking creatively involve providing open-ended tasks, challenges, problems or issues to be thought about or acted upon. These should be presented within a range of subject contexts. Students should be encouraged to use a wide range of mediums through which to solve the problems, engage in the tasks or present their outcomes. They should be encouraged to personalize connections and transfer their thinking from the school context to other life situations.

Characteristics of open problem solving that should be encouraged to support thinking creatively:

- Ensure it is authentic.
- Present it in a stimulating and motivating way.
- Celebrate variety and diversity of solutions.
- Ensure all know that there is no one fixed 'right' answer.
- Encourage recognition of tasks and subtasks.
- Explore opportunities for the development of unique ideas.
- At decision making junctures, value subjectivity
- Apply existing knowledge to new situations throughout the process (not just at the onset or after completion).

Other, more general pedagogic, tactics that can be used to stimulate creative thinking include using questions to stimulate articulation of alternate viewpoints:

- 'What else …?'
- 'How to make it (something) better …'
- 'What would happen if?'
- 'What do you think will happen next?'
- 'How can we …?' and 'describe the different ways you could …?'
- 'Are there any other different approaches/types you could think of?'

Other approaches in lessons, that can support more creative thinking in classrooms include:

- Using creative play/games.
- Using a continuing story concept.
- Using props to create/generate alternate/cross connecting new ideas.
- Using role play/drama/skits/movies.
- Using cartoons/humour/jokes.

- Using pictures/photographs/maps.
- Using music/rhythm/lyrics.
- Using artwork/sculptures/unusual artefacts.

Conclusion

The extent and nature of creative thinking varies immensely. It can be artistic, aesthetic, sensitive, musical, scientific, mathematical, historical, geographical and even involve emotional resonance. This chapter has begun to consider how thinking creatively differs to thinking critically. There are suggestions about how teachers may support and nurture its development. Opportunities in existing programmes and pedagogic approaches that could develop this kind of thinking are suggested. When inspectors visit classrooms to assess teaching and learning they are looking for evidence of 'critical thinking, creative thinking and imagination'. Fisher (2000) asks 'which teaching methods best achieve these kinds of thinking?' This chapter begins to address this question, by drawing attention to the differences between thinking creatively and critically and associated pedagogies.

Key ideas

Creative thinking is not a special characteristic that only a few talented people possess.

Creative thinking can be nurtured through a variety of techniques.

Thinking programmes can be used to develop creative thinking.

The subjective or objective nature of learning activities can influence whether creative thinking is naturally encouraged.

Increased teacher awareness of the nature of creative (and critical) thinking can help them support development of it.

Pedagogic tactics or strategies that can support creative thinking include:
- providing more open learning or problem solving opportunities
- more open-ended questioning
- expecting varied solutions
- allowing more time for incubation of ideas
- celebrating differentiated outcomes
- encouraging more extension and exploration of initial ideas
- using open questioning more supportively

9 Development of critical thinking

The Answer

We're looking for the answer,
We're searching high and low.
We're doing what we can, Sir-
We really want to know.

We've ransacked desk and drawer, Sir,
Basket, bowl and bin.
We've scrutinised the floor, Sir –
You couldn't hide a pin.

We've been out on the street, Sir;
We've been up on the roof.
And even when we cheat, Sir,
This question's answer-proof.

We've cudgelled all our brains, Sir.
And still we're in the dark.
Got nothing for our pains, Sir,
Except a question mark.

We've thought ourselves to death, Sir.
With 'What?' and 'Where?' and 'Who?'
We're beat and out of breath, Sir,
So how about a clue?

The teacher tapped his forehead.
At last! The children cried.
The answer, Sir's in your head ...
What a perfect place to hide.

(Ahlberg, *Heard it in the Playground*)

Ahlberg's (1989: 18) poem illustrates how we do not wish children to view learning, perceiving that the teacher or an expert adult always 'holds' the correct solutions or answer to their problems. Ultimately education should aim to support the development of independent thinkers who are discerning problem solvers (in the broadest sense, able to resolve their own scholastic, work and life challenges) and can use a range of cognitive skills and strategies, including critical thinking, to resolve problems. This chapter begins by considering a range of views and definitions of critical thinking. The types of critical thinking developed through different programmes and pedagogical approaches are then described and contrasted in more detail.

Defining critical thinking

There are widely contrasting views of critical thinking. Some of the views described here highlight the range of perspectives developed around this aspect of education. Many definitions concerned with critical thinking have developed from Dewey's early writings (1910) about the nature of thinking in education. He described how, in an educational sense, 'thought denotes belief' and this may or may not be based on 'grounds that have been considered'. In other words he described how what we believe influences what we think, and we base our beliefs on evidence we have evaluated (implicitly or maybe even explicitly). He goes on to describe how 'thinking in its best sense is that which considers the basis and consequences of beliefs' (Dewey 1910: 5). Many definitions of critical thinking expound the notions of evaluating information, ideas or propositions and considering consequences of actions or thoughts before judging whether they are plausible or useful. Glaser (1941) extends this early notion of critical thinking to include 'knowledge of the methods of logical enquiry and reasoning'. He also describes how it requires 'persistence to examine beliefs' or ideas 'in the light of the evidence that supports it and the further conclusions to which it tends' (Glaser 1941: 5), and involves a disposition (or inclination) to consider in a thoughtful way the problems and subjects that come within the range of one's experience.

Facione (1998) explicates the idea of *core* critical thinking skills, and provides much more detailed descriptors of associated characteristics. He identifies these as analysis, inference, explanation, evaluation, self-regulation and interpretation. Analysis is 'to identify the intended and actual inferential relationships' between things (including statements, questions, concepts, descriptions, evidence, experiences, information or opinions). Inference means to 'identify and secure elements needed to draw reasonable hypotheses', which may require consideration of relevant information, and to deduce the consequences flowing from data, statements, principles, evidence, beliefs opinions, concepts,

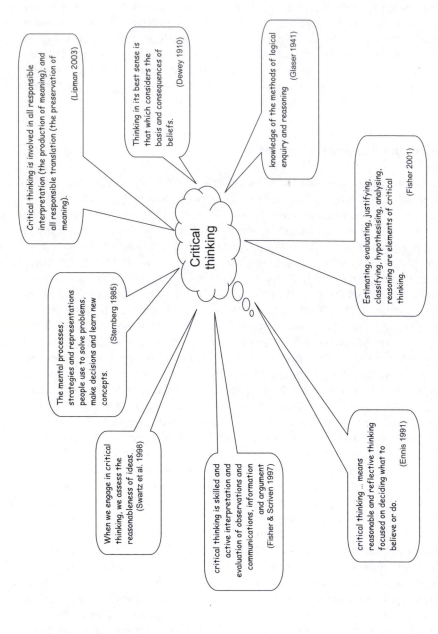

Figure 9.1 Definitions of critical thinking

descriptions or judgments. Explanation is being able to 'state results of one's reasoning in terms of the evidential, conceptual, methodological, criteriological and contextual considerations upon which one's results were based; and to present one's reasoning in the form of coherent arguments'. Evaluation is the assessment of the 'credibility' of statements or other representations that are accounts or descriptions of a person's perception, experience, situation, judgments, belief or opinion. Self-regulation, he maintains, means to 'self-consciously monitor one's cognitive activities, and the results deduced, particularly by applying skills in analysis and evaluation to bring one's own judgements with a view toward questioning, confirming, validating or correcting either one's reasoning or one's results'. He (and many others) describe good critical thinker, those who are as able to interpret, analyse, evaluate and infer from information or evidence given and then also explain what they think and how they arrived at their conclusion. In so doing they are making and explaining reasoned judgments. He also highlights how development *and* practice using these six core cognitive skills is important, just as accomplished dancers or musicians would lose their 'touch' if they did not continue using their established skills. Critical thinking is pervasive. There is hardly a time or place where it would not seem to be useful. As long as people have purposes in mind, have to decide how to accomplish things, wonder what is true or not and consider what to believe and what to reject, good critical thinking is essential. Fisher and Scriven (1997) also recognize the important pervasive nature of critical thinking and develop their notion of it as an academic competency, almost as important as reading and writing: 'critical thinking is skilled and active interpretation and evaluation of observations and communications, information and argument' (Fisher and Scriven 1997: 21). Alec Fisher (2001: 8) further elucidates on the core constitutes of critical thinking skills, which he defines as fundamental to:

- identify the elements in a reasoned case, especially reasons and conclusions;
- identify and evaluate assumptions;
- clarify and interpret expressions and ideas;
- judge the acceptability, especially the credibility of claims;
- evaluate arguments of different kinds;
- analyse, evaluate and make decisions;
- draw inferences;
- produce arguments.

He describes how skilful critical thinking contrasts with 'unreflective thinking', which accepts evidence, claim or decision at face value. It can be carried out at various intellectual levels, particularly when clarity, relevance, adequacy, coherence and other critical skills are involved. He emphasizes how critical thinking clearly requires interpretation and evaluation of observations, communications and other sources of information. This type of thinking also requires skill in thinking about assumptions, in asking pertinent questions, in drawing out implications, reasoning and arguing issues through. Fisher describes how a good critical thinker, before deciding what to think or do, will employ reasoned and reflective thinking and will select the appropriate methods. He also indicates that the ultimate aim of effective critical thinking is 'to see a better model' and try to move 'practice towards that better model'.

Fisher's (2001) approach, in developing critical thinking, is to involve students discussing critically specific situations or scenarios and then presenting that particular thinking skill to others themselves. His method is very much one of describing a situation that students can relate to and then consider. He scaffolds how his pupils should think critically through posing a sequence of questions. In this example a student fails a test. He says 'That test was unfair. I studied for days, reading the material four times, underlining important details and then studying them. After doing all this I should have got a good grade. That test was unfair.' The questions the students are encouraged to contemplate include: *What is the 'conclusion' of his argument? What is he trying to persuade the teacher to accept? What reasons does he give in support of his conclusion? Does he make any implicit assumptions? Does he assume anything without actually saying it? Is it a good or bad argument?*

Robert Ennis has probably produced the most detailed and comprehensive descriptions of critical thinking (Ennis 1986, 2001), its nature and the kind of characteristics a teacher might wish a critical thinker to develop. In his description of dispositions (arguably typical behaviours and inclinations) of good critical thinkers he emphasizes how they wish to get things 'right' as much as possible, they have the ability to objectively empathize with others' views, take account of personal beliefs and even consider emotional aspects of dignity and worth. He also identifies core abilities or facets that depict good critical thinking, which includes being able to clarify (which involves identifying, defining and analysing); decide (about credibility), infer (through deducing, judging and explaining), consider, reason and be able to integrate all these abilities to defend decisions. Other traits that he describes as useful include proceeding in an orderly manner, being sensitive to the feelings and knowledge of others as well as being able to rhetorically present ideas. Interestingly the latter traits are the kinds of skills that Lipman defines as *maieutic*.

Swartz et al. (1998) highlight how information is often accepted from one (or more) source(s) without considering corroboration and reliability. They describe how when learners are engaged in critical thinking, they are assessing the 'reasonableness of ideas'. They present questions relating to everyday life that require critical thinking to answer them. For example, *'Should I accept the idea that eating red meat regularly is a health hazard, or should I believe that it is risk-free?' 'Should I embrace the idea of teaching thinking or should I concentrate on teaching just the facts?'* They suggest that accepting ideas and acting on them is the primary way we progress through our lives and in our professional work. Underpinning much of their teaching approaches is the basic philosophy that critical thinking is crucially important to ensure that the judgements to be made are more likely to be correct than incorrect, and that sound judgements cannot be made if all information heard and read is uncritically accepted. Good critical thinkers scrutinize ideas (with an open mind) and consider the positive and negative aspects of propositions before making judgements. Swartz et al. have developed a range of graphic organizers (explained in more detail in Chapter 6) and a series of questions to support the teaching of critical thinking skills. These skills are summarized in Table 9.1. There are two types of critical thinking they support: skills relating to assessing the reliability of basic information (from the Internet, textbooks, other people, personal observations and so forth) and skills relating to how conclusions are developed from inferences about evidence.

To engage skilfully in causal reasoning they highlight that students need to reflect on evidence with the following processes in mind:

- generating ideas about possible causes;
- considering what evidence would be necessary to show which is the probable cause;
- considering the extent of the evidence;
- making a judgement about the cause based on the evidence.

Swartz et al. (1998) extend their discussion about the lack of critical thinking in the context of thinking about possibilities or potential outcomes. As McGregor (2003) also found, students do not spontaneously predict or hypothesize when investigating problems. McGregor and Gunter (2006) also found that teachers did not regularly ask students to make projections about possible or potential findings in a variety of situations until they *understand* the 'thinking' value of students generating propositions. When thinking about making predictions students also need support in considering the likelihood of possibilities and what evidence they already have or know about that can support

Table 9.1 Outline of critical thinking skills developed by Swartz et al. (1998) (examples have been modified or generalized to connect more appropriately to UK situations

	Critical thinking
1 Assessing basic information	
a Accuracy of observation	This approach can be used to assess the accuracy of newspaper and magazine articles, reports, textbooks etc. The detailed guiding checklist of questions includes having the students think carefully about the experience, expertise, state of mind, physical ability, vested interests etc of the observer. They are also guided to critically review the conduct of the observations made (and reported on) and the nature of the report itself.
	E.g. Critically reviewing the accuracy of claims for previous Life on Mars; historical writings by different people of battles and past life.
b Reliability of sources	This approach can be used to assess primary or secondary sources of information. The guiding checklist of questions is designed to focus on the source of information, the nature of the publication, where and when it was published, whether it is reputable … is the author expert? Is there bias? Is it secondary or primary information? Is there any corroboration or confirmation with other sources?
	E.g. critically review articles about the same incident in *The Times* or the *Sun* newspapers.
2 Inference	
a Use of evidence	
Casual explanation	The guiding questions:
	What are the possible causes of the event in question? What could you find that would count for or against the likelihood of these possibilities? What evidence do you already have that is relevant to determining what caused the event? Which possibility is rendered most likely based on the evidence?
	E.g. critically review 'why did the plague spread so quickly in medieval Europe?' and 'why did the dinosaurs die out?'
b Prediction	The guiding questions:
	What might happen? What evidence might you get that would indicate that this prediction is likely? What evidence is available that is relevant to whether the prediction is likely? Based on the evidence, is the prediction likely, unlikely or uncertain?
	E.g. What will happen to crops if global warming continues? What will happen if the human population continues to increase at the current rate?
Generalization	The guiding questions:
	What generalization is suggested? What sample is needed to support that generalization? Is the sample being used large

enough? Is the sample representative of the whole group? Is the generalization well supported by the sample? If not, what

additional information is needed to support generalization?

E.g. All people living in Bourneville like Cadburys chocolate, so it must be the favourite chocolate in the UK. Everyone living in Bournemouth will vote for the Conservatives at the next election, so the Tories will be the next government.

Reasoning by analogy   The guiding questions:

What things are similar to the object or idea you are trying to understand? Which is similar in significant ways? What do you know about these things that you don't know about the thing you are trying to understand? What can you conclude regarding what you are trying to understand based on this analogy?

E.g. Is the postal service or the heating system in a house similar to the blood circulatory system? Why?

In studying perspective in Van Gogh's work is it useful to think about pixels that constitute graphics on a computer or how a camera works?

b Deduction

Conditional reasoning   The guiding questions:

What topic are you trying to get information about? Formulate a conditional statement that you know about that topic. What information do you have about the components of the conditional statement? What conclusion are you considering? Is it valid to reason from the conditional statement and the given information to the conclusion?

E.g. How important is the pituitary gland for growing?

Notes: Goal: critical judgement. Core skills: skills in assessing the reasonableness of ideas.

their suggestions. Swartz et al. also highlight how causal explanation, prediction, generalization and reasoning by analogy are all strategies based on evaluating and using the evidence available.

Lipman (2003: 56) highlights characteristics of those who think critically as 'keenly analytical', 'scrupulously accurate' and 'clear headed'. He also indicates how, more recently, 'critical thinking has come to denote *any* thinking that, when applied to an instance of thinking, could make it more efficient and more reliable'. He lists, almost as extensively as Ennis, a wide variety of characterizations that reflect how critical thinking should strive to be 'impartial, accurate, careful, truthful, abstract, coherent and practical. Sternberg (2003) connects practical critical skills with adapting to and reshaping a problem situation to develop a solution and subsequently act wisely.

Supporting teachers to understand the nature of critical thinking

The various ways of classifying and categorizing critical thinking skills (Figure 2.1, Figure 1.3, Table 2.1, Table 9.1) that constitute a significant proportion of 'thinking skills' offer contrasting insights into how mental activity can be perceived. What educators need to appreciate is the nature of thinking critically to begin to recognize how various cognitive processes can contribute towards thinking skilfully in that way.

Puzzles, games and many activities in the various thinking programmes can be used to highlight and emphasize the nature of critical thinking. A simple thinking activity, developed from a children's puzzle book, is 'Finding the Photo' (see Figure 9.2). This activity is fun and authentic. It can provide much material for discussion about critical thinking. The cognitive processes that could be applied to *figure out* not only the correct sequence of the photos but also subsequently which one might be fabricated and not real includes comparing, contrasting, sequencing, inferring, analysing, synthesizing and hypothesizing. The cognitive processes and the problem solving strategies that are developed and used, become clarified through metacognitive discussion. Further consideration of the contrasting experience of the origami activity, described in Chapter 8, can enhance the understanding of the difference in nature between creative and critical thinking. Typically the differences that classrom practitioners identify are those summarized in Table 8.2.

Table 9.2 Examples of the potential for critical thinking in some of programmes reviewed

Programme	Nature of critical thinking potential
CA suite of programmes	In KS3 CASE programme:
	Reflection of all reasoning achieved (e.g. understanding variables; proportionality and ratio; probability; classification; correlation; equilibrium; compound variables).
	Analysis of the activities and what they mean; synthesis of reflections about activities.
	Prediction through asking students what will happen next?
	In CATE programme:
	Control and exclusion of variables – exploring characteristics of objects, their similarities and differences, not just through observation, but also drawing; processing information from multiple sources (or factors) to solve a variety of problems within technology and everyday life
	Logical reasoning – application of truth tables, sequencing and analysis of controversial evidence to deduct solutions to tasks and mysteries.
	Gathering and organizing information – thinking about what is important and relevant in connecting the pieces of information together, tasks set within the context of technology tools, everyday objects, machines and materials.
	Recognizing and defining problems – clarifying what is to be explored or investigated in the context of solving a mystery or sequencing actions of people (in different roles) or processes (of a technological context).
	In ARTs programme:
	Classification – applying consistent criteria to classify attributes or objects into groups or categories using criteria, such as chronology, loudness, medium.
	Frames of reference – recognizing and applying predefined notions of rhythm, balance, symmetry, equilibrium, style etc to pieces of drama, music or art. Includes reasoned assumptions.
	Symbolic representation – includes using analogy and metaphor, gesture and mime, or signs and symbols to communicate ideas and messages
	Critical reflection – includes reflection of artistic intention of others, justifying opinions and actions, recognizing and explain bias, justify arguments.

Table 9.2 *continued*

Programme	Nature of critical thinking potential
	Causality – explore and explain cause and effect in music, drama and art scenarios Narrative seriation – includes sequencing, ordering stories, drama or musical pieces and even using flashbacks to develop complex narratives.
ACTs	The following are infused into learning activities across the curriculum: • Making predictions and formulating hypotheses. • Drawing conclusions, giving reasons for conclusions, not jumping to conclusions. • Distinguishing fact from opinion. • Determining bias. • Being concerned about accuracy and checking. • Relating cause and effects, designing a fair test.
Thinking Together	The pupils are expected to 'reason' about their ideas throughout all the activities. They are often asked about their views. Questions are asked frequently, some of which can help develop critical thinking; e.g. 'What kind of character is X?' 'What choices does X have?' 'Why should …'? There is also activity comparing contrasting poems purposely designed to develop critical thinking; and a game where the pupils are encouraged to develop their own critical questions.
TT series (Geography; History; Religious Education; English; Science etc)	Information processing skills involving: • Locating and collecting relevant information; • Sorting, classifying, sequencing, comparing and contrasting; • Analysing part-whole relationships. Reasoning skills involving: • Giving reasons for opinions and actions; • Draw inferences and making deductions;

- Using precise language to explain what they think;
- Make judgements.

Enquiry skills involving:

- Asking relevant questions;
- Defining problems;
- Predicting outcomes and anticipating consequences;
- Testing conclusions.

Evaluation skills involving:

- Evaluating information;
- Judging value of what is seen, heard and done;
- Develop criteria for judging their and others' work or ideas;
- Have confidence in their judgements.

Are all developed through the 5Ws; Odd one out; Classification; Living graphs; Mystery; Taboo and Maps from memory teaching strategies used across the subject areas.

IEP/STS/TTTT	Very wide range of processing skills including analysing, synthesizing, recognizing relationships and patterns, etc. Reflective generalizations about what is perceived through activities and recognizing where possible application of problem solving skills to real world.
P4C	The following critical skills are developed within the discussions after reading the various novels: Making judgements; classifying; distinguishing; recognizing; exemplifying; reversing ideas; connecting evidence; extending rules to be more inclusive; recognizing.
De Bono's six thinking hats/action shoes	Black-hat thinking – recognizing poor ideas or the disadvantages in some suggestion or idea. White hat thinking – looking for and describing benefits in suggestions or ideas. Each of the shoes – hypothesizing about possible actions and critically assessing consequences of carrying out one thing or another.

Table 9.3 Summary of reasoning, critical and creative thinking potential in Let's Think (CA) activities

Reasoning Focus	Lessons	Context of activities that are used to promote the reasoning	Critical thinking skills needed to succeed in the lesson activities	Potential creative thinking opportunities
Seriation	1, 2, 3, 10, 11, 15	Sticks, flowers, marble run, stones, boxes, library books	Sorting, sequencing, ordering, comparing, contrasting	Bridging to why, where and when this type of reasoning (thinking to put things in sequence or progressive order) would be applicable in everyday life.
Classification	4, 5, 6, 7, 9, 13, 14, 19	Shapes, farm animals I & II, buttons, cars, living, guess what, bricks	Comparing, contrasting, sorting, grouping, classifying	Creating (modifying/refining/developing) criteria for group characteristics. Bridging to why, where and when this type of reasoning (putting things together in groups with similar characteristics) would be applicable in everyday life.
Time sequence	8, 12, 21, 27	Lost boot, cooking, the cat and snail story, the ice cream story	Extrapolating, inferring, deducting, analysing synthesizing, rationalizing	Creating narratives and explanations for the living characters and placement/movement of objects in the stories.
Spatial perception	16, 17, 18, 26	crossroads I and II, looking at shapes, farmyard	Analysing, synthesizing, ordering, connecting, empathizing, changing perspective, making assumptions, deducting	Bridging to why spatial perception is useful in everyday life.
Causality	20, 22, 25	Rolling bottles, shadows, transformations	Analysing, synthesizing, generalizing, extrapolating, predicting	Creating reasons for observable happenings. Bridging to cause and effect in own life.
Rules of a game	23, 24	In this town, making a game	Analysing, synthesizing, generalizing hypothesizing, sequencing	Creating new rules. Bridging to own life where adhering (or not) to rules.

- The following pictures have been taken.
- They are not in order.
- One of them is not real, it is a digital recreation … use your logic to try and work out which one it is.

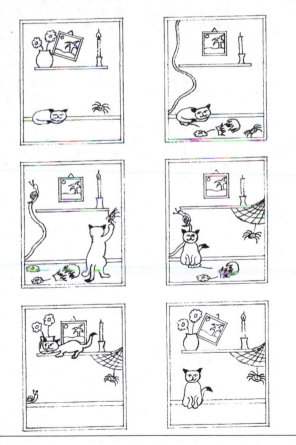

Figure 9.2 Find the photo activity

Enabling educators to experientially compare and contrast creative and critical thinking, helps them realize how *what* they do as teachers strongly influences the kinds of cognitive processing and problem solving approaches their own pupils can experience in learning. To critically review, *what* and *how*, teaching thinking programmes *can contribute* to the development of critical thinking in learners, teachers themselves need to become critical thinkers. Table 9.4 suggests how

Table 9.4 Compilation of vignettes to emphasize how students' thinking can be supported to become more critical

Context	Task that involves critical thinking	Development of task to develop *more skilful* critical thinking
Maths	Following instructions to calculate the dimensions of the school hall (for new flooring).	Choosing the best method (of at least two or more) ways of measuring and then calculating dimensions of the school floor. Being able to give a variety of reasons (practical and theoretical) as to why the method chosen is the best and the method(s) rejected are not so useful.
English	Reading a poem about winter and explaining it to someone else.	Comparing and contrasting two poems about winter. Developing a set of criteria by which each poem could be judged. Being able to use the criteria and explain how mood, style and other aspects are different between the poems.
Science	Matching full descriptions of parts of a plant to the diagram of a flower.	Being able to name and recognize the parts of the plant from the name labels (with extra descriptors/incomplete descriptors/wrong descriptors) and offer explanation in own words why each part is structured the way it is. Contrasting different plants to identify similar structures (e.g. stem, carpel, pollen, stigma etc.)
Shopping	Budgeting better on a low income to purchase food. Which is the best low price store?	Considering more influential factors on the efficacy of shopping (e.g. amount of money, time, quality of products etc.) before doing it, and reflecting afterward. Logically arguing which are the most important criteria to save money. Time efficiency, quality of goods or total amount of money spent?
Football	Practising for an hour, repeatedly, as the trainer instructed, the new 1,2,3 offensive move with two team members.	Consider what offensive moves are possible in this situation? Which is the best to use? How can we improve them? Which do we need to practice most? When should we use the move? Do each of us understand our contribution to the move? When to use it or when to revert back to an established manoeuvre?

teachers might review and modify learning activities to support *more skilful* critical thinking.

Active experience, engagement and guided reflection in thinking tasks is often needed before practitioners can critically (and creatively) review and develop appropriate tasks to encourage more skillful specific cognitive processing. Reflecting on activities in this way may help educators better recognise where thinking opportunities lie in their curriculum. As Dewey (1910: 39) indicates:

> any subject, from Greek to cooking and from drawing to mathematics, is intellectual, if intellectual at all, not in its fixed inner structure, but in its function – its power to start and direct significant inquiry and reflection. What geometry does for one, the manipulation of laboratory apparatus, the mastery of a musical composition, or the conduct of a business affair, may do for another.

Critical thinking and thinking programmes

Cognitive Acceleration approach

The suite of programmes within the CA approach all focus on development of understanding of various reasoning patterns (or Piagetian schemata). These understandings are usually reached in a reflective way through questioning after engaging in some kind of activity. Transfer or bridging to the real world is a metacognitive strategy to help learners connect their thinking to other contexts. This also involves some critical thinking to compare and contrast possibilities and evaluate their reasonableness. In the *Let's Think* programme for Year 1 children, in an activity on classification, they consider living and non-living things and their associated characteristics. The children are given different picture cards of objects and living organisms. In turn they have to place their card, with a reason, in either the living or non-living pile. The first child has a picture of a fish. He reasons it should be placed in the living pile because it moves. The second child has a picture of a hand-knitted jumper. She reasons it can not be placed in either pile because 'it is not alive, it doesn't move or eat; but the wool it is made of came from a living animal, a sheep … so could it go in a different pile?'

The first child demonstrated, clearly, critical thinking, applying what he knew about a characteristic of living things to the fish. He determined that fish could belong in the group 'living'. The second child demonstrated both critical and creative thinking. Critical in that she mentally compared and contrasted characteristics of living and non-living things with an object that she knew something about. Her suggestion that it had characteristics that didn't conform to established criteria and that a third pile or group should be considered indicated some creative originality in her suggestion. If she extended her reasoning to describe or suggest characteristics of this third group, that included 'once alive' or 'part of an animal that lived', arguably she was generating another possibility. In learning activities there are often a variety of cognitive processes that are required to reach a solution. Therefore several cognitive skills may be applied to complete the activity. Table 9.3 suggests the range of cognitive skills that young children may apply when engaging in learning activities, with specific examples (see also Table 4.3) emphasized from the Let's Think CA programme.

ARTs programme

Yates and Gouge (2002) include critical reflection in their thinking arts programme. The learners have to act as 'critics' and in so doing develop their skill in judging (art, drama and music). The intention within the programme is to support students maturing from a subjective and constrained view of objects and situations to a more imaginative but comprehensively objective perspective requiring explanations for judgements. Other additional opportunities to think critically are listed in Table 9.2.

Activating Children's Thinking

McGuinness (2000) in her ACTs programme emphasizes how thinking critically includes learning how to scrutinize and examine one's own thinking and to adopt a sceptical stance. In so doing pupils need to check the reliability of sources, to assess the reasonableness of ideas and to examine cause and effect. The process of determining the authenticity, accuracy, or value of something is characterized by the ability to seek reasons and alternatives, perceive the total situation, and change one's view based on evidence. This is also referred to as 'logical' or 'analytical' thinking. McGuinness et al. (2003) emphasize that for pupils to engage in critical thinking they need:

- to develop habits of mind or depositions for thinking critically;
- to be open minded and questioning about conclusions;
- to examine reasons for and against argument and not to 'jump to conclusions';

- to show concern for accuracy in using evidence and be ready to check the reliability of their sources;
- to practise relating reasons to conclusions for causal reasoning, making predictions, using evidence and drawing generalizations.

Thinking Together

This programme has focused some activities around critical thinking. One lesson looking into poems encourages children to critically question. They have to reason why they like one or other of the three very different poems. They are encouraged to consider different criteria to make judgements, including the types of words used, whether it is challenging to understand, whether it is funny or clever and even if after listening to others' views they change their minds about what is good or not.

Thinking Through ... (TT) series

As outlined in Table 4.4 and 4.6, these teaching strategies offer multiple opportunities for students to think critically. As indicated through the analysis of the thinking opportunities in Table 9.2, in many learning activities there are several cognitive processes that may be applied. The TTRE lesson on the Seder table used the approach of 'maps from memory'. Some students observe a prepared Seder Table for a short time and then have to return to their working groups to relay information about the contents and arrangement of objects on it. The other members of each working group have to produce a diagrammatic representation of the table. There may be a temptation by teachers to cue and clue to direct the groups to reproduce an accurate drawing including everything that is on the table.

STS/FIE/TTTT

These activities can provide very interesting ways to develop many cognitive skills. The modules titled 'comparative thinking', analysing and synthesizing' and 'understanding analogies' provide very rich opportunities to stimulate critical thinking. The materials are very open to interpretation, deliberately, so many kinds of cognitive processes that support thinking critically can be activated. In one activity the students are provided with a diagram of a dustbin containing a variety of rubbish (a black bin liner containing *clean* household rubbish can be even more motivatory). The purpose is for the students to work out, through various deductive means, whatever they can about the occupants of the house from whom the rubbish bin is taken. They have to connect their predictions or hypotheses about the occupants using the rubbish as evidence. Although predominantly critical, creativity is involved too. Hypothesizing and connecting items or objects with activities or the lifestyle of a family requires much critico-creative thinking.

De Bono's thinking hats

De Bonos' black and blue hats, require critical appraisal of information or development of reasoning about an idea or suggestion. Black-hat and yellow-hat thinking could stimulate critiquing a proposition by assessing its positive and negative aspects. The green hat is more critico-creative. The blue hat is reflective and requires appraisal of the thinking that has led up to the decision making or the conclusion reached in a task or discussion.

Challenging ideas to critique and critically consider with different thinking hats might be 'all clothes should be made of recycled materials' or 'all cars should by fueled by methane' or 'fast food will become very expensive'.

Conclusion

Many of the learning activities pupils engage in at school can be developed, honed or modified in some way to apply an aspect of critical thinking. The chapter began by outlining various views of thinking critically and ended with brief accounts of some activities that can support this kind of cognitive perspective. Educators understanding what constitutes critical thinking should be better informed about how to nurture this in their students and look for a range of contrasting opportunities where it can be activated, emphasized and subsequently developed over time.

Many forms of critical thinking have been described, some of which are more comfortably developed in specific programmes, types of lesson or subject matter. Most of the programmes support some development of critical thinking, but some require more demanding thought than others. The varied ways in which pupils can be encouraged to engage independently more widely and deeply with critical thinking depends upon curricular and pedagogic choices that schools and teachers make. These programmes, however, do offer insights into how to develop critical thinking and some offer a systematic way of doing so. Emphasizing affective aspects of these approaches is imperative to encourage independent critical thinking. We do not wish pupils to think (as the poem above suggests) that teachers *always* hold *all* the *answers*!

Key ideas

Thinking critically is the mental act of reviewing, evaluating or appraising something (including a picture, play, information, evidence, or opinion) in an attempt to make judgements, inferences or meaning about that something in a rational, reasoned way.

Thinking critically is more concerned with objectivity as opposed to thinking creatively, which is more subjective in nature.

A wide range of cognitive skills that contribute to the process(es) of critical thinking have been expressed. Core critical skills include:
- inferring
- explaining or reasoning
- analyzing
- synthesizing
- generalizing
- summarizing
- evaluating or judging

Thinking programmes support development of different kinds of critical thinking:
- the CA programme generally supports thinking about Piagetan schemata, what the reasoning patterns mean and how they can be applied in the context of learning particular subjects
- the ARTs programme can also provide the opportunity to think as a *critic*
- thinking Together provides specific activities to be critical
- ACTs offers a way of infusing thinking critically across the curriculum
- P4C extends critique to moral, ethical and social contexts

Skilful critical thinking may also require skills that could be deemed more creative and may be referred to as critico-creative thinking, for example, generating criteria by which to judge something or refining, modifying or improving an idea.

10 Development of metacognition

> ... pedagogy of mutuality presumes that all human minds are capable of holding beliefs and ideas which, through discussion and interaction, can be moved toward some shared frame of reference. Both child and adult have points of view, and each is encouraged to recognise the other's, though they may not agree. They must come to recognise that differing views may be based on recognizable reasons and that these reasons provide the basis for adjudicating rival beliefs. Sometimes you are 'wrong', sometimes others are – that depends on how well reasoned the views are. Sometimes opposing are both right – or both wrong. The child is not merely ignorant or an empty vessel, but somebody able to reason, to make sense, both on her own and through discourse with others. The child ... is capable of thinking about her own thinking, and of correcting her ideas and notions through reflection – by 'going meta', as it is sometimes called.'
>
> (Bruner, *The Culture of Education*)

This chapter considers a range of views that exist regarding metacognition in teaching, learning and thinking. It then elaborates on how those views and various pedagogic approaches support the development of metacognition.

'Meta' in the sense that Bruner (1996: 56) uses it above, is concerned with learners reflecting on their own views and those of others about something, and developing a more *reasoned* idea through that reflective process. Enlightenment or elucidation of ideas through reflection is further supported by Dewey.

Dewey (1910: 6) describes reflective thought as 'careful consideration of any belief or supposed form of knowledge in the light of the grounds that support it, and the further conclusions to which it tends'. He connects the process of reflective thinking to the development of beliefs. Consideration of the basis of beliefs, being able to reason why an idea is so, is an important aspect of metacognition.

Statt (1998) defines metacognition as 'having knowledge or awareness of one's own cognitive processes'. Roberts and Erdos (1993: 259) extend it from the awareness of one's own thinking to being able to articulate and define it. They describe how metacognition refers to knowledge about cognition itself, cognitizing about cognition. Smith (1994: 22) highlights how implicit cognitive processes can become more explicit through metacognition to indicate where improvements can be made. 'Metacognitive processes are presumed to take place when we think about our own thinking, for example, when we reflect upon whether we know something, whether we are learning, or whether we have made a mistake'. Larkin et al. (1980) reiterate this, because, arguably, 'It is only after one has solved a problem that one can learn most effectively how one should have solved it', or could have solved it. As Nickerson et al. (1985) emphasize, 'the training of such skills, if done effectively, should have considerable payoff. In particular, in as much as these skills are very general, a successful effort to improve them should beneficially affect performance on a wide range of tasks'.

Flavell (1976: 232) indicates how thinking reflectively can become a monitoring technique that serves to guide and focus subsequent thought. He says 'Metacogntion refers, among other things, to the active monitoring and consequent regulation and orchestration of these processes in relation to the cognitive objects or data on which they bear, usually in the service of some concrete goal or objective.' Cobb et al., (1997) extend metacognition to thinking reflectively through social (re)construction of collective ideas. They consider how each participant may influence or change the dimensions of another's view. He describes how collective exchanges, focused on descriptions of mental acts to complete tasks, can lead to conceptualization about thought processes – something that Sternberg and Wagner (1982) indicated was not prevalent when children were asked about why they solved problems in the ways that they did. In educational programmes designed to enhance thinking skills, metacognitive approaches have been shown to impact positively (Swanson 1990; Lucangeli et al. 1994; Schwanenflugel et al. 1994; Marzano et al. 2001; Higgins et al. 2004, 2005) on the learning experience. Hartman explains:

> Metacognition is especially important because it affects acquisition, comprehension, retention and application of what is learned, in addition to affecting learning efficiency, critical thinking and problem solving. Metacognitive awareness enables control or self-regulation over thinking and learning processes and products.
>
> (Hartman 1998: 1)

Teaching and learning and thinking programmes, however, interpret and apply metacognition at different levels and in different ways.

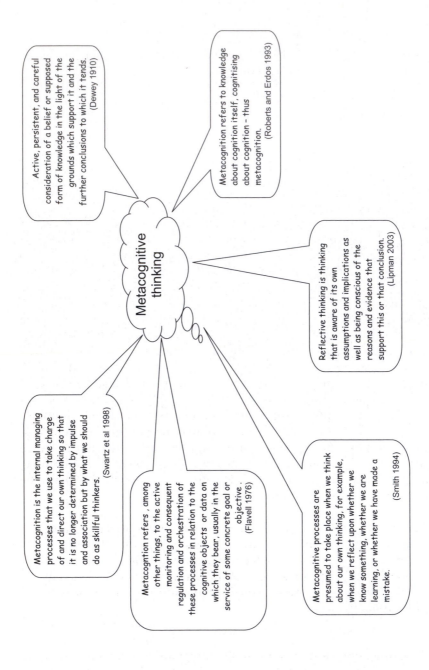

Figure 10.1 Definitions of metacognition

The CA approach uses Adey's (1997) view of metacognition as 'thinking about your thinking, becoming conscious of your own reasoning'. This is what is expected to arise towards the end of a thinking lesson. Piaget (1950) viewed 'reflected abstraction' as an individual's generalization regarding the external stimuli perceived and the observations resulting from it. Adhami et al (1998: xiii) describe how the teacher has to intervene and engage the whole class in elaborating on what they have achieved and why or how it worked, often recording the processes involved in the pupils' own words. The TT series advocates reflection in the debriefing section of the lessons that support understanding about the process of learning. This is the time when teacher and students discuss and evaluate the thinking and learning that has taken place (Butterworth and O'Connor 2005: 3). The aim is to help them think about how they can improve their learning in future, by being informed sufficiently to take control of their learning processes in subsequent situations.

Nickerson et al. (1985) suggest that it is through metacognition that one becomes 'a skilful user of knowledge'. The P4C approach corroborates this and highlights how metacognition should also promote thinking carefully and constructively about how to improve one's thinking. It emphasizes how the students should have a 'clear perception of oneself and the contents of one's consciousness' (Lipman et al. 1980: 204). The children are encouraged to recognize and reason about different standpoints from which to view ideas. Artists or scientists, for example, may make very different judgements about colour or works of art, because they may be more objective or subjective in the criteria they apply; a perpetrator of a criminal act will perceive fair punishment in very different light from a victim.

ACTs highlights how metacognition is the kind of thinking least familiar to teachers, but nonetheless is crucial for the development and enhancement of thinking skills. McGuinness et al. (2003) reiterate that metacognition is 'thinking about your thinking' and emphasize how reflection and evaluation are key in helping students coming to realize the thinking they have employed to solve a problem or tackle a task. Although recognizably challenging, ACTs provides prompts, which can support teachers in focusing students on reflection. This infused approach greatly values classroom dialogue and suggest ways in which students can be questioned, to 'go meta' at different points in a learning task (see Figure 10.2).

McGuinness at al also emphasize how developing a vocabulary for talking about thinking facilitates metacognition. They suggest that students be introduced to appropriate words, such as 'guess', 'predict', 'conclude', or 'estimate'. The words should be elaborated, the use of

Figure 10.2 Providing students with a rich thoughtful palette of cognitive skills

them modelled and posters describing them could even be displayed in the classroom. The process of metacognition also involves asking pupils to describe their plans or strategy before beginning a task, review it when the task is complete and compare different strategies that groups use and ask them for improvements to their plans. McGuinness (2005) suggests that this metacognitive perspective makes thinking more visible in classrooms and optimizes adoption and transfer of learning. Swartz et al. (1998) describe how the thinking used in a task has to be identified before it can be analysed, evaluated and improved upon. They have designed a graphic organizer that asks about the kind of thinking used in a task, the steps taken in the task and how then the thinking engaged in can be used again in a different situation. The STS approach also emphasizes how students should be able to describe the thought processes they use when solving problems so that they can apply appropriate techniques and methods in similar situations in future.

Nickerson et al. (1985) indicate how, as STS advocates, metacognition is about knowing how to use what you know and knowing how to improve how you learn. Dewey (1910: 220) likens knowing what techniques to use in solving problems with the artistic ideal. 'When an artist is preoccupied overmuch with means and materials, he may achieve wonderful technique, but not the artistic spirit *par excellence'*. Therefore if we wish our students to think skilfully, perhaps we should consider how to provide them with a rich, thoughtful, palette of cognitive skills, so they can respond reflectively and flexibly in future to problem situations by artfully selecting appropriate thinking strategies (see Figure 10.2).

Levels of metacognition

Learners can be asked to reflect on the thinking that they did to solve a problem or answer a question at different levels and can be prompted by different kinds of questions (see Table 10.1). Asking students how they compared the lives of Lincoln and Douglas, a simple response would be just to reply and say 'I read the two pages and looked for what was similar and then what was different about the men's lives'. A more sophisticated response might be 'I read about Lincoln first. Then I read about Douglas. Then I reread the information and compared when they were born, what they did as children, how they became qualified, then what they did politically'. This second level of metacognition is describing the strategy used to compare and contrast the men's lives. Evaluating and then making a judgement about whether the strategy used was good or not requires metacognition at a deeper level. Comparison with others' strategies can support a wider evaluation of a variety of more-or-less successful approaches. Other students might have just searched from the beginning, in parallel, for key words in both texts, scanning for birth information, then childhood, then adulthood. Elicitation of different thinking approaches is needed before they can then be compared and evaluated. The students describing their tactics, for others to be aware of what they learned through their method, is key to enabling others to perceive that there are alternative cognitive strategies that can be used to reach a similar or acceptable solution to a problem. This is particularly important for teachers to engage in to realize how thinking programmes, activities and pedagogy can influence the kinds of thinking developed. This influence of pedagogy on the nature of metacognition is explained in more detail in Chapter 13.

Any thinking activities, such as games, poems, novels (Fisher 2001), or *Let's Think* (Adey et al. 2001) narratives to put in order,

Table 10.1 Varying depths or levels of metacognition

Level	Metacognitive level	Teacher mediation to focus metacognition at this level
1st	Becoming aware of thinking and being able to describe it.	Describe what you have done. Describe to me how you are doing it. What words can you use to describe the way you tackled the task?
2nd	Developing cognizance of thinking strategy/cognitive processes being used and after used.	Why did you do it that way? How did other people do it? Could you have done it a different way? How did you decide that this was the best way?
3rd	Evaluative reflection of procedure (before/during/after).	How well did your approach work? How did you/do you know your strategy is working? Did you change anything as you did it? Does the order of steps matter? How could you improve the strategy?
4th	Transfer of procedural experience and knowledge to another context.	Where else would this strategy be useful? Why? What kind of problem was it? What kind of solution did you develop? How would you approach a similar problem next time?
5th	Connecting the conceptual understanding with the procedural experience.	How did approaching the problem this way help you understand what (subject concept) you were learning about? What information/data/evidence was most important in helping you figure out the solution? What thought processes did you use to solve this kind of problem? What happened along your thinking journey that helped you understand?

TTG (Leat 2001) the mind movies or the living graphs, *Thinking Maths* roofs (Adhami et al. 1998) – in fact, all the thinking activities – could be approached in different ways, thus potentially offering multiple ways of solving them. How the teacher presents the task and the kinds of reflective questions posed about thoughtful involvement and progress can influence the extent and nature of the metacognition engaged in. Exploring the range of strategies learners use to solve problems is key in metacognition. Explaining why a task was approached in a particular way presents others with alternative thoughtful insights. Sharing implicit decision making enables others to appreciate a wider range of mental tools that can be used. Taking the next step in reflection, to evaluate the different possible strategies, really is becoming 'meta' cognitive. Evaluating thinking strategies, tactics or approaches to problem solving and then considering when these strategies were used before and where could they be useful or applicable in future is becoming reflexively metacognitive. As Karmiloff-Smith (1991) indicates, becoming 'conscious of our own thought processes ...' is key before being able to develop the '... ability to be reflexive'. Some programmes employ this kind of thinking; it is, however, an approach that could be used more widely and even more powerfully. It is frequently referred to as self-directed learning in US.

Metacognition and questioning

McGuiness et al. (2003) in ACTs prescribe the questions that teachers should ask to focus student reflections during learning tasks:

1 *When pupils are planning a task they can be encouraged to reflect on previous experience and think ahead.*
   - How are you going to do this task?
   - Is it similar to anything you have done before?
   - Is it *one of those ...?*
2 *When pupils are completing a task, they can be encouraged to reflect on their progress.*
   - What do I understand so far?
   - Do I need to ask a question?
   - Am I on the right track?
   - Am I still on track?
3 *When pupils have completed a task, they need to evaluate ...*
   - How did I do it?
   - What methods did I use?
   - Did my plan work out well?
   - Can I learn from my mistakes?
   - Can I do better next time?

Questions that prompt pupils to reflect on the mental processing they have used to reach a solution requires them to stand back from involvement in the learning to reflect more objectively and consider what was done and how it was done. The nature of these and the level of metacognition that can be developed are suggested in Table 10.1. Claxton (1999: 191) describes this becoming reflective as 'the consciousness of good learning'. He goes on to say that: 'Being reflective means looking inward as well as out, making explicit to ourselves the meanings and implications that may be latent within our store of originally unreflective know-how'. It also includes influences of others that shape our beliefs and understandings. In this sense he says: 'In periods of reflection ... ruminating on experiences ... to see what larger significance they may have. At the same time ... theories ... can be re-examined in the light of personal history'.

Intervention is critical to raise awareness of and development in reflective thinking. Reflection of thinking outcomes and thinking processes engaged in during the lesson should be shared. The nature of applied thinking (creative, critical, metacognitive) and the associated specific cognitive skills involved should become overt, for example 'What kind of critical thinking was needed to analyse the key factors influencing the course of the Second World War or the life of the Mayor of Casterbridge or the way continents have moved over that last few million years?' Important generalized metacognitive questions that a teacher can ask include:

- What did you think at the beginning?
- What do you think now?
- How did you find that out?
- What strategies did you use?
- How has your thinking changed/developed?
- How is your thinking about this different or similar to some one else? Why do you think your ideas are different?
- What has influenced your thinking (doing something; listening to someone; explaining to someone; reflecting on something)?

Metacognition is not just about teachers asking pupils questions, it is also about students questioning themselves and/or each other. Meta-cognition through questioning can arise through collaborative exchange and development of exploratory talk (described in collaboration and talk section). Students can be guided to use self-reflective questions that support metacognition in thought as well as action. Schoenfeld's view (1985) extends the notion of metacognition being solely cognitive. He indicates how it should involve reflection on action too. It can relate to actions, in a very general sense, not just within scholastic contexts of learning an academic subject. Students learning to evaluate and steer their own progress regularly ask questions such as:

- What am I doing here?
- Is it getting me anywhere?
- Am I doing it the best way possible?
- What else could I be doing instead?

These are very general reflective questions, but they can provide support to help students avoid persevering with unproductive approaches to a problem or challenge.

Metacognition and the curriculum

Leat and Lin (2003) and McGuinness (2005) indicate that it is evident that metacognition consistently features as a critical part of interventions to raise achievement and improve approaches to learning. Current reforms demand that teaching thinking is taught in the National Curriculum in England so that pupils can reflect on *what and how* they have learned and transfer their learning to new contexts. To do this pupils must develop metacognitive knowledge. The DfES (2003a) National Strategy describes metacognition, as one of four ways to improve thinking. Metacognition is described as the ability to monitor, regulate and select strategies in doing a task. It can be facilitated by developing reflection on thinking and learning that can:

- articulate the cognitive processes used;
- recognize why they were appropriate skills to use;
- connect the thinking skills to the learning outcomes;
- suggest creatively where else these thinking skills could be usefully applied.

These are processes that the DfES would like supported in schools. What, hopefully, will also be stimulated, to a greater or lesser extent in some pupils, over time, is private reflection. Intrinsically stimulated reflective thinking (or even self-directed learning) may result in pupils applying cognitive skills and strategies to problem solving in life, or to even solve scientific technological, or social problems of the future.

Leat and Higgins (2002) indicate that metacognition and transfer are in danger of becoming overconceptualized and underrealized. They highlight why it is important that teachers are supported in realizing what metacognition means in a pragmatic sense in the classroom and that they recognise its value in helping students understand *how and what* they learn. The main issue, however, that remains to challenge teachers, is the overcrowded curriculum and little time for professional development and refocus of pedagogic approaches. There are further suggestions made about how to support teachers understanding the nature of a thinking pedagogy in Chapter 13.

Metacognition and generalization

Reflecting on a theory of education, Bruner (1986), asks how the learning experience for the pupils could be improved. He suggests that teachers should reflect on their impact on students' learning as well as supporting students to reflect on their personal learning experience. He elaborates that the process of reflection is better if one distances oneself from one's thoughts. Reflection to gain better insights or perspectives of one's learning experience requires standing back from the experience itself. He explicates how 'transaction' of self and knowing requires reflection, (implying a reflecting agent) and 'metacognition requires a master routine that knows how and when to break away from straight processing to corrective processing procedures' (Bruner 1986: 129). His view indicates that a temporal or spatial gap is needed to reflect and generalize effectively about a learning experience. He also suggests that some kind of routine method of reflection is useful to inform individuals about how to improve.

Reflectivity is about, as Dewey (1938) would say, moving from 'routine action' to 'reflective action'. Schon (1983) would say that it is about moving beyond 'habitual action' to consider other factors. Flexible reflection or metacognition is what Sternberg (1997) highlights when he discusses 'practical intelligence' (one of three basic facets in his triarchic view of successful intelligence).

Claxton (1999: 131) describes metacognition as a way of encouraging the development of people so that they can manage their minds more productively and deploy their resources most effectively. Dyer (1995) has indicated that

> from an early age (five upwards) children are able to engage meaningfully in dialogue about their own learning, and can use frameworks offered by the teacher to access their own intuitive understanding of themselves as learners. This seems to indicate that teachers could now desist from treating children as passengers in the voyage of their own learning ... and treat young learners as pilots.

Vygotsky (1978) emphasized the role of metacognition to connect scientific thinking with everyday referents, to enable concepts to 'come to life' and be applicable across a range of situations.

> Vygotsky made it a point to argue that scientific concepts far from being assimilated in a ready made form, actually undergo substantial development which essentially depends on the

existing level of a child's general ability to form concepts. This level of comprehension in its turn is connected with the development of spontaneous concepts. Spontaneous concepts in working their way upward toward greater abstractness, clear a path for scientific concepts in their downwards development toward greater concreteness.

(Kozulin 1986: xxxiv)

Howe (1997) explains this by arguing that whereas pupils may be able to define or explain a given concept on a verbal level and be able to use words to express their understanding, a concept remains an abstraction and is not fully understood unless or until it can be applied to specific examples. In applying generalized concepts to specific examples student thinking becomes concrete, moving from the plane of abstract thought to the phenomenon represented by the words or symbols. In contrast, everyday concepts develop outside a definite system; therefore to be understood in relation to what has been learned in school, thinking about a given phenomenon must move upward from the known specific example toward abstraction and generalization. The child must eventually come to see everyday concepts as part of a system of relationships and at, the same time come to see how the experienced object or phenomenon fits into the scientific system he or she has been taught. In other words, as teachers, a metacognitive aim should be to support and encourage the learners to make lateral and vertical connections with prior learning and life experience to enable gradual construction of generalizations of the world-to-be-learned-about.

Metacognition and transfer

Adey and Shayer (2002) describe this as Act 4 in a CA lesson. They describe how bridging, the finale in a thinking lesson, is the process of linking the type of thinking developed to the broader curriculum and real life. Ashman and Conway (1997) indicate that the nature of the link between situations must be cognitive, so that the learning is not fixed to one task. They indicate how the role of the teacher is not to provide examples of bridging, but to have students draw on their personal experiences or prior knowledge to explain where else the thinking would be applicable. The aim is to ensure the contexts that students connect are more relevant to them than the teacher (see Figure 10.3).

The issue of transfer is still seen as very fraught. Desforges and Lings (1998) point out that transferring knowledge from one context to another is not straightforward, illustrated by the famous example of

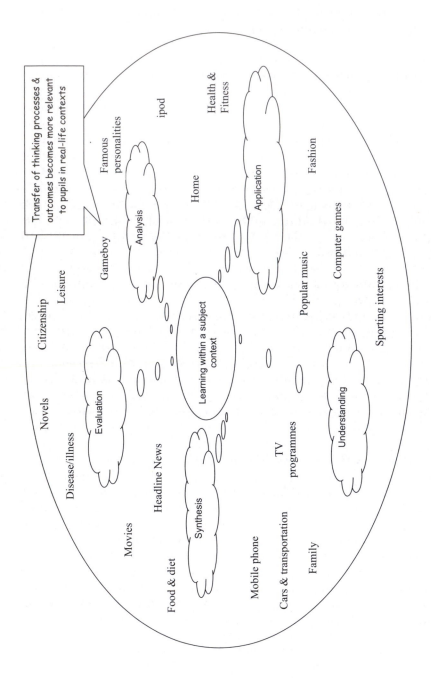

Figure 10.3 Possible contexts for far transfer of thinking processes or products

accomplished child street traders who cannot apply their knowledge to simple classroom tests (Nunes et al. 1993).

Transferring thinking processes

Blagg et al. (1988: 52) highlight how transfer is a key aspect of the STS approach. He indicates how this overlaps with Feuerstein's notion of 'transcendence', that is, the purpose of each activity transcends beyond the immediate demands of the thinking task. The aim is to facilitate pupils acquiring skills and strategies that can be deployed flexibly in novel situations. Progression is built into the tasks for each module. They become more challenging through presenting more information to be processed, making the tasks more abstract or changing the style and content. To develop generalization, to be able to transfer thoughts, the teachers are guided to ask:

- What is similar about this activity compared to previous ones?
- What is different?
- Have you learned anything previously that will help you with this task?

The intent is to mediate the transfer of skills and strategies until students themselves spontaneously apply them in problem solving situations with no prompting. This view is corroborated by Mayer and Wittrock (1996: 48) who define transfer as 'when a person's prior experience and knowledge affect learning or problem solving in a new situation.'

Mayer and Wittrock argue that transfer is enhanced when students have learned general and specific processes or skills and the ability to select and monitor them. As Shayer and Adey highlight (2002), generalization is the key to students being able to transfer these formulated ideas. Furthermore, they propose, on the basis of research evidence, that effective instruction ensures that students select relevant information, build internal connections between the information and build external connections to other contexts and subject matter. They report a range of studies in which metacognitive ability has been linked with better performance. Mayer and Wittrock effectively underline the interdependence of metacognition and transfer.

Transfer thinking outcomes

Greenfield (2002) describes thoughts as ideas that can be explained physiologically as 'hubs of ... [neural] ... connections that were previously independent ... hooking up with each other'. This coalescence, can result in new and perhaps unusual 'juxtaposition of association'. She goes on to explain that an extreme example would be Linus Pauling, who imported the principles of physics into chemistry, with his mastery concept of the chemical bond, or Australian immunologist Macfarlane Burnett, who saw a similarity between the principles of Darwinian evolution and the immune system (Greenfield 2002: 54). Thus, for learners of any age to translocate their understanding of one idea into a new context is a really thoughtful act. In the CA programme, an example of bridging or transferring understanding could be a 14-year-old who has understood the (unlikely) likelihood of 250 consecutive heads (rather than tails) from the flip of an unbiased coin and can apply that realization to the probability of a smoker or non-smoker developing lung cancer.

Hatano and Inagaki (1992) provide a somewhat juxtaposed insight into transfer. Drawing on the work of Gentner and Stevens (1983) they describe the importance of mental models in transfer. They contrast 'routine experts', who can apply set procedures, with 'adaptive experts', who have conceptual knowledge of the major objects in a domain or topic. The conceptual knowledge allows the expert to run mental simulations, or models, and make predictions for situations that have not been experienced and transfer to new contexts. Their study population was nursery children who looked after goldfish. These children developed conceptual knowledge concerning the need to feed the goldfish and clean their environment by changing the water. This gave them the basis for superior performance on questions about how to look after other animals, thus apparently affecting their problem solving in a new situation.

Metacognition, talk and collaboration

Black and Wiliam (1998) highlight how challenging pupils to think independently and explore understanding through thoughtful reflective dialogue is key in raising standards. Bereiter and Scardamalia (1989) suggest that explaining one's thinking to another leads to deeper cognitive processing. Bruer (1997), in describing distributed cognition, hypothesized that more success could be achieved in group work because the group is able to draw upon a larger collective memory and has access to variety of strategies for solving problems.

A social constructivist view emphasizes that value of dynamic talk in developing a greater appreciation of the thinking engaged in by collaborating peers because, as Vygotsky (1978) illustrates: 'talking provokes a representation of one's thoughts – a process which inevitably raises them to a more conscious plane of awareness so that they can become the objects of reflection and modification'.

Gauvain and Rogoff (1989) suggested that the experience of working in a collaborative situation encourages the development of metacognitive abilities such as planning. McGregor (2003) has shown how pupils engaged in carrying out practical tasks, who have previously been guided to discuss ideas openly, question each other, make collaborative decisions and reason more spontaneously. They elaborate on why they chose a particular course of action and openly reflect on the nature of what they have achieved. In this kind of mutually supportive learning situation they appear to spontaneously metacognate at various points during the problem solving process. These metacognitive episodes can render the thinking and rationalization that the students are applying more explicit. However, as Joiner et al. (2000) indicate, this does not arise across all small groups working together. A cultural way of working collaboratively together requires nurturing. As Wegerif (2002) notes the 'ground rules of exploratory talk open up and maintain intersubjective space', but a willingness to engage in intellectual exchange and develop intersubjectivity requires more open expectations (McGregor 2003) to be communicated from the teacher. Teachers themselves need to be metacognitive to support and nurture these abilities in their students. They need to recognize how to support effective reflections, to elucidate cognitive processes and outcomes.

Near transfer and far transfer

Driving a car involves transferable skills. Similar skills are needed when driving different cars, or driving in another country that has different rules of the road. Driving in these situations requires, arguably similar skills and could be perceived as near transfer (see Table 10.2). If, however, the context was very different, and involved piloting a small motor boat, there are some similar skills that could be applied and others that would need enhancing to apply in a new context. This is arguably an example of far transfer. Differentiated transfer is acknowledged by McGuiness et al. (2003) and considered a little more deeply by Swartz et al. (1998). They perceive transfer as the last part of an infusion lesson (Figure 6.4), the application of the thinking that has occurred. Transfer can be broadly categorized as near or far activities. Application of the

Table 10.2 Bridging thinking and learning: near and far transfer examples

Description of learning activity	Conceptual context Near transfer	Procedural context Far transfer	Near transfer	Far transfer
Learning about particulate theory and having pupils create their own 'models' for explaining changes of state	Explaining why when cooking, making gravy or custard, the longer you heat it the lumpier and solid it becomes because the liquid has evaporated.	The changing form of money. It retains its value, but in the bank it can appear as a statement in an account book, if you transfer some it then can appear on your current account card or your telephone card … you could withdraw money from that account … or you appear as a balance on your phone card … or you could withdraw the money in different forms (as coins or notes)?	Observing closely and creating a model that explains things (at a micro/macro level) that are not observable, e.g. a young child creating a model to explain night and day; or why, over time, frogspawn develops into an adult toad or mist appears often in a morning. Explaining physical phenomena but not all detail is clearly available to explain it.	Creating an abstract model to explain something logically based on observable evidence. Developing economic models (like elasticity of demand or explaining why house prices suddenly drop or rise) or developing a model that explains why some adolescents are more violent or disrespectful.
Kabbdii game: the offensive move.	Fast break in basketball.	In any team sport, played with ball, important features of rapid transition from defensive to offensive play.	Talking about rules of play. Playing for a few minutes and applying the rules. Stopping and theorizing about why offensive moves are successful (or not). Useful when learning a new team game or applying new rules or manoeuvres.	Trying out any new skill (cooking; singing; drama; art; photography). *What are the rules (aspects of it necessary)?* Try it out. Theorize how it was done and whether it was successful or not? (within the constraints adhered to)

thinking within the same class session to a content similar to that of the initial activity in the lessons is described as 'near transfer'. 'Far transfer' is described as a context that is considerably different from that of the original thinking. Transfer can be about the procedure or process or concerned with the conceptual understanding. In the *Titanic* example (Figure 13.3) asking the questions connecting floating and sinking to swimming or a larva lamp is a way of encouraging and supporting transfer in pupils about a scientific concept. This is concerned more with the thinking outcome or conceptual understanding. However, the Moebius strip exercise (see Chapter 13) focuses more on the process of developing thinking, rather than conceptual outcomes. The Moebius strip exercise (Figure 13.4) is related to a learners experience as a way of transferring understanding about the process of learning as a novice (not knowing the answers) rather than an expert teacher of subject material.

In these far transfer contexts, asking students to create their own *bridges* ensures that they have 'made the connection'. Teachers can model examples, but ultimately the students provide (formative) evidence that they have realized the connection between the conceptual understanding 'what have I learned' and procedural understanding 'how did I get there'. Supporting the development of far transfer in this way could connect more clearly for students *why* they are studying *what* they are studying in schools. More regular (not all the time – its too effortful and exhausting!) interventions that review scholastic learning and make thoughtful connections with contexts important and relevant in children's lives (for instance, through movies, ipod, headline news, mobile phones, latest books, music, leisure, home life). It is not easy for pupils to do this, they need time to develop their transferable under-standings. Often seeding at the onset of lesson, that a suggestion is expected by the end of the activity can give them sufficient time to nurture a proposition; or providing discussion time with others or even allowing them to sketch or map ideas can act as tools to facilitate the thinking. As Dewey suggests active, persistent, and careful reflection is effortful rather than passive (as is any purposeful and skilful thinking). The 'process of consideration regarding the *grounds* or information supporting an idea or belief may require concentration or focus for some time before understanding, implementation or application of the notion is complete' (Dewey 1910: 6).

Conclusion

Watkins (2001) reviewed 66 studies and concluded that a focus on learning and thinking processes enhanced learning performance,

emphasis lies with improvement of academic performance, ultimately the aim of education should be to prepare children for a successful and fulfilling adulthood.

The nature of problem solving

Bentley (2000) describes that this should be helping children to think flexibly and develop the skills needed to face any challenge after school in everyday life. Resnick (2001: 5) describes how the nature of thinking should extend to problem solving, which she views as the 'new basics of the 21st century'. Sternberg (2003) highlights how problem solving is connected with development of practical intelligence and nurturing wisdom depends on the context of problems considered. Costa (2001) discusses how developing particular approaches to problems can illustrate intelligent behaviour. All these perspectives recognize how learners have to be flexible and adapt to the situations in which they find themselves.

Lochhead and Zietsman (2001) identify how problem solving is something we do every day. In an adult context this could involve deciding where to park the car, how to deal with the leaking roof, how to deal with a misbehaving son, which financial package to invest in or even where to buy the healthiest food. For children the problem solving they engage in, in an everyday life context, might be: *When, how or in what order shall I do my homework? How can I finish early so that I can get outside to play football? How can I persuade my parents that I want to watch the game/film that finishes late on TV tonight? How can I get the latest tracks onto my ipod? How do I beat X to win the – game?* More maieutically, they might consider . . .*What is the tastiest and healthiest food to eat? Are GMs really affecting my life? Will it really matter if more animals and plants become extinct in my lifetime? Should we spend so much money on space exploration when there are people, who, through no fault of their own, are starving or destitute?*

And then, as a young adult . . . *How can I persuade her to go on a date with me? Where can I get the latest fashion clothing or sportswear kit? How can I get a job? What kind of job am I best suited to? How can I earn enough money to buy a car?*

And as an adult . . . *How do I find the best mortgage? Where is the best place to live? Why? How should I invest my money wisely? Which is the best to buy for economy? Speed? Style? Family outings? Why does the baby keep crying? When do I wean the baby? What nappies are best to buy . . . for the environment? . . . for economy? . . . for keeping the baby dry? How can I help sustain natural habitats or conserve energy? How do I do my job to the best of my ability? How should I conduct my life so that I ensure the environment is kept safely for future generations? Which politician should I trust? Why? Who should I vote for?*

All these questions are open ended, in that there is no one correct answer. True problem solving poses dilemmas of this kind, which involve development of options and choices to be made to reach a solution.

Polya (1948) has written much about problem solving within mathematics. He explains that:

> A great discovery solves a great problem but there is a grain of discovery in the solution of any problem. Your problem may be modest, but if it challenges your curiosity and brings into play your inventive faculties, and if you solve it by your own means, you may experience the tension and enjoy the triumph of discovery. Such experiences at a susceptible age may create a taste for mental work and leave their imprint on mind and character for a long time.
>
> Thus a teacher of mathematics has a great opportunity. If he fills his allotted time with drilling his students in routine operations he kills their interest, hampers their intellectual development, and misuses his opportunity. But if he challenges the curiosity of his students by setting them problems proportionate to their knowledge, and helps them to solve their problems with stimulating questions, he may give them a taste for, and some means of independent thinking.
>
> (Polya 1948: v)

He suggests a simple framework for tackling problems which highlights four phases:

1 You have to understand the problem.
2 You have to devise a plan.
3 You have to carry out the plan.
4 You have to examine the solution obtained.

He explicates the phases:

> It may happen that a student hits upon an exceptionally bright idea and jumping all preparations blurts out the solution. Such lucky ideas, of course are desirable, but something very undesirable and unfortunate may result if the student leaves out any of the four phases without having a good idea. The worst may happen if the student embarks upon computations or

Candle Race

John noticed that when Jo lit a candle in a small lantern it often flickered and went out.

When Sue lit a candle in a much larger lantern it usually burned brighter and for much longer.

Jo said 'I bet a candle with more air around it will burn better than one in a small space'.

Can you design an experiment to find out if this is true.

Equipment you might use:

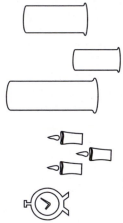

Open candles task sheet

Candle Race

John noticed that when Jo lit a candle in a small lantern it often flickered and went out.

When Sue lit a candle in a much larger lantern it usually burned brighter and for much longer.

Jo said 'I bet a candle with more air around it will burn better than one in a small space'.

Can you design an experiment to find out if this is true.

Equipment you might use:

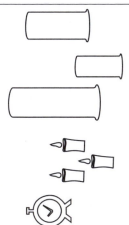

Think carefully about the following before you start to carry out the experiment.

• How can you accurately measure how long the flames burn in different sized jars?
• How can you make sure that your tests are fair?
• How will you present your results?
• How many times do you need to repeat the experiment so you know your results are reliable?
• What do your results mean?

Scaffolded candles task sheet

Three Candle Race

John noticed that when Jo lit a candle in a small lantern it often flickered and went out.

When Sue lit a candle in a much larger lantern it usually burnt brighter and for much longer.

Jo said 'I bet a candle with more air around it will burn better than one in a small space'.

This is an investigation to find out if the amount of air available in the lantern affects how long it remains alight.

You will need:

3 candles of the same size   bunsen burner
small jar   safety mat
medium size jar   goggles
large jar   spill
stopclock

1 Light the bunsen burner (remember you must have goggles on).
2 Set out each of the candles, with a jar close by, ready to light with a spill.
3 Light each candle.
4 Start the clock and at the same time place the jars over each candle as in diagram above.
5 Record how long each flame burns for, and fill in the results below.

6 After each try turn the jars upside down several times before repeating the experiment.

Time that candle burns for	Small jar	Medium jar	Large jar
1st try:			
2nd try:			
3rd try:			
Average of all three tries:			

7 Can you explain your findings?

Prescriptive candles task sheet

Cognitive outcomes
- More critical thinking that focused on the nature and patterns within the findings
- More confident metacognition of the findings
- Much less creative thinking – no modification or refinement of the procedure

Cognitive outcomes
- Creative thinking to develop a range of alternate strategies to solve the problem
- More critical thinking in applying scientific concepts to explain the findings
- More critical thinking in evaluating application of scientific procedures to explain anomalies in evidence
- More metacognition and critical thinking evident in approach to verification and validation of evidence collected
- More metacognition evident through exploration of propositions from others in the group

Cognitive outcomes
- More creative thinking developing a very wide range of strategies to solve the problem
- Metacognition limited to developing a resolution, little or no consideration of quality of solution

Source: Based on McGregor (2003).

Figure 11.1 Influence of differentiated task support on cognitive outcomes of independently working groups

Issues connected with developing problem solving skills in classrooms – an example from science

Consider a typical, well-performing and well-resourced school. The students have just been taught how to measure 'density' of objects in a classroom, by immersing objects in water, measuring the change in volume, then weighing the object and recording the mass. The students are then shown by illustration and step-by-step procedures on the board how to use these two pieces of information to calculate the density of various objects. The challenge to the pupils is then to 'think' and work out how to 'design a life raft that floats'. The students are given various pieces of equipment including popsicle sticks, foam, thin balsawood and a hot-glue gun. They work cooperatively together, there is very little argument or discord between them. However, quite typically, a dominant student will manipulate the resources and the others watch, sometimes offering suggestions, occasionally taking hold of some materials and proffering them for inclusion in the raft building. There is usually little productive, collaborative discussion involving the different ideas (and experiences) each of them holds about raft (or boat) structure and what makes it sink or float. Talk often revolves around movies, music or social engagements of some kind, but there is an air of business in the classroom. There is a lot of creating in a 'hands on', trial-and-error, sense. The lack of explicit guidance about how to work together, share ideas, weigh up plausibility of each proposition, test each idea out and systematically assess for the best design is obvious when observing a lesson of this nature. The students' lack of understanding about the collective power of collaboration is not evident. The application of theory that has been learned about density is completely forgotten in the concentrated, concrete, try-it-out-and-see process of creating a floating craft. This generalized description of a problem solving approach in a typical lesson that might culminate in the teaching of floating and sinking, lacked key questions for the students to answer in the process of figuring out what was the best raft design. These students are without scaffolding and have little or no experience of working together effectively to solve an open-ended problem. Interestingly, to an outsider, the students appear to be on task, with some actively working toward their goals but not engaging in a cognitive way with the act of 'doing'.

Reflection on learning to promote problem solving skills

Pupils are not usually guided to think about *how* what they are learning can be applied to solve problems. Neither are they generally guided to think about *how, where, when* and *why* they could apply the cognitive and affective skills developed in school in an everyday context. The nature of the interactional mediation between teacher and pupils influences how, where and when problem solving skills can be activated and applied.

Vygotsky's view of the teaching-learning interaction is described by Brown and Ferrara (1985):

> Vygotsky's theory of cognitive development rests heavily on the key concept of *internalization* ... The child first experiences active problem solving activities in the presence of others but gradually comes to perform these functions independently. The process of internalisation is gradual; first the adult or knowledgeable peer controls and guides the child's activity, but gradually the adult and child come to share the problem solving functions with the child taking the initiative and the adult correcting and guiding when she falters. Finally, the adult cedes control to the child and functions primarily as a supportive and sympathetic audience.
>
> (Brown and Ferrara 1985: 281)

Mediation in the form of scaffolding can help or support pupils who cannot solve a problem unaided. Mediation can take many forms including a cue of some kind (be it a verbal, written or actional), a psychological tool, which could be a series of progressive questions or a gesture toward equipment to be used; or a psychological sign such as a nod or shake of the head or symbolic diagrammatic representations of experimental work. Task design and the nature of teacher mediation can therefore significantly influence cognitive processing during task resolution. As Vygotsky (1978) describes:

> Children solve practical tasks with the help of their speech, as well as with their eyes and hands. This unity of perception, speech and action, which ultimately produces internalisation of the visual field, constitutes the central subject matter for any analysis of the origin of uniquely human forms of behaviour.
>
> (Vygotsky 1978: 26)

So it is also important to consider how the learning tasks appeal to the senses to engage and motivate pupils thinking through and about

Steps in problem solving process (and key questions to think about and focus on)	Potential thinking opportunities/cognitive skills to be developed
'Is it what was anticipated?'	• Making decisions • Testing solutions • Determining bias • Checking for reliability of evidence
Step 8. Describing the solution: *'What does the solution look like?'*	• Analysing • Synthesizing • Reviewing • Evaluating • Connecting (nature of relationships, whole/parts, etc.) • Elaborating • Decision making
Step 9. Was the problem solved? *How far did our method solve the problem?* *What else could be considered?* *How would we do it again better?*	• Evaluating • Reviewing • Reflecting • Reasoning • Comparing projections and outcomes • Sequencing • Synthesizing
Step 10. Transferring/bridging the thinking processes and outcomes: *Where else would you use this kind of problem solving strategy?* *Where else would this kind of outcome arise?*	• Reflecting • Synthesizing • Analysing • Comparing • Reasoning • Extrapolating

Note: It is not intended that pupils should necessarily 'progress through' all these stages in a kind of chronological order – but it is a systematic way of making the 'thinking steps' explicit in the process of problem solving. This list is not necessarily exhaustive, just indicative.

> • consider how the process and product or outcome could be improved
> 10 Connect the thinking processes used to other real-life contexts for:
> • the product or outcome; and
> • the strategy or tactics developed.

Consider these three contrasting situations of open problem solving. In each case there is no, one correct procedure to follow and no one

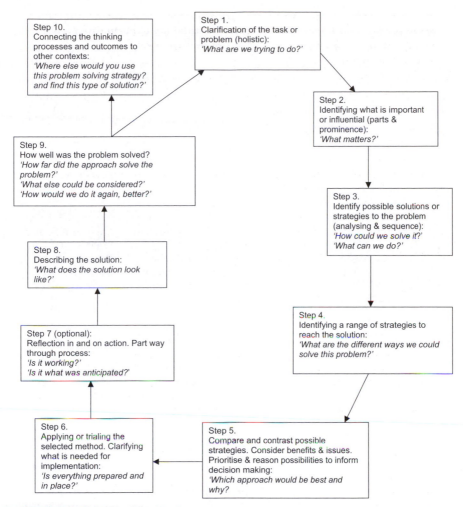

Figure 11.2 Connecting the incremental thinking and associated focus questions involved in supporting (open-ended) problem solving

successful outcome. Obviously, though, some outcomes will be better than others. The first is a scientific investigation to find out 'which training shoes are best to wear for running the 100 metres'; the second is a PSHE-type activity where pupils have to create a brochure saying 'No to Drugs' and the third is adults planning to buy a house. To develop problem solving skills, various studies have shown that pupils working collaboratively together (Light et al. 1994; Howe 1997; Murphy and Spence 1997; Mercer et al. 1999) reach task resolution by focusing on various aspects of the problem solving process (see Table 11.2). Collaborating problem solvers may engage in these different aspects of problem resolution (McGregor 2003) for differing lengths of time and perhaps not even in a strict logical sequence (left unguided), but the nature of the exchanges revolves at some point around these 'processing' issues (or potentially *key* junctures) arguably achieving higher quality cognitive outcomes (McGregor 2004).

Table 11.2 Generalizing thinking processes involved in problem solving

Problem solving steps	Investigating 'which training shoes are best to wear for running the 100 metres'	Creating a brochure on drugs	Buying a house
1	Clarifying what the task means should be done. What does the task imply? Will it have to be carried out? How many shoes can be used? Are runners needed? Should timing be important? These will all need to be considered.	Clarifying. What does the task imply by 'drugs'? What does 'NO' mean (not ever or not regularly; what about when ill)? What kind of brochure? What emphasis? What style of presentation? What materials should be used?	Clarifying. What kind of house with what kind of facilities? What is feasible? What is this project likely to involve?
2	Consideration of the problem to identify what is important, e.g. not necessarily the whole shoe, but the sole and the nature of the grip it can provide on the running track.	Developing a view that 'no' is important and the negative of drug taking or positive of not taking drugs has to be portrayed visually, somehow within a constrained space.	How could sufficient funds be raised? Selling the current house has to happen before buying can proceed.
3	Development of different strategies, focused on changing the surface area of the shoe, or the nature of the grip, or the mass of the shoe.	Development of different ideas that may focus on negative of taking drugs or positive of health without drugs or using key words or visual images.	Development of strategies to sell one house, advertising in various places, agents, email at work and/or continue looking for less expensive house in paper, Internet, etc. or even consider renting for interim.
4	Decision making to focus on one variable that can be changed (rather than several simultaneously).	Decision making that involves the nature of design as well as the message(s).	Decision making. Should all, several or only that one tactic(s) be used?
5	Detailed planning, involving identification of the steps (this could include gathering	Planning the relational location of information/graphics.	What should be done? In what sequence should it be done (are there any fixed points

Problem solving steps	Investigating 'which training shoes are best to wear for running the 100 metres'	Creating a brochure on drugs	Buying a house
5 (cont.)	materials/resources and considering what evidence should be gathered/how it should be analysed) to be taken and in what sequence.		of action around which the sequence has to logically fit)?
6	Carry out the planned investigation.	Create the planned brochure.	Carry out the planned selling/buying steps.
7	Part way through reflection . . . consider is the process working toward the solution/product as hoped? Are refinements or modification needed?		
8	Description of findings related to investigating training shoes and running success.	Presentation of brochure communicating why we should say 'no to drugs'.	Sale/purchase communications, clarifying what has been agreed, what is/is not included in the price.
9	Reflective evaluation of task including how well the task question was answered; how the resolution compares to others; how could both method and findings be improved?	Reflective evaluation of the brochure to consider how well it persuades readers to 'say no'; how the brochure compared to others; how could the process by which the brochure was developed as well as the brochure itself be improved?	Reflective evaluation of the strategy and tactics used to sell/buy. Did you achieve what you set out to? Are you going to get a fair price/good deal? Do other people achieve selling/buying similarly? How could the process and outcome be improved?
10	Where else (in life) would knowing about trainers and success in running be useful? Where else (in life) would a similar approach to *investigate* something like this be useful?	Where else (in life) would knowing about saying 'No to drugs' be useful? Where else in life would you use similar approaches to *developing* the brochure?	Where else (in life) is knowing about buying/selling useful? How transferable is the *process of* or the *strategies* for buying/selling similar?

The process of problem solving, the associated cognitive processing and the ways in which pedagogy can support development of this kind of thinking will be considered further in Chapters 12 and 13. Although the different contexts described here can facilitate generalizable problem solving steps, there are many other considerations concerning further criteria (such as, when selling a house, how much each part of the process costs), there may also be 'unpredictable' and uncontrollable happenings in selling a house that would influence the outcome (as is the case in real life). However the intention here is to illustrate that there are some recognizable steps in open-ended problem solving that require similar kinds of thinking skills and cognitive processing. In schools these kinds of thinking can be encouraged with a view to supporting problem solving skills for lifelong learning.

Developing a problem solving 'tool' kit

Figure 10.2 suggests how planned cognitive development should provide students with a repertoire or palette of a range of cognitive skills implied in Table 11.1. Students should understand how to use these cognitive skills for problem solving skilfully. Like an artist, the learner needs to know what the skills (or colours) are available and how they could be blended, sequenced and applied to solve problems (or create a picture). To become skilful and artful in applying the range of thinking skills needed to solve problems, firstly students need to be *aware* of the skills; then they need to *understand* how to use them; then they need practice in *applying* them. Metacognition is key in raising their awareness, developing their understanding and enhancing their recognition of potential opportunities to use thinking skills. *Practice* in applying them in a *range of contexts* (across the curriculum) and developing a lexicon to be able to describe their use, will help them generalize about *how, where and when* they would be appropriate to use elsewhere, in problem solving situations.

From a pedagogical perspective teachers should bear in mind, the psychological steps through which to guide their learners and use key questions (Table 11.1) to mediate pupils' thinking. Teaching strategies such as de Bono's six thinking hats or Swartz and Parks' graphic organizers can also act as initiating or practice material to support development of thinking to problem solve.

Critical, creative and metacognitive thinking in problem solving

In problem solving situations there is much critical thinking. The processes of defining and clarifying 'what does the task really require?' and discerning 'what really matters?' involves scrutiny and interpretation of task information. More creative thinking is needed when possible tactics, methods or approaches to the problem are developed and proposed.

In the ongoing process, however, of making judgements about the plausibility of ideas and ranking the worth and value of suggestions, new (or modified) ideas may emerge. The seesawing between propositions and weighing up the positive and negative aspects of each can result in the evolution of a newer, more innovative idea that involves what Fisher (2001: 13) describes as critico-creative thinking. He uses this term to describe the positive, imaginative aspects of critical thinking. He argues that sometimes-critical thinking is seen as rather negative, often because it is used to describe how other people's ideas, propositions or arguments are critiqued or criticized. However, to be a good evaluator of ideas and arguments one needs to be imaginative and creative to consider other possibilities, alternate perspectives and different options. To be a good judge of issues it is not enough to just see faults in what other people say, judgement needs to be based on the best arguments (in the time available). This often requires that other relevant considerations need thinking about that have not been presented. Imagining alternative scenarios, empathizing with different viewpoints requires creative thinking.

Problem solving for teachers who wish to teach thinking

Application of the problem solving steps could extend to teachers who have to make discerning decisions about how to develop thinking more explicitly in their lessons. They have to clarify what kinds of thinking they wish their students to be skilful in using. Which type of programme or approach would best (FIE, STS, TTTT, CA, TT series, using de Bono's CoRT materials or infusing strategies ... and applying the Swartz and Parks approach)? How, when and where are they going to implement the chosen approach? How will they (formatively, part way through and summatively) assess the success of the new approach? How will they present and communicate their success? How will they modify or adapt the programme for future use? Where else in the curriculum (or in or out of school) can the approach(es) and outcomes be applied?

Conclusion

Children (and teachers) becoming aware of and more practised in the use of particular cognitive processes required to think critically, creatively and metacognitively will develop important skills to solve problems. The nature of the problems posed, as well as the mediation that teachers use (mostly through questioning), can influence the extent to which pupils apply different types of thinking. Practice in problem solving, in scholastic contexts that is then extended into real-world or everyday life situations will support development of core, flexible, transferable, twenty-first century skills. The development of problem solving skills is arguably the best life long education, educators can provide, to help children learn how to think *and* act intelligently.

Key ideas

A problem solving approach in learning promotes:
- understanding of the subject matter
- motivation, engagement and intrinsic interest in the subject matter
- appreciation of the (cognitive) processes and thinking involved in solving open-enquiry
- recognition that there is often no, one, correct answer; that some solutions, however, are better than others

Problem solving offers potential for application of wide range of cognitive skills and ways of thinking (including critical, creative and metacognitive).

The nature of tasks pupils are given to solve can constrain or provide wide potential for the development of thinking skills.

It is possible to generalize about steps that can, inform a psychological framework to, support development of flexible and adaptable thinking to solve problems.

The questions that teachers ask can be key in focusing thinking at important junctures of the problem solving process.

Recognize importance of varied resolutions and processes of 'getting there' in problem solving in school and then connecting these to life out of school and life after school.

12 Synthesizing the general from the particular

Billy McBone

Billy McBone
Had a mind of his own
Which he kept mostly under his hat
The teachers all thought
That he couldn't be taught
But Bill didn't seem to mind that.

Billy McBone
Had a mind of his own,
Which the teachers had searched for for years.
Trying test after test,
They still never guessed
It was hidden between his ears.

Billy McBone
Had a mind of his own,
Which only his friends ever saw.
When the teachers said, 'Bill,
Whereabouts is Brazil?'
He just shuffled and stared at the floor.

Billy McBone
Had a mind of his own,
Which he kept under lock and key.
While the teachers in vain
Tried to burgle his brain,
Bill's thoughts were off wandering free.

(Ahlberg, *Heard it in the Playground*)

As Ahlberg's (1989: 32) poem indicates, some pupils do not readily share their thoughts for others to glimpse into their internal world and their personal understandings. To develop pupils' thinking and learning, however, teachers do need some insight into the workings of their minds.

Appreciating what and how pupils think can inform teaching approaches to enhance and develop their cognitive abilities. This chapter attempts to synthesize from the various programmes and approaches described, generalized principles about the tactics or strategies that teachers could use, to encourage pupils to develop their thinking. From previous chapters, it should be obvious to the reader that the various programmes and approaches described support development of a range of differing kinds of thinking. The designs of learning activities inviting certain kinds of cognitive activity and the interplay of teachers' pedagogies ultimately influence the nature of pupils' thinking. The tasks within a programme or approach and the varied pedagogic emphasis can affect what kind of thinking the pupils engage in, when, where and how. Figure 12.1 indicates the contrasting intentions of most of the thinking programmes reviewed. To teach specific cognitive skills, FIE, STS or TTTT can be applied to model and explicate thinking in a non-curricular context, emphasizing logic, spatial, numerical, sequential, categorical and analytical types of thinking. All intended to support the general development of problem solving skills. Teaching, which aims to improve the general processing capacity through focus on and development of specific types of under-standings (or schemata), taught in a subject context, is the general intent of the CA programmes. These also involve action or kinaesthetic activity embraced within the thinking lessons.

Philosophy for Children focuses on the cognitive and intends to encourage thinking in a philosophical way, contemplating possible courses of action and their consequences. It does not test out propositions in any real experiential sense. Infusing thinking in the ways that Swartz and Parks (1994) and McGuinness et al. (2003) describe involves refocus and redesign of current content lessons (see Figure 12.2). Teachers are expected to reflectively emphasize thinking skills needed for the learning activities. The content material influences this kind of approach, because teachers have to make judgements about the systematic explication of thinking skills and support progressive, coherent experiences for learners toward thinking outcomes. The *Thinking Through* ... series (Leat 2001) provides a range of innovative strategies for supporting the development of thinking skills in several subject contexts. Leat identifies the kinds of thinking skills that are developed through the various pedagogic strategies used throughout the series (Butterworth et al. 2005: 138).

This chapter considers, in turn, a variety of factors that can influence the nature of thinking learners can be encouraged to engage in:

1   An open and thoughtful classroom ethos.

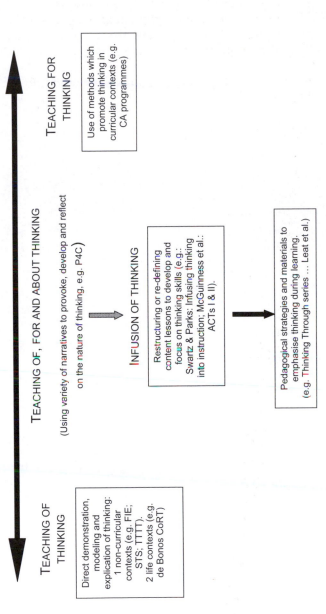

Figure 12.1 Approaches to teaching thinking

2 Explication of thinking objectives including processes and outcomes. Pupils need to understand teacher expectations.
3 Structure of a purposeful and connected programme or approach.
4 Task design of learning and thinking activities.
5 Teacher mediation through pedagogic strategies or tactics.

These factors are summarized in Figure 12.2 and elaborated upon in this chapter.

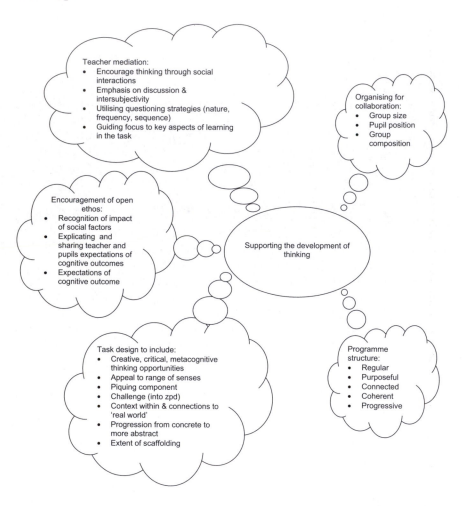

Figure 12.2 Factors that can significantly influence the kinds of thinking learners engage in.

Encouraging an open thoughtful ethos

Pupils in classrooms need to know what the teachers' expectations are. The purpose of a lesson might be for the learners to *know* the periods during which particular kings and queens ruled or *know* the names and locations of all the European countries and their capital cities. The learner expectations would in these situations involve *knowing the right answers*. The teacher emphasis, even if encouraging familiarization or consolidation via an innovative strategy, would be that students should 'know' (and recapitulate) particular information by the end of the lesson. In lessons where 'thinking' outcomes are more prominent, students need to understand that the expectations are different. The learning objectives in these kinds of lessons should emphasize cognitive processing and celebrate the range of ways that learners can achieve understanding and create the time for the pupils to do so. Emphasizing cognitive activity, such as comparative thinking, evaluating bias in an argument or developing alternative methods for problem solving where there is no, one, correct answer requires pupils to feel confident about contributing towards these more pluralistic outcomes. Students need to recognize when there may be several plausible solutions to questions or problems posed. The aims and objectives for lessons that emphasize 'thinking' or development of cognitive skills, therefore, contrast sharply with those that pursue 'knowing' specific facts or information. Teachers need to convey clearly when and where they 'expect' such different kinds of cognitive or learning behaviours so that pupils realize that 'conforming' with others' views, or the teacher's perception of the 'correct' answer is no longer the assumed expectation. Just telling pupils that they should be 'thinking more', 'focusing on their thinking' or 'there is no right answer to this' or 'you must share your ideas with others' does not necessarily create and develop an open ethos resulting in the kinds of thinking communities that Lipman (2003) and Fisher (2000) describe. Teachers need to support and foster thinking classrooms through a multifaceted approach (aspects of which are elaborated throughout this chapter) which involves being more 'open minded' to create opportunities to develop an ethos as a 'learning community' (McGuinness 1999).

Design of a purposeful and connected programme or approach

Research evidence suggests that those programmes with a structured approach (for example, CA, FIE, P4C, CoRT) appear to have most evidence of success (Cotton 1991; McGuiness 1999; Wilson 2000; Higgins et al. 2004, 2005). The nature and extent of the impact these programmes have, however, is not similar. What is apparent is the regular interventional nature of these approaches. Each of these programmes involves weekly or fortnightly lessons or activities (for about an hour) that serve to stimulate, focus, practice and elaborate upon children's thinking in particular ways. The approaches that they adopt require different pedagogical tactics that contrast with transmission teaching. Thinking and learning experiences that learners engage in when participating in these programmes diverges considerably from the usual scholastic diet that pupils normally consume.

Contrasting approaches

The CA approach clearly focuses on the development of schemata or particular kinds of cognitive functions that Piaget recognized as challenging for pupils at particular ages; FIE and STS deliberately offer context-free tasks, which can stimulate thinking in a wide variety of ways, often initiated in a very abstract context that subsequently develops toward the concrete; philosophy for children emphasizes philosophizing about a wide range of possible, plausible and unfettered perspectives and CoRT offers many opportunities to consider problem situations by applying particular cognitive techniques.

Regular interventions

Regular interventions that contrast with everyday transmission or less interactive forms of learning can stimulate pupils to engage in and reflect upon the thinking developed during learning activities. The KS3 CASE and CAME lessons are designed to focus on a way of thinking (such as classification, proportionality, or variables) every two weeks. Although the activities are carried out in subject settings, the subject *matter* is not of paramount importance. The prime objective is the thinking process of classifying or developing proportionalistic understanding. The STS programme also proffers weekly open-ended stimuli to purposely solve problems and consider the strategic thinking developed. In P4C the weekly reading of a mini-novel, to consider, as a group of philosophers, what the characters could or should do rather than critique for construction and grammar is the cognitive aim. The regular, intermittent nature of the interventions can result in pupils making more meaningful long-term connections that are progressively accrued and developed.

Figure 12.3 Major contributions to teaching thinking.

Successive and progressive components

Building progression, connectivity and succession into a programme is key. The CA approach gradually develops from the concrete to the abstract to achieve the aim of the programme. This is based on Piaget's notions about chronologically linked cognitive stages of development. Within the lessons, too, there is inherent progression. The thinking is set within a concrete context, for example shapes of roofs, rules of a game or looking for rhythms in a piece of music. The pupils are guided to engage in an activity within the context introduced and ultimately generalize about the cognitive processing required to complete the activity in that circumstance and then relate it to another situation. Within the FIE and the STS approach in particular, pupils are introduced to a range of successive skills, often within a more abstract context, which they then relate, in a more concrete way, to a life situation. The STS programme provides a tree-like analogy (Blagg et al. 2003: 47) to describe how each successive cognitive skill builds up from 'Foundations for problem solving', through 'Analysing and synthesizing', 'Comparative thinking', 'Positions in time and space', 'Understanding analogies' and finally to 'Patterns in time and space'. Philosophy for Children develops progressively each successive year by considering increasingly intricate novels with characters facing more complex situations and dilemmas.

The infusion approaches do not clearly indicate how progression in thinking should be organized. McGuinness et al. (2003) and Swartz and Parks (1994) do indicate, however, that curricular mapping can provide a plan for infusion (see Figure 6.1):

1 Identify potential themes and key ideas that students should understand.
2 Identify thinking skills and processes that offer insights about these key ideas.
3 Examine curriculum objectives for appropriate contexts to emphasize selected thinking skills or cognitive processes.
4 Schedule each theme where it seems appropriate in the school year.
5 Ensure the introductory lesson on each thinking skill or process is early enough in the year to allow sufficient transfer opportunities.

As Leat (2005) indicates, whole school planning should avoid problems of students being overexposed to a particular strategy and becoming bored. Infusion approaches need to be carefully coordinated in an effort to introduce particular sets of skills and then practise the use of them (see Figure 12.4) and finally connect them to other out-of-school contexts.

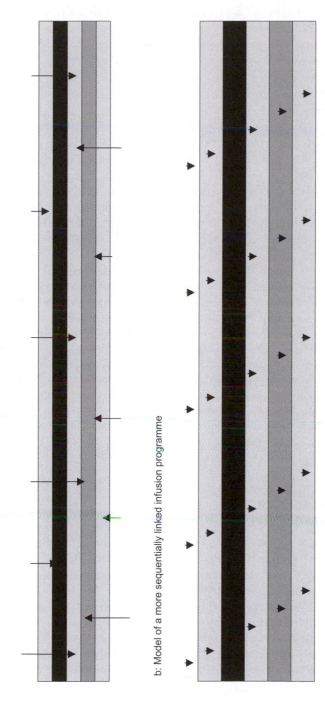

a: Model of a typical infusion approach

b: Model of a more sequentially linked infusion programme

Notes: The shaded bands represent the different subjects taught in the curriculum. The arrows indicate infusion of varied thinking skills into different curricular areas. The longer and shorter arrows indicate more or less time spent focusing on and developing associated kinds of thinking at that time in that particular subject area.

Figure 12.4 Model of a typical infusion approach

Thinking programmes or approaches should support progressive development of critical, creative and metacognitive thinking as well as providing open problem solving opportunities where the thinking skills previously developed are applied in a variety of contexts.

The design of tasks

Murphy and Spence (1997) suggests that 'tasks used in classrooms influence the kinds of thinking in which children engage and this in turn influences learning outcomes'. Tasks that pupils are asked to engage in therefore need to foster and support thinking, reasoning and sense making. This is because 'tasks influence learners by directing their attention to particular aspects of content and by specifying ways of processing information' (Doyle 1983: 161). Howe (1997: 20) identifies how small variants in task structure can have major implications for interactions and subsequent learning. Task design includes *what* are students are asked to do and *how* are they instructed or guided to do it? More detailed guidance will constrain the thinking opportunities and open tasks will offer unfettered opportunities (McGregor 2006). The extent of the scaffolding or support, within a task, to achieve particular thinking outcomes requires careful consideration if the programme aim is to develop autonomous thinkers (McGregor 2003). Tasks should connect with real-life contexts and be designed to provide opportunities for critical, creative and metacognitive thinking (described in previous chapters).

Progressive development of more sophisticated thinking could be supported through designing increasing complex learning tasks. Simple steps to consider when planning for incremental growth of thinking skills would include:

1   Introducing or activating the skill(s);
2   Practice using and applying the skill(s);
3   Extending the contextual applications within which they are used;
4   Applying them to open problem solving situations.

This developing level of sophistication in using a range of identified thinking skills could be applied during a school year, over a whole key stage or even throughout a school.

Chapter 11 highlights how task structure and thinking to problem solve can be closely connected (McGregor 2003, 2006). The ways in which tasks can provide more or less support can influence the extent to which pupils engage in exchange of perspectives, identify and negotiate

differences in opinion, consider the relative merits of various propositions, reach reasoned solutions and subsequently reflect on the thought
journey taken to arrive at a successful resolution. Teachers providing
tasks that do not require decision making opportunities are likely to
constrain the potential for thinking.

Authentic, purposeful and challenging tasks

Learning and thinking tasks for pupils should be authentic. The pupils
should perceive genuine value in engaging in a task to find an answer or
resolution to the problem posed. For pupils to see value in a problem
posed it needs to have direct relevance to their lives. Connecting the
thinking to solve a problem then has true meaning and worth (see Figure
10.3), rather than an abstract activity that cannot be related and
connected to what pupils already know will seem purposeless to them.
As Dewey emphasizes:

> Nothing can be more absurd than to make a plea for a variety of
> active occupations in the school while decrying the need for
> progressive organisation of information and ideas. Intelligent
> activity is distinguished from aimless activity; by the fact that it
> involves selection of means-analysis-out of the variety of
> conditions that are present, and their arrangement synthesis to
> reach an intended aim or purpose.
>
> (Dewey 1974: 383)

Tasks should not be boring, pointless, confusing or too trivial (Lee
and Anderson 1993) or they may not provoke cognitive growth or
development. Young children, for example, can be given an assortment
of stones varying in size. Asking them to place them in rank order would
seem a pointless exercise from their perspective. However, giving them a
reason for putting them in size order would give meaning and purpose to
the task. Imagining they have to be placed across a shallow local river to
provide stepping stones for children to walk from one side to the other is
more engaging. (An aquarium could provide a simulated model for this
exercise.) Explaining that the river is shallow at each side and gradually
gets deeper in the middle provides the stimulus and motivation to
achieve the task, because it is deemed to be of value. Some of these kinds
of activities are presented in the CA materials, especially the materials for
KS1 and KS2. Thinking objectives are not always clear to learners so
teachers may need to provide a clear rationale or challenge to the pupils
to clearly authenticate the tasks. Bridging and transfer, promoted at the

end of the CA lessons, provides the vehicle to connect the tasks to situations outside the lesson or even school. As Lave (1988) emphasizes, cognition or thinking should apply to the 'real world'.

The *Thinking Through* ... series tasks are quite different in nature. They usually provide information, facts or texts to consider, analyse or use in a variety of exciting, intriguing and engaging ways. The teaching strategies applied, including taboo, odd one out, mysteries, living graphs and mind movies, focus on authentic material such as earthquake information, population data, religious artefacts or biographies.

The P4C approach provides a mini-novel (although Robert Fisher has developed other literacy contexts, for example poems, stories and even games to be used in a similar way to extend thinking opportunities) which usually centres on a child of a similar age with realistic school, family and peer experiences. The nature of material to be philosophized about is authentic, involving societal issues of violence, moral and ethical behaviours, and so forth. The dialectical approach and Socratic reasoning is purposeful in that pupils are invited to consider what should or could be done in particular situations and what the consequences of particular actions might be. Pluralistically they consider the views of others from sociological, ethical, moral and other standpoints.

These philosophical questions can provide challenges, because of the increasingly complex situations and dilemmas that the characters in the novels face. Challenge in CA is deliberately included through application of Piaget's ideas about cognitive conflict. Most tasks have 'surprising' or 'unexpected' trip-ups in them.

Presentation of thinking tasks

Swartz and Parks (1994) and McGuinness et al. (2003), in their infusion approach, provide numerous graphic organizers, which act as a scaffold and visual guide to the thinking anticipated during task engagement. These graphic organizers are generalized, so could be used in a variety of thinking situations. The *Thinking Through* ... series contains a range of photocopiable materials, including cards for sorting in odd one out; graphical axes for living graphs and fortune lines; newspaper articles for storytelling; photographs and diagrams for maps from memory. The CA approach provides worksheets for older students and most approaches (except CATE, some CAME and some ARTs) require equipment and props of various kinds. These thinking activities highlight how it is not just the cognitive that is important because thinking and action should be interrelated to improve general problem solving and associated mental capabilities.

Multisensory stimuli to encourage engagement in learning will, as Costa (2001) highlights involve the brain processing the information. Simulating children to think about what they see, hear, feel (emotionally), touch and possibly taste to make sense of the world and phenomena around them should be encouraged. Presenting tasks that require visual, auditory, logical, musical, mathematical and kinaesthetic processing is therefore likely to activate intra- and inter-thinking.

Using computers to present thinking and learning tasks provides an alternate sensory approach (which can involve a raft of visual and auditory stimuli) in contrast to writing or reading. Wegerif et al. (2002) and McFarlane (2003) have indicated that certain kinds of thinking can be stimulated through the use of particular software programs.

Thinking tasks, then, should provide the opportunities for students to answer or respond to questions or problems that are purposeful and authentic, piquing and challenging and designed to support pupils collaborating to construct understandings rather than teachers transmitting predetermined theories, concepts, solutions or answers (Selley 2001: 41). As Lee and Anderson (1993) found, the nature of tasks depends on the totality of the interactions between students' agendas and understandings, teachers' agendas and understandings and the curriculum materials.

Pedagogic strategies

Leat and Higgins (2002: 72) refer to methods such as Taboo, Odd one out, Living graphs as 'powerful pedagogical strategies'. Leat and Higgins (2002) describe how these can be perceived as ready-designed techniques or tools that can support the development of thinking. They highlight how these approaches are generic, flexible, creative strategies for making lessons more challenging. They describe the key characteristics as:

- being manageable for teachers and pupils;
- being adaptable for a wide range of age groups, abilities and subject matter;
- being open ended and encouraging a variety of working methods and reasoning;
- encouraging pupils to use what they already know to grapple with new information and situations;
- encouraging talk; and
- providing a useful experience upon which to focus metacognition.

Other specific pedagogic techniques include de Bono's CoRT materals, his six thinking hats and six action shoes (described in Chapters 5 and 6). These can be perceived as pedagogic techniques or tools because the ways in which they should be used are clearly defined and described.

Pedagogic tactics

Tactics are more generalized intentions. In the encouragement of thinking, this might include intent to question more rather than giving away answers (easily), to ask more open-ended questions or to only answer pupils' questions with another question. Mediational intent could include not leading or guiding students to the *right* answers but intentionally to scaffold to encourage thinking and not cue for a particular answer. Teachers can mediate to lead the learner deliberately (for example, the nature of questions in the problem solving process in Chapter 11) through a series of thinking steps and deliberately open up the possibilities for pluralistic reasoning or explanation of a phenomena or idea. Mediation can manifest as a variety of pedagogic behaviours. Vygotsky describes mediation as the means by which mental processing is invoked, usually between a more expert other (often a teacher) and a novice learner. Wertsch (1985) elaborates Vygotsky's ideas further to illustrate how speaking (and the use of language) is important in explicating inter- and intra-mental ideas. Vygotsky strongly believed that articulating thoughts was an effective method to process connected or random thoughts in a conscious way to raise the awareness of mental activity and subsequently create organized logic and meaning for oneself and others from these utterances. The nature of dialogic exchange in learning is thus essential because it can transform the way in which children learn, think and understand.

Mediation can be demonstrated in a variety of ways, often dialogic, but also visual and actional, to help or support pupils who cannot solve a problem unaided because, as McGregor (2003: 144) has shown, some teachers do not regularly 'intervene' to support learning. Supporting teachers developing more mediational techniques to nurture more effective learning is pertinent, because as Murphy (2000: 158) identifies,

> currently models of practice available to teachers and learners are narrowly conceived. Hence practices have not been developed to support negotiation in social interaction in subject cultures. The issue is whether there is potential to reconceptualise approaches to science education in ways that recognise the cultural process of meaning making.

Asking questions is a key skill in mediation and teaching generally (Kyriacou 1997: 124) to promote thinking. Brown and Wragg (1993: 98) describe a question, simply, as a 'request for information'. In a thinking context a question is a statement intended to evoke a thoughtful, usually verbal, but possibly actional response. Questions can be also be used to arouse interest or curiosity or even stimulate pupils to ask questions themselves, which can support further participation and involvement in learning. Brown and Wragg (1993) in a study of various subject teachers, found the most common reasons for asking questions were encouraging thought and checking for understanding. Morgan and Saxton (1991: 12) have also identified that certain kinds of questions encourage particular kinds of thinking. Hargreaves and Moyles (2002) demonstrated how teachers could be encouraged to become more interactive by increasing the ratio of questions asked. Kirkwood (2005: 97) has indicated how the nature of questions posed in classrooms can influence the kinds of thinking encouraged and engaged in. The approach she describes has been generalized and applied from a mathematical context to computer studies classrooms. It is metacognitive, in that students reflect on what happened when they were involved in producing a computer program. They are guided to consider. Was it expected? How can you change it to improve the situation or make it work as you hoped? Throughout this book there are descriptions and illustrations about how questions can be used to guide and generate thinking, for example, in the ARTs programme (Figure 4.2), generally in problem solving (Chapter 11) and in the STS approach (Chapter 5). The following suggestions describe how particular kinds of questions can be posed to mediate thinking at key junctures in a lesson.

1 Preparing for thinking

The setting of the task should be introduced. Thinking objectives achieved are metacognitively articulated in most thinking programmes. This is unlike teaching where Ofsted (2000) expects the learning objectives to be clearly stated at the onset of a lesson (a characteristic indicative of high-achieving schools). Unfamiliar equipment, new terms or words, an unfamiliar context of the task) may also need introducing. Pupils may need practice in becoming familiar with the pragmatics of the activity (which table or form to fill in; how to distribute the cards or how to orient the picture). The initial part of a thinking lesson should be perceived as the preparation or 'setting the scene' for the activities(s) and thinking. Typical questions that could be asked here include:

- What do you already know about ...?
- What do you think about ...?
- What could we do here?
- What do you think this is going to be about?

2 Challenging thinking

This aspect of a lesson may involve presenting 'unexpected' data or information. This should support pupils in the development of their ZPD. Engagement in learning can also become more memorable through very dramatic 'conflicting evidence or information' being presented to the pupils. The CASE approach describes this as the 'cognitive conflict', the stage of the activities or lesson where information does not 'fit' preconceived ideas – it provides 'conflict' in the mind of the pupil. The next stage is the phase where the pupil mentally 'wrestles' with the 'new' unexpected evidence and tries to 'make sense' of it. For instance, in the Thinking Science Lesson 1, pupils are presented with card objects that are blue or red in colour; large, medium or small sized and either a triangle or a square. The pupils need time to consider that the way they vary is in colour, size and shape. From the card objects pupils are asked to consider whether any variables are 'linked'. After discussion it becomes apparent that the variables 'shape' and 'colour' are related because blue objects are squares and red objects are triangles. The pupils are then given another set of objects with similar variables but this time the relationship is between size and colour, not shape and colour. The 'sorting out' in their minds about how the relationship has changed and the recognition of a new connection and the explanation required to overcome this initial 'cognitive conflict' then offers opportunities to reconstruct the second relationship through experience of the first. This is an example of structural conflict. Other programmes, like P4C, introduce socio-conflict through exploration of the dilemmas that characters in the novels face. The pluralistic nature of propositions that the members of the mini thinking communities will proffer will engender some socio-conflict within the group. Consideration of possible courses of action (for the characters), the consequences of actions and the differing perspectives each child will suggest can augment the challenge within the thinking. In the Thinking Through lessons this stage or aspect to challenge thinking would be obvious in the odd one out, where patterns of conformity and additional information that doesn't fit is purposely sought. Typical questions that could be asked here include:

- What information appears not to fit what we already know?
- How is that possible?

- What can it mean?
- Why do you think that?
- Can you explain it?

3 Organizing your thinking

Within a thinking lesson there should be an opportunity for pupils to collate their experiences and attempt to transform them into under- standings and make meaning out of them. This is where activity should promote development of the zone of construction. This may well arise over a period of time or successive lessons, and not just within a single lesson. In the living graphs (Leat 2000: x) activity based around population growth (illustrating the birth rate, death rate and total population numbers), for example, in placing some provocative statements (for example, more children share a bed or there are more grandparents celebrating golden wedding anniversaries) in appropriate places on the graph, pupils should be stimulated to envisage life in the 1800s compared with life now. The impact of rising standards of living should activate their meaning making out of the activity. Typical questions that could be asked here include:

- What does it mean?
- How can it be described and explained?
- What sense can I make of the information?

4 Reflecting on your thinking

This stage involves mentally looking back over actions and cognitive processing that developed as a result of engaging in the thinking (and learning) task. It is therefore best after the task has been completed (although metacognition part way through a problem solving task can be useful to gauge the likely extent of success in pursuing the current course of action). Whatever task pupils have been involved in working on involves reflection focused on the cognitive aspects of reaching a conclusion. Reading about and creating the lifeline for Muhammed (Baumfield 2002: 43) involves comparing and contrasting, analyzing, synthesizing and empathizing about factors that influenced his life and how he might have felt at that time. Each learner will interpret his biography in different ways and proffer varied suggestions to construct the happy, sad or ambivalent stages in Mohammed's lifeline (see Figure 12.5). In the CA and STS approaches, pupils are encouraged to reflect metacognitively on the thinking they do to succeed in completing a task. This stage in thinking illustrates why pupils need to already know how to describe different kinds of thinking.

Figure 12.5 A small group collaboratively working on Mohammad's lifeline

Figure 12.6 Teacher gathering reflections about thinking during a learning activity

Typical questions that could be asked here include:

- What did you think about ... before you did the activity?
- What did you think after you had done the task?
- How did your thinking develop?
- How did your thinking change?

5 Comparing thinking

This aspect of a thinking lesson is important because the teacher should carefully and sensitively support comparative thinking to illustrate how differing approaches *can* each reach good quality solutions.

Typical questions that could be asked here include:

- How did your thinking compare to that of others?
- How did your ideas develop differently to some one else's?
- Can you explain why ... thought this, and ... thought that?

6 Transferring thinking

This aspect of a thinking lesson connects directly with organizing and reflecting. Once pupils have 'constructed' some meaning from an activity, to illustrate how they really understand a principle or concept, they should transfer or bridge to another context. As described in Chapter 10, there are several forms of transfer, the process and the outcome, and also near and far transfer.

The example of the dinosaur activity (Table 12.1) indicates how the pupils might transfer classifying an object in two groups (for example, a CD classified and lodged under the singer's name and the bargain bin in the local music shop) or transfer how they reached the solution, comparing, contrasting, grouping similar things together, then one object fitted both groups, which can be represented by overlapping circles (or a simple Venn diagram). Typical questions that could be asked here include:

- What kind of thinking have you done here?
- How did your thinking change or develop?
- What caused you to change or develop your ideas?
- Where else would you use this kind of thinking?

Chapter 10 focuses on metacognition, suggesting further considerations about reflection and transfer.

Transferring thinking to another context is often cited as the most difficult aspect for students to develop (Perkins and Salomon 2001).

Table 12.1 Questions posed and associated cognitive activity involved in a classifying dinosaurs activity (after *Let's Think* lesson 7 on farm animals)

Description of different stages in learning activity	Typical questions posed	Associated cognitive processing
Variety of dinosaurs (plastic models or laminated cards). [1] Each type of dinosaur should be represented in various colours.	How are these similar? How are they different? What could we call them (a name based on their characteristics)?	Close observation Comparative thinking Analysis of range of prominent characteristics Synthesis of names based on physical characteristics of the dinosaurs; eg fan-backed (Dimetrodon); long-tailed (Diplodococcus); two horned, frilly-necked (Tricerotops); two-legged erectus (Tyranosaurus) etc.
Sorting the dinosaurs Place all the red dinosaurs in one circle. Place all the blue dinosaurs in another circle.	Where should we put the other dinosaurs? Why? What is your reason? What can we say about the group of dinosaurs in the first circle? How are they similar/different to the dinosaurs in the second circle? What do the dinosaurs in the second circle have in common? What could we call this group? What do the dinosaurs outside the two circles have in common? What could we call this group?	Observation and synthesis of grouping organisms with a characteristic in common together. Comparative and categoric thinking. Constructing the understanding that if the dinosaur is nether red nor blue it can be placed anywhere outside the two circles.
Mix up dinosaurs again Place all purple dinosaurs in one group in the first circle. Place all the brachiosaurus in one group in the other circle.	What should we do with the purple brachiosaurus? (suggestions include: place it outside the two circles; put two circles immediately adjacent to each other and place it where the two circles touch; create a third circle; overlap of two circles to create a simple venn diagram – it goes in the overlap	Consternation regarding the position of the purple brachiosaurus. Reasoning. Justifying where the purple brachiosaurus should be placed.

		Synthesizing a name of a group based on the characteristics of the members of the group.
	between the two). Explain which position of the purple brachiosaurus best and why? Why was it difficult to decide which group to put it in? What kind of dinosaurs are not in either group? What should each group be called? Why?	Reflection. Analysis. Synthesis. Application (buying a Beyonce record in WHSmith; should you look at top 10; under B for Beyonce or in the bargain basket?)
Reflection after participation in the activity	What kind of thinking have we done here? How did we arrive at our solution? Where else might we apply this kind of thinking? For example, Trying to group things, but it is difficult to decide where it should go because it actually has charactertistics of two different groups.	

Note: [1] For example, a red, blue, green, yellow, purple, orange dimetrodon, tyranosaurus, triceratops, stegosaurus and brachiosaurus.

Witschonke (2006) made connections with the Harry Potter novels. Witschonke's ideas connect most closely with philosophy and have broad moral and intellectual themes. He uses the novels to highlight particular notions: *Harry Potter and the Philosopher's Stone* (1997) reflects on greed, self-sacrifice, fear of the unknown and self-confidence; *Harry Potter and the Chamber of Secrets* (1999) focuses on connections related to heritage, pride and prejudice; *Harry Potter and the Prisoner of Azkaban* (1999) connects with notions of revenge, justice and mercy; *Harry Potter and the Goblet of Fire* (2000) relates to pride, prejudice and the power of the media; *Harry Potter and the Order of the Phoenix* (2003) highlights racism and the power of the media.

Transferring processes or outcomes of thinking (see Figure 10.3) to novels that interest pupils, or the latest movies they may have seen, or electrical gadgets that they are likely to have (such as ipods or mobile telephones) or even connecting in some way to a favourite TV programme can help bridge understanding. Having pupils apply the thinking processes (Perkins and Salomon 2001; Swartz and Fischer 2001) and outcomes to a context that has relevance and direct meaning for them can be very powerful (Leat and Higgins 2002).

Supporting pupils to help them engage in sharing their thoughts, to consider alternative perspectives and even reflect on the co-construction of ideas, methods or propositions means that they need to be asked open questions (as described in Table 12.1).

Posing closed questions (in the sense that they have a single right answer or a very narrow range of possible right answers) constrains the thinking pupils are likely to engage in. As Bricheno et al. (2000: 146) indicate pupils, often expect there to be right factual answers in lessons and responses other than that required by the teacher is 'wrong'. Sometimes pupils even appear to try and 'guess' what answer the teacher is searching for (Wellington 1998). Pupils generally appear to be reluctant to offer alternative resolutions and usually perceive that problems have only one possible solution.

Hodson (1998: 107) also indicates how there is much use of 'closed' questions and that most questions are pitched at too low a level of cognitive demand to form the basis for useful discussion and too little time is allowed for students to formulate responses, and that silence is assumed to indicate incomprehension or lack of understanding. As Selley (2000) argues that accepting wrong answers requires a particular pedagogic tactic, as outlined earlier, especially if the intent is to encourage more higher order thinking. Posing more open questions (in the sense that they may have several very different, plausible and acceptable answers) can provide more opportunities for pupils to develop their thinking. Recognizing a pedagogic intent to encourage higher order thinking, involving development of understanding, ability to apply ideas, to analyze and evaluate (Bloom et al. 1965) demands that teachers carefully compose their questions. Pursuing a line of thought, challenging preconceptions, deliberately 'twisting' ideas or misunderstanding pupils statements, focusing on misconceptions, asking for rationalization, justification and explanations and inviting reflective or metacognitive thinking all require higher order questioning as well as higher order thinking to provide a skilful reply.

Peer collaboration

Tactically supporting peer collaboration can support development of pupils' thinking. Adey and Shayer (1994: 119) recognize the value in peer collaboration, Leat (2000: 161) recognizes that students around a table doing the same task and working *as* groups is successful. He also elaborates that group composition requires some thought, suggesting that mixed ability groups are desirable 'because of the value that variety brings'. Fisher (2000: 54) suggests that regularly meeting in a group (as a thinking circle) can support the development of more searching and thoughtful questions. As Roth (1995: 11) explains, 'we make sense in various ways, and understand the world not merely by means of one theory ... or interpretative repertoire, but in a multi-faceted way and from different (ideological) positions.' Juxtaposed with Piaget's more individualistic perspective of learning, Vygotsky (1978, 1986) perceived these higher mental functions: thinking, reasoning and understanding as social in their origin. He emphasized how children engaging in social construction can mutually support each other's cognitive development. Stobart and Stoll (2005: 230) indicate from their survey of the effectiveness of the KS3 National Strategy, that when 2000 pupils were asked 'What helps you learn?' The most frequent response was working in groups. McGregor (2003: 173) also found from a survey of almost 900 pupils that they recognized the intellectual value of working together in small groups. Teachers can tactically encourage social constructivism in their classrooms to promote sociocognitive conflict arising through dissonance with others. Mediating to encourage pupils to solve problems through social interaction can support development of comparative thinking, analytical thinking, synthesis, reasoning, rationalization and many other cognitive functions, all leading toward a reasoned solution and contributing to the collective decision making process. As Durkin (1995) states, 'cognition' can be perceived 'as a product of social interaction'. The nature of social interactions that can nurture cognitive development are not purely dialectical (McGregor 2003), however, a vast number of studies (Doise et al. 1990; Edwards 1997; Mercer et al. 1999;

Mercer 2000; Leat and Higgins 2002) emphasize talk and language as the means by which pupils communicate and render their thinking explicit. Light et al. (1994) have highlighted how having to use language to make plans explicit, to make decisions and to interpret feedback seems to facilitate problem solving and promote understanding. In these studies talk and language are considered integral to make explicit egocentric thought. Vygotsky (1999: 248) proffered that speech was 'a distinct plane of verbal thought'. Inter-'actions' such as dealing cards, shifting apparatus, moving transient labels or scribing collective ideas are social inter-'actions'. Bruner (1986: 72) describes how language is important in thinking, but should also take account of action. 'Language is (in Vygotsky's sense as in Dewey's) a way of sorting one's thoughts about things. Thought is a mode of organising perception and action'. 'Talk' alongside 'action' can both implicitly and explicitly illuminate pupils' cognitive processing. It is through this (often jerky) seesawing of ideas, suggestions, clarifications that collaborating pupils can dialogically expose their strategic or tactical approaches, with the implicit understandings (or misunderstandings) becoming obvious through actional and linguistical manifestations. Emergence of procedural and conceptual understandings (often interwoven, like the DNA double helix, with two visible, inextricably linked, threads) often occurs in staccato-like reactions to each other's utterings and actions. Thus through both talk and actional interactions, the development of understanding is accrued in a spiral-like fashion, between the pupils gradually attributing and accumulating their 'public' knowledge and understanding. Rogoff (1990: 150) describes how teachers who do not appreciate a more social and cultural perspective of thinking may limit learners' cognitive development.

Collaboration and intersubjectivity

Intersubjectivity is the dynamic, ongoing, exchange between co-learners of ideas and thoughts to resolve an issue, problem or task. The interactions involve clarifying how each idea is juxtaposed with the other. The collaborators use the diversity of their propositions to gauge value, amend suggestions and eventually reach a reasoned solution. Intersubjectivity is fundamental to developing shared understandings about the nature of the task itself, as well as agreement about how to perform the task and any interpretations that may be accrued through engagement in the task or findings or outcomes developed through reflection of the task. As Ding and Flynn (2000: 11) suggest from their work on the theory of mind, in order to collaborate effectively pupils (and the teacher) must have a shared understanding of the task and goals. Intersubjectivity thus underpins effective collaboration.

Lave and Wenger (1991) describe how the process of intersubjectivity is pivotal for learning:

> Learning is a process that takes place in a participation framework, not in an individual mind. This means, among other things, that it is mediated by the differences in perspective among co-participants. It is the community, or at least those participating in the learning context, who 'learn' under this definition
>
> (Lave and Wenger 1991: 15)

How collaborators are orchestrated to work together and their collective perspective thus impacts on the nature and extent of the thinking developed.

Teacher tactics clearly communicated to group collaborators to support cognitive development are therefore important.

Composition and size of collaborating groups

The number of participants in a collective can impact on the extent to which individuals engage in working together. Too large a group or too small a group may not productively support affective intersubjectivity. McGregor (2003) has shown how the application of Mercer's (1995) ground rules, forming the basis for the early Thinking Together materials, can be successful with triads. Promoting development of 'exploratory' talk *and* developing an explicit expectation that there should be symmetrical contributions from *all* participants is emphasized. Questions are posed to groups collectively; immediate individual responses are not anticipated. The collaborators are expected to engage with each other's ideas and share what they consider to be salient (Murphy and Spence 1997). Salient is taken to mean the pupils subjective interpretation of the relevant and important aspect(s) of the task. Proposals are considered and discussion centres around issues of significance in a task as intersubjectivity progresses. Each group is encouraged to reach a majority decision.

If mediation of differences supports learning then pupils of differing sociocultural backgrounds should be encouraged to collaborate. Collaborative working should therefore recognize the impact different groupings may have on the nature and quality of thinking.

Conclusion

Philosophy for Children encourages the students to engage in becoming a community of learners. The approach involves the whole class, usually between 20 and 30 children sitting around in a circle to engage as a community of learners. In TTG, CASE, CAME the students are encouraged to work in groups of about five or six and in the Thinking Together approach students are encouraged to work in trios.

Charles Crook (2000: 162) draws parallels with 'ecology' the 'study of the interactions between organisms and their environment'. Arguably in a classroom, there are several small communities of learners or collaborators when teachers assign working groups. Thinking about how to nurture social interactions effectively to develop intersubjectivity in each of these communities requires a number of pedagogic tactics and mediation techniques.

As Dewey indicates, it is not just the materials used or the programme followed, it is the *way* that these are used by teachers in classrooms that can really make a difference in the thinking and learning that they do:

> Everything the teacher does, as well as the manner in which he does it, incites the child to respond in some way or other, and each response tends to set the child's attitude in some way or other ... with the young, the influence of the teacher's personality is intimately fused with that of the subject; the child does not separate not even distinguish from the two.
>
> (Dewey 1910: 47)

The ways that teachers present, encourage, challenge, scaffold, mediate and reward thinking are all influential factors that will determine whether or not the student perceives the task or challenge as valuable and worthwhile. Perhaps educators should think more carefully about tactics for developing thinking capability and become more strategic in their approaches (so that even Billy McBone would collaborate!)

Key ideas

Clear cognitive objectives are required to inform emphasis (for teachers and students) in thinking activities.

Creating an open thoughtful ethos is important to encourage thinking.

Thinking programmes can developed to be progressive and sequential.

Thinking within lessons can be progressive.

There are identifiable and generalizable phases in thinking lessons:
- preparing for thinking
- challenging thinking
- organizing thinking
- reflective thinking
- transferring thinking

The interplay between the teacher's views, the pupils' views and the nature of the task can influence the thinking developed.

The nature of tasks (and scaffolding provided) can influence the type of thinking pupils develop.

Supporting thinking requires a range of pedagogic strategies and tactics (which contrast with transmission teaching or direct instruction).

Insightful psychological perspectives of learning can inform how to encourage more skilful thinking.

Teacher mediation can significantly influence the nature and extent of thinking.

Mediational strategies that can strongly influence thinking include:
- questioning techniques (frequency, nature and sequence)
- encouraging peer-peer collaboration (through various means)
- scaffolding purposely for cognitive development
- encouraging reflective discussion

13 Professional development to support thinking classrooms

He that knows not, and knows not that he knows not is a fool.
Shun him.
He that knows not, and knows that he knows not is a pupil.
Teach him.
He that knows, and knows not that he knows is asleep
Wake him.
He that knows, and knows that he knows is a teacher.
Follow him.

(Arabic proverb)

This proverb highlights how it may not be apparent to teachers that they do not know something. It does not mean they are foolish (unlike the proverb) it highlights how they may be unaware of something. A meta-analysis that Joyce and Showers (1995) carried out indicates how the nature of professional development that teachers engage in can raise their awareness, skill *and* practice (see Table 13.1) of new initiatives at differing levels. This chapter introduces some of the issues connected with educators understanding pedagogic practice to nurture thinking in their classrooms. The chapter then proceeds to describe the type of professional development (PD) that can support teachers understanding how social and cultural factors as well as their practice, can influence pupils' thinking. The chapter ends by attempting to summarize the important facets of PD for teachers wishing to support skilful thinking in their classrooms.

Curricular imperatives

Recent curricular changes in England and Wales brought about by a raft of National initiatives, not least the regular revisions of the National Curriculum, have not necessarily brought about all the pedagogic reforms envisaged. As Stobart and Stoll (2005) identify, the National Literacy Strategy (NLS) and National Numeracy Strategy (NNS) have been identified as ambitious large-scale educational reforms, and are perceived

Table 13.1 Effective INSET provision for teachers: a meta-analysis by Joyce and Showers (1995: 112)

Nature of INSET provision	Impact on teachers' ...		
	Knowledge (being *aware* of new developments)	Pedagogic skills (developing awareness of the *things* they can *do*)	Practice (*transferring* the new developments to the classroom)
Given theory	Low	Low	None
Given theory and demonstration	Low	Low	None
Given theory, demonstration and opportunity to practice	Some	Some	None
Given theory, demonstration, opportunity to practice and feedback	High	Some	Low
Given theory, demonstration, opportunity to practice, feedback and coaching	Highest	High	High

to 'have worked' (Stobart and Stoll 2005: 228), although the lack of attention to pedagogy has been criticized (Alexander 2003). The KS3 National Strategy, based on the success of the NLS and NNS, also intended to improve teaching, has placed special emphasis on Assessment for Learning and Thinking Skills, which are both whole-school initiatives (DfES 2003). The thinking skills aspects have been based primarily on the CA work by Adey and Shayer (1994, 2002) and Leat's (1999) work on professional development. As Stobart and Stoll highlight the reform has focused on what should be taught and how. There are various barriers to teachers changing their pedagogies, not least, the rate of frenetic national policy developments Leat and Higgins (2002). To support curricular change, teachers need time to reflect, plan and act. Joyce et al. (1997) indicate how time is an issue and that curriculum initiatives often fail because there is insufficient PD to support teachers. As Craft (2000) indicates, how teachers view learning (and therefore thinking) is implicit in the way they choose to organize their classroom. Each choice a teacher makes about the physical layout, the curriculum content, the structure of assignments, the availability and use of resources, the nature of classroom interactions and relationships reflects to some degree that teachers view of learning. Teacher understanding can therefore strongly influence their pedagogical approach and the tactics they may develop to foster thinking skills. McGregor (2003: 218) shows how, before inservice-training (INSET), teachers perceived learning in a somewhat constrained way. They did not recognize the potential impact of pupils discussing ideas and working collaboratively on problems. Teachers appeared to believe that learning occurred predominantly as information *given from them*, the more 'expert' teachers. Pupils working together was not perceived as an effective way to learn primarily because many could 'opt out', but it was a necessary strategy to share valuable or limited resources and materials.

Significant features of INSET

Features of INSET that are important to support teachers' understanding of how to nurture cognitive skills include the philosophy of the course, the ways that inset offers experiential insights, connections with classroom practice and theoretical understandings, demonstrations of good practice and coaching provision that offers guidance and feedback.

Teachers can be supported to appreciate that thinking skills are more than just an antidote for the instrumentalism of prescribed curricula (Leat 1999). Pedagogical approaches that encourage thinking can be described, modelled, deliberately demonstrated, but none of these approaches help teachers understand or empathize with their pupils' thinking dilemmas unless they are placed in the position of novice learner themselves.

The approach that McGregor and Gunter (2001a, 2006) used involved experienced tutors enacting a cognitively sensitive pedagogic approach, using a variety of tactics to mediate learning through social interactions to ensure that teachers 'experience' learning together. In reflective discourse and collective reflections the teachers are encouraged to objectify and make explicit the cognitive purpose of the activities *and* social exchanges. As Cobb et al. (1997) explain, teachers engaged in actions or processes, who are then guided to reflect on their involvement realise how ideas can be transformed into conceptual (subject principles) and cognitive objectives.

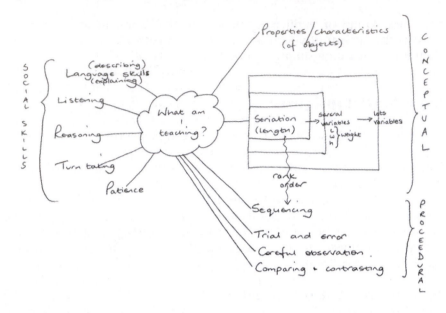

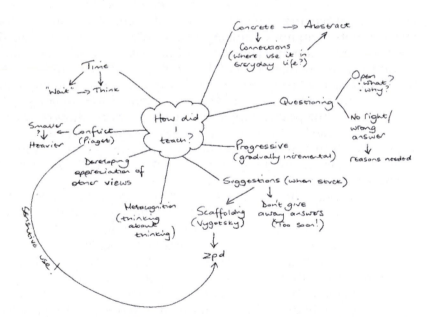

Note: The first set of notes illustrates discussion about *what* was understood by the learners the second *how* the teacher taught.

Figure 13.1 The collective nature of making explicit the cognitive and social in a thinking lesson (seriation described in Table 4.3) through notes on a whiteboard

These kinds of explicit reflections of the modelled experience provide the opportunity for the teachers to empathize, as learners, with their pupils' learning situations (see Figure 13.1).

Experiential insights

Educators of teachers should be experienced in supporting the thinking approaches with pupils so that they can make legitimate knowledge claims. Having 'lived' and 'experienced' the 'material in some fashion' (Collins 1990: 232) they are in a position that is 'empowering and illuminating'. They can discuss different pedagogical approaches with teachers because they can 'reflect on' and 'speak about' their experience in ways not available to someone 'outside' the activities. Experience is crucial for teachers to be able to enact pedagogic practices to enlighten and empower them in *understanding* the learning processes engaged in by *their* pupils.

Practice connecting with theoretical understandings

Effective inset activities should be authentic, purposeful, stimulating and include facets of a pupils' thinking task (see Chapter 12) but refocused for the adult learner. The essential methods to develop pupils cognitively, which Adey (1997) describes as those that provide tasks that encompass challenge, reflection, construction and bridging, should be transferred to adult learning. Thinking should be centred on placing the learner in 'the position where she has to construct herself – slowly and often painfully – the type of thinking needed to tackle all sorts of scientific problems and investigations' (Adey 1997: 71). To illustrate the pedagogical tactics that teachers could use to develop cognitive skills McGregor and Gunter (2001a, 2006) devised a series of activities. These activities provided the 'arena' within which to 'enact' (Lave 1988: 179) nurturing cognitive development. The teachers became the 'persons acting', and their 'active participation' in small groups, enabled them to *see* and *feel* how to support mini-communities of learning in thinking classrooms. The mediational tactics and questions developed within these types of activities can be generalized, for teachers to apply in other learning situations for cognitive purposes. A wide variety of professional development activities were developed to highlight characteristics of thinking tasks, but only a few are described here: Fs, *Titanic* and Moebius. The origami activity (Figure 8.5) and finding the photograph were (Figure 9.2), used to illustrate to teachers the development of critical and creative thinking, are described in Chapters 8 and 9 respectively.

Fs activity

This is a good introduction for teachers new to supporting thinking for pupils. The Fs activity (see Figure 13.2) sensitizes teachers to the thinking that a learner may engage in when posed a simple question like 'how many fs are in this sentence?' It is a closed question; there is only one right answer. The activity clearly demonstrates how well-qualified teachers with much educational experience do not all respond with the correct answer after several attempts at reading one paragraph of text. Carter's (1998) work on how the brain functions when doing this specific task illustrates that the information is processed by individuals in very different ways. How learners perceive and interpret the same information in various ways illuminates why they tackle similar tasks, process information and reach conclusions that differ. Connections linking the unique physiology of the brain to individualized cognitive processing and personalized learning could be discussed and pursued from this point.

Titanic activity

The *Titanic* activity is used to illustrate a range of mediational strategies that can be used tactically to support the development of thinking. It is also useful to illustrate the social and cultural impacts on teachers' (and students') thinking and learning. Triads of teachers from differing schools, and consequently with varied life histories, can work together. Participants can then contribute their perspective, equitably, to group discussions. The experience provides conceptual 'evidence' for collective reflections on rationale for deliberately grouping and organizing pupils working together in particular ways to achieve cognitive aims.

The context of the activity is floating and sinking. Influences on the buoyancy of several liquids (cooking oil, coloured water, syrup) and solid objects (grape, nuts, rice, pasta, tomato, raisins) are considered. Real-life relevance is integrated through the adoption of the *Titanic* movie as a theme.

Distribution of questions

Each collaborating group has questions posed to it collectively, in a sequential way. The worksheet (Figure 13.3) is best not given immediately but instead revealed a question at a time on Powerpoint (or similar). This is because presentation of information that will be relevant later may constrain the initial thinking in the activity. This technique

> ## Introduction to thinking ...
>
> ### Finished files are the result of years of scientific study combined with the experience of many years

Steps in the activity:

1 The teachers are presented with this text to read, in silence.
2 They are then asked, text removed, without discussion to recall how many Fs were in the paragraph? 0, 1, 2, 3, 4, 5, 6 or 7.
3 The responses of the teachers are written on a flipchart at the front for collective appraisal.
4 No feedback is given.
5 The text is presented for reading a second time. Again the teachers are asked to recall how many Fs are in the paragraph.
6 Again no feedback is given.
7 Again the collective responses are collated on a flipchart for all to see.
8 The text is presented a third time for reading. The teachers are asked again how many Fs are in the paragraph.
9 The responses are collated for all to reflect upon.
10 Typical responses are:

	Number of Fs in paragraph		
No. of Fs	After first reading	After second reading	After third reading
0			
1			
2	Several folk		
3	Most folk	Most folk	A few folk
4	Some folk	Several folk	Several folk
5	A few folk	A few more folk	Some folk
6	One or two folk	Several folk	Most folk
7	Occasional folk		

The reflective discussion includes:

- A simple question is posed with *One* right answer, not *All* teachers present responded correctly after three readings!
- Consideration of the range of responses (to simple question) illustrates the uniqueness of the ways in which each person's brain functions.
- Consideration of the CAT scan evidence that indicates certain types of processing occur in the Broca's and/or Wernicke's area of the cerebral cortex (Carter 1998: 150–1).
- Each pupil in a class will perceive the tasks and questions asked of them in differing ways that we, as teachers need to take account of.

Figure 13.2 A professional development (PD) activity to emphasize non-conformity in thinking

illustrates the importance of progression and sequence in questioning. Each time a question is posed the collaborating groups are encouraged to

- Take turns to describe to the others what they think.
- Consider, compare and contrast each contributor's ideas.
- Agree as a group what is the best response to the questions posed (i.e. discuss, debate and decide).

The first question, 'What will happen when I add the two liquids to the syrup?' invites participants to consider previous relevant experience. It is not typical of school science; therefore teachers are likely to be unfamiliar with the predictable 'right' answer. Even some experienced science teachers are not sure what will happen. Collaboratively 'considering' the question, each participant's suggestions, then weighing up the advantages and disadvantages of propositions before responding to the tutor/teacher provides an opportunity for each to contribute their experience and expertise. Examination of the liquids may lead to suggestions that because the oils appears 'thicker' than the water it will rest on top of it. Experience or knowledge about oil pollution, for example, may result in a suggestion that the oil will float at the top because participants have seen evidence (or pictures of oceanic oil spills). Someone who pays attention to the oil seepages from cars and notices it floating on the surface of puddles may suggest that oil floats on water. Someone who has perhaps used jam or syrup in the bottom of a jar, topped up with water, to attract (and then drown wasps) in summer may suggest that the syrup sinks. Life histories and previous relevant observations or experiences will influence proffered ideas. Distribution

The TITANIC Activity

- ☐ *What will happen when I add the two liquids to the syrup?*

- ☐ *What will happen when I drop in Leonardo di Grapio?*

- ☐ *Why do you predict this?*

Discuss why this happened

What will happen with these objects?

- ☐ *Nut Winslet?*

- ☐ *Billy Grain?*

- ☐ *Jenny Pasta?*

- ☐ *Tom Harto?*

What would happen if I dropped a raisin into the jar? Explain your

prediction.

Discuss, debate and decide as a group what you think.

- ☐ *What about a glass of water?*

- ☐ *What about sparkling water?*

Now try it.

- ☐ *Can you explain how this happened?*

Discuss, debate and decide as a group what you think.

Explain the following:

- ☐ *How does a lava lamp work?*

- ☐ *Why is it easier to swim in the sea than in the swimming pool?*

- ☐ *Which of these two questions was a better 'bridge' to everyday life and why?*

Discuss, debate and decide as a group what you think.

Source: After McGregor and Gunter (2006).

Figure 13.3 Example of the worksheet used to develop teachers' understanding of social and cultural impacts on pupils thinking

of questions for collaborative consideration, before propositions are collected, is a technique to share subjectivities. Individually targeted questions with little or no time for deliberation will curtail the rich nature of peer-mediated discussion.

Nature of the questions

The second question is 'What will happen when a grape is dropped in?' (humourously named Leonardo di Grapio) and 'Why do you predict this?' Any open question asking 'what' provides for a plethora of responses, but followed up by 'why' invites rationalization of the 'what'. In this instance asking for predictions about what happens to a grape dropped into the jar of three layers of liquids (and why) invites reflective consideration of previous experiences. Many would argue the grape is made up of mostly water and therefore will float in the middle water layer. Some may argue that it contains sugar; therefore, it will sink to the syrup. Others suggest that it is light and has air in it therefore it will float on the water. (These kinds of propositions can provide formative information about understandings of scientific concepts.)

More open-ended questions are asked deliberately to pose much less 'leading' challenges and thus provide opportunities to develop more diverse cognitive processing. The opportunity to also predict or respond to 'What happens next?' provides the challenge of constructing sense out of what has happened so far. Asking learners to predict can be a very powerful mediational strategy that invites synthesis and analytical processing of relevant information or data provided to project and extrapolate what could happen next.

Questions with this prefix, 'What will happen?' can create very open-ended possibilities, with no fettering or constraints on the anticipated response. Frequent use of this type of question engenders a more reasoned 'open' culture of offering proposals with justifications. Less 'knowing' teachers may readily ask 'Will the grape sink or float in the water?' This type of closed question, where there are two possible answers, requires much less thought. Closed questions constrain the opportunity for cognitive processing. Teachers experiencing the cognitive demands of open, 'what' and 'why', questions understand how to mediate better learning through questioning.

Later on in the *Titanic* activity learners are asked to 'explain' ideas. Teachers can mediate students' learning to provide good-quality explanations by allowing them to rehearse propositions with each other in their collaborative groups. They can evaluate others' contributions, prioritize ideas and co-construct resolutions. Generating a learning culture so that collaborating teachers engage in this unique dynamic process provides enlightenment about the social influences on learning together.

Metacognition on the nature of social construction

After participation in the *Titanic* activity teachers are guided in collaborative reflections. Purposeful questions such as 'How did your thinking and understanding change as the task proceeded?' 'Why?' 'What influenced you?' 'What happened between members of the group as the task unfolded?' 'How did you support or influence each others' thinking?' 'What kinds of questions were asked?' 'Were there more or less effective questions posed at particular junctures of the task?' 'How would you have taught about different densities/buoyancy/floating/ sinking?' 'How did this learning activity differ from the way you would normally teach?'

The intention of the reflective discussion is to provide the opportunity for all group participants to share how their constructions and understandings developed as a result of both engaging in the activity and entering into discursive consideration about meaning and explanation. Teachers reflect on how their experience of relative densities of 'foodstuffs' has never been formally taught, therefore they don't 'know' the answers. They recognize that engaging in an activity where they are 'novices' means they can enter into learning and constructing new knowledge together (social construction). They reflect on how each participant has contributed differing facets of their solution(s) and how the collaborative nature of their interactions contributes to shared referents and the development of mutual under- standings.

Exploring the connections between thought and language

In responses to what will happen to the various pieces of food dropped into the liquids, each participant in turn offers a proposal that contributes to the group goal of a negotiated and commonly agreed prediction. Through articulating a prediction involving 'unknown' influences (not knowing the exact composition of a grape, nut, tomato and so forth, it is impossible to calculate the absolute densities) thus attempting to reason where the object may (eventually) come to rest invites more thought and thus more explicit (and probably extensive) linguistic description and explanation. Reflective consideration of the likely quality of written responses from students compared with the rich nature of the group discussions illustrates to teachers the spontaneity and importance of language in developing thought and consequent learning. They note, too, that insistence on learning in a 'written form' constrains thinking.

Importance of socio-cognitive conflict

This involves asking a question knowing dissonance will arise between co-learners because they have little or no prior knowledge to draw on, or because the phenomenon explored is unpredictable, or because the subject matter is unfamiliar, for example 'What will happen to the tomato?' Most people would predict that it is denser than the water and so will sink to the syrup/water interface. However, in young, fresh firm tomatoes more air is trapped in the tissue, which can result in it floating in the oil layer. Attempting to explain this can then be vexing but a biologist may support developing plausible suggestions. The raisin dropped into tap water will sink; in sparkling water it cyclically rises and falls – this is unlikely to be predicted. Creating deliberate conflict in an activity is a factor that can stimulate curiosity, contribute to on-task 'engagement' and stimulate discussion of subjectivities. Teacher mediation can intervene to twist or change suggestions deliberately to check for 'firm' volition of understanding. Teachers (before professional development of this kind) often offer positive reinforcement clues indicating to learners what the 'correct' solution is and this tends to curtail deeper, reflective thinking about the task in hand. Students tend to halt their thinking once they perceive they have achieved the 'right' answer.

Authentic task

The questions regarding floating or sinking foodstuffs provide a familiar context that requires more difficult scientific ideas to be applied: relative densities; surface tension; density versus viscosity; buoyancy and upthrust. Dropping various objects of everday relevance into different liquids should mean that participants could offer some suggestions based on life experience. For example, cooking risotto may contribute to predictions about rice grains (single and clumped); peanut tossing in the local hostelry may contribute to notions about peanut buoyancy; having boiled dried pasta, or washed tomatoes or experience of food preparation and/or cooking could contribute to learners' ideas being readily generated regarding pasta and (small cherry) tomatoes. The food objects being associated with a character name or actor from a movie provides a humourous perspective, giving an additional cultural dimension to the reflective discussions.

The social and cultural influences each participant brings to bear during group resolution are starkly demonstrated through experience in this in-service activity. Teachers begin to understand better how social and cultural experiences can influence learners' perceptions, interpretations and understandings in their classroom. This then underpins why a societal mix of co-learners is useful if the aim of a lesson is to support cognitive development.

Moebius strip activity

This is another powerful PD activity (see Figure 13.4) providing experiences that help teachers to appreciate learners' difficulties when facing abstract challenges in their lessons. Students often find it difficult to comprehend abstract ideas that subject teachers understand, such as particulate theory of matter in science, algebraic equations in maths, sophisticated character and plot analysis in English. More experienced and expert teachers often forget how naïve their pupils may be and the limited social and scholarly experiences they may have to draw on to think about things. The reflection on the challenging thinking required for this activity highlights how novice learners may be overwhelmed; generate novel ideas; create insightful but misconcieved explanations or consider only a part of the information given to solve the task.

Concrete and abstract

The activity begins in a very concrete way and gradually unfolds to extend participants to engage in challenging abstract modelling. Initially the teachers have to decide how many faces and edges a sheet of paper has. Some perceive it as a 3D object, with the same number of edges and faces that a flattened cuboid would have; others describe it simply from a 2D point of view. Focusing on the faces and edges of the paper, which is held together as a loop and then eventually adhered together as a Moebius strip, provides the teachers with frames of reference that can be applied to begin to unravel the subsequent happenings when handling the strip. This clear example of progression in thinking highlights the simpler, more direct, concrete thinking from the very challenging more abstract forms of thinking.

Preparing for thinking

This activity also illustrates how to prepare learners for thinking challenges because linguistic terms and understandings have to be negotiated before the real thinking can begin. The introductory part of

Steps:

1   Teachers are given a sheet of A4 plain white paper. They are asked to dddd their group ideas regarding the faces and edges of the sheet of paper.

Some will perceive the paper in a 3D way, as a flat cuboid like structure, others will see it as a 2D object. There is likely to be some differences of opinion regarding the number of faces and edges. Agreeing, however, with plausible reasons, that there are, for the sake of the rest of the activity, two faces and four edges is preparation for the following steps.

2   The teachers are the instructed to cut down the longest edge of the paper a 5 cm width strip. They are asked again to dddd the number of faces and edges. There is likely to be conformity in the thinking this time (as they reflect on the previous step).

3   The teachers are then instructed to hold the two ends of the strip together so a loop is formed. Again they are asked to dddd the number of edges and faces. There should be conformity in agreement again, with two edges and two faces:

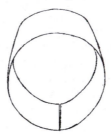

4   The teachers are then shown how to twist one end through 180 degrees and given tape to stick the ends together to form a Moebius strip:

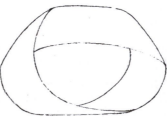

Without touching or moving the Moebius strip they are asked to describe how many faces and how many edges it has. There is likely to be differences of opinion here. The reasoning and discussion to help teachers appreciate that there is one face and one edge is useful preparation for the next steps. Some may have to trace the path of the face to check out their understanding.

5   The teachers are asked to think about the Moebius strip and consider what would happen if the strip were cut down the centre. It is important that they have time to develop a reasoned prediction.

6   Once the predictions from each group are articulated on the flipchart (or IWB). It is important to have some moments for reflection to consider the diversity and rationale behind the propositions. The teachers can then cut the strip.

7   Reflections on the product of the cutting and the differences (and similarities) with predictions contributes to important metacognition.

8   Further development of thinking can be to have the teachers predict again what would happen if the strip were cut one-fifth of the way in from the edge.

9   Explicating predictions and reasons and comparing and contrasting the range of ideas is important in teachers beginning to appreciate the issues that face pupils when they do not 'know' the right answers!

Metacognition, on the nature of the differences between predictions and the product of the cutting, as well as the social and cognitive processes involved in this activity is important to parallel with pupils learning processes and outcomes. There are obvious junctures where what the teacher asks for, for example predictions and reasons, can be very powerful in provoking thinking. The nature of the open questioning is also explicated.

Notes: When each question is asked, consider in your collaborative groups what you think is the best response to the question. Remember to describe your ideas to the all others in your group, discuss, deliberate on the suggestions made and decide which is best and why. Describe, discuss, deliberate, decide (ddd).

Figure 13.4 Using the Moebius strip to help teachers empathize with pupils' thinking

the activity is about establishing common understandings of 'faces' and 'edges' so that all participants subsequently use those terms to mean the same thing when describing and explaining their future propositions. This illustrates that talking about ideas cannot only shape and influence the thinking all collaborators are engaged in, but it also helps them recognize how pupils need experience and subsequent guidance in developing and using an appropriate lexicon to explain thinking and ideas more exactly and precisely.

Illustrating forms of metacognition

Reflection-on-action and reflection-in-action are also key in this activity. Once teachers have made their initial predictions (see Figure 13.4) about what will happen when the strip is cut down the centre it is imperative to reflect on the range of differing predictions (for example, a Moebius strip twice as long, two separate Moebius strips) with the actual findings (a longer loop with two twists). It is unusual to have anyone predict correctly. Reflection-on-action then focuses on 'what did we find?' and 'why was it different from what we expected?' Discussion about the nature of these differences supports the teachers when they make a second prediction. The second time they can be asked (after making another Moebius strip) 'what do you think will happen when it is cut about a third in from the edge?' The collaborators now have a common experience, or frames of reference, upon which to draw and inform reflection about what they think will happen next. Not ever divulging or suggesting to the teachers what they *will* produce next conveys how the nature of questions can steer, guide and support thinking.

As Roth (1995, 1999), Cobb (1994), Cobb et al. (1997) and others describe, these learning activities are authentic in that they are used to help teachers make sense of and develop meaning for theories about thinking and learning. The PD activities are purposely humourous too because, as Dewey (1910) advocates, a balance of fun and intellectuallualism alleviates bias. 'To be playful and serious at the same time is possible ... it defines the mental state. Absence of dogmatism and prejudice, presence of intellectual curiosity and flexibility, are manifest in the free play of the mind upon a topic' (Dewey 1910: 218).

Teachers are encouraged to compare, contrast and analyse their juxtaposed perspectives and to reach a group goal collectively. As Mercer (1995: 104) illustrates the approach to encourage 'inter-thinking' appears to absorb participants in exploratory talk, rejecting inferior ideas, proposing and negotiating superior views. Through conflict (of a social and evidential nature) and the development of an open thoughtful ethos, the application of Mercer's ground rules appeared to help teachers see how to develop explicit agreement, which precedes decision making and action. Teachers' collective reflections on how they discussed, negotiated meaning and developed understanding through their active in-task engagement provided 'real' experience to empathize with pupils' learning (and cognitive) frustrations and successes. Teachers removed from their usual 'expert' role and resituated as 'novices' in collaborative learning situations, allows them through 'learning in practice' (Wenger 1998: 95) to recognize how to sustain 'mutual engagement' of participants in pursuing an enterprise. Developing teachers' appreciation of the nature and importance of their role in enculturating this kind of autonomous, mutually beneficial way of learning together is essential to nurture cognitive skills.

Joyce and Shower's review of effective INSET suggests that changed practice cannot be affected by central PD alone but in combination with coaching it is more likely to support pedagogical changes. Supportive coaching can be provided in a variety of forms including teacher practice and post-professional discussions, demonstration teaching, collaborative planning and team teaching or even professional dialogue focused around videoed teaching. All these components continuing to corroborate the view that the interactive, collaborative nature of INSET can influence practice significantly. McGregor (2003) and McGregor and Gunter (2001a, 2006) explored the impact that PD of this kind has on teachers' practice. Some of the findings from teacher reflections, of personal pedagogical impact are reported here.

Before PD, many teachers infrequently 'grouped' their pupils to work together. In professional discussions with them they frequently mentioned that, after INSET, they considered a raft of issues (including a variety of capabilities, gender and cultural background) when placing pupils in particular groups to work together. They realized that dialogue was likely to be richer if pupils changed working partners regularly; they recognized how boys made quite different contributions from girls in discussions as a result of varied life histories, as Ball (1993) indicates, they took account of learners' heritage; they found that mixing abilities could support ZPD development through the divergent exchange of ideas and reasoning. Teachers appeared to develop their questioning tactics. They generally asked more questions, regardless of type, indicating that they perceived this was a useful strategy to engage pupils cognitively. The proportion of open questions was markedly increased, complemented; it appeared, by a significant decrease in the proportion of closed questions.

Table 13.2 Summary of significant pedagogic changes

Teaching characteristic	After participation in professional development focused on thinking
Preparing for thinking	Recognition that diversity in co-thinkers can influence the nature of cognitive activity.
	Grouping pupils more often in triads.
	Purposefully grouping for cognitive outcomes.
Questioning	More frequent.
	More open (*why*, *how* and *what*) questions.
	Wider range of questions asked.
	More time given for pupils to think and respond.
	More attention paid to nature of pupils' answers.
	More asked between peers.
Discussion	Encouraged much more in problem solving situations.
	More time spent considering each others ideas and group findings.
	More credence given to verbal contributions in class.
Hypothesizing	More opportunities generated for prediction.
	Asked 'What do you expect next?' more often.
Explaining	Expect more justifications for ideas.
	Expect more elaboration and explanation of findings and ideas.
Transferring	More encouragement to transfer ideas to other contexts.
	Specifically asking 'Where else?'
	More connections from classwork to real-life situations.
Intervention	More purposefully proffering conflicting propositions.
	More spontaneous use of anomalous information or surprising data.

Source: After McGregor and Gunter (2006).

The more open nature of questions included 'what do you think?' and 'why?' more often to elicit from pupils reasoning behind their answers to questions. Rather than revealing immediately whether the responses were right or not, teachers developed the strategy of collecting a range of possible replies or responses, to reflect on possibilities, before giving any negative or positive replies. Although there was no opportunity on the questionnaire to explain why they reduced the proportion of closed questions asked, previous interviewees (McGregor and Gunter 2001b) understood that 'closed' questions constrained the thinking, because 'answers' required a selection from limited possibilities. Many teachers increased their 'wait time' (Tobin 1984), better described as cogitating time, after posing questions to provide pupils the opportunity to elaborate (and discuss) their responses before expecting a reply – a technique noted to support development of reflective habits of mind (Zessoules and Gardner 1991). Many teachers encouraged prediction and reasoning about what might happen next more often. Teachers realized how this tactic elucidated pupils' current understandings and provided formative assessment for learning (Black et al. 2003). Teachers more frequently intervened to suggest or present non-conformist ideas to provoke cognitive ponderings into 'what does it mean?' When appropriate, they created more space and time to contemplate meanings of things, evidence, data or happenings. There were many more opportunities to discuss, explain, justify, clarify, reason and generally think about ideas with peers.

McGregor (2003: 152) noted that teachers began to encourage more discussion and consideration around planning, the meaning of evidence and post-activity attempts to explain findings. These points of focus, previously ignored by teachers, were subsequently recognized as appropriate junctures at which to encourage exchange of subjective views. It appears that they recognized these were effective tactics to use strategically to engage and stimulate pupils cognitively and conceptually to develop and apply their understandings.

There appeared to be a dramatic shift in teachers' practice in classrooms, presumably underpinned by their change of views and understandings about how to develop pupils' cognitive development and subsequent learning. Their practice, as Craft (2000) and Leat and Higgins (2002) suggest, was influenced by their changed beliefs and understandings. A range of pedagogic strategies, overtly modelled to support teachers' developing pupils thinking and understandings through social interactions are those that support: clarification of the tasks; collective consideration of solutions to tasks and proposition of likely outcomes (prediction); consideration of learner (pupil) responses encouraged through different types (and frequency) of interventional questioning; consideration of conflict through evidence that provides dissonance with likely preconceptions; exaggeration of socio-conflict (through description of others' alternative views); deliberate teacher misinterpretation of descriptions, explanations or propositions; the need to reach for a common goal, prediction or hypothesis through the process of dialogic reasoned argument and negotiation participated in by all members of the group; intragroup post-task evaluative reflection of conceptual and procedural processes; influential contributions by participants in the group to the final collective solution.

The INSET activities described in this chapter should indicate to teachers what to do when faced with developing not just thinking skills, but a thoughtful ethos within thinking classrooms too. The discussion within this chapter (and in other chapters of the book) is intended to support educators planning and developing thinking lessons. Issues such as 'What is an effective working group?' 'When should the pupils be questioned?' 'How should they be questioned?' 'What is appropriate reflection?' 'What is the value of prediction?' 'Why is it relevant?' 'What kind of discussion should be encouraged?' 'Between whom?' 'When?' 'What is it about the structure and nature of the activity that is important?' 'What are the key elements of the activities?' are all pedagogic concerns that have been addressed in this book, but ultimately teachers need to clarify, practice and implement in the ways that best suit themselves and their students.

Key ideas

Enacting what 'thinking' feels like can help teachers, as participants in learning, to realize how to develop their practice to support thinking.

Authentic, interactive learning tasks can be used to support the elicitation of critical, creative and metacognitive thinking for teachers.

Reflections of participation in learning activities can objectify and connect cognitive procedural processes with development of the conceptual under-standings.

The importance of purposeful questioning to develop thinking is reiterated:
- proffered to collaborating groups
- open nature
- careful progression and sequencing
- differing nature of questions that invite critical, creative and metacognitive thinking

---

Recognition that inviting pupils to hypothesize and reason, and to engage in many other kinds of thinking, can provide formative assessment for learning.

---

14 School development to support thinking communities

Finishing Off

The teacher said:
Come here, Malcolm!
Look at the state of your book.
Stories and picture unfinished
Wherever I look.

This model you started at Easter,
These plaster casts of your feet,
That graph of the local traffic-
All of them incomplete.

You've a half-baked pot in the kiln room
And a half-eaten cake in your drawer.
You don't even finish the jokes you tell –
I really can't take any more.

And Malcolm said
. . . very little.
He blinked and shuffled his feet.
The sentence he finally started
Remained incomplete.

He gazed for a time at the floorboards;
He stared for a while into space;
With an unlined, unwhiskered expression
On his unfinished face.

(Ahlberg, *Heard it in the Playground*)

This book is not the complete story on teaching thinking and this chapter is only a brief outline of the ways in which schools might think about nurturing thoughtful communities of learning. Some obvious issues and concerns are highlighted for consideration but the complete solution is in the hands of the managers of schools. Ahlberg's (1991: 40) poem about a young boy who is obviously struggling in school and never completes his work connects with the current narrative on teaching thinking. As McGuinness (2005) emphasizes, there is no general agreement or conclusion about the most effective way to develop cognition. Generalizable features of an effective programme have not reached closure but there are commonalities in perceptions of thoughtful pedagogy. There is common agreement that metacognition is key, although there are differences in the ways that metacognition is conceived and enacted. The story about how schools should implement a thinking programme or approach to nurture a thoughtful culture of learning is not complete either. In her (1999) review for the then DfEE, now the DfES, McGuinness (1999: 28) suggested that there was sufficient evidence for a general framework for teaching thinking, which would include the need to:

- make thinking skills explicit in the curriculum;
- adopt a coaching style to teach thinking;
- operate within a metacognitive perspective;
- develop collaborative learning in both face-to-face and computer-mediated learning;
- encourage good thinking habits or general dispositions.

She also suggested that infusing thinking in subject domains could develop 'thinking classrooms' and 'thinking schools'.

In 2005, she added comments regarding the nature of the pedagogy required in thinking classrooms. As illustrated in Chapter 13, teachers need to understand the cultural changes that are necessary to nurture thinking, to focus more on dialogue (and other interactional exchanges) and to engage collaboratively in open-ended activities to co-construct meanings. Teachers need support to empathize and understand better how to create thoughtful environments that nurture collaborative processes (McGregor 2003). As Kirkwood (2001b) corroborates, the goal is to aspire toward teachers becoming more knowledgeable thinkers about how best to nurture children's thinking. As Perkins (1992: 17) highlights, to become *smart schools*, educators need to be informed to foster thoughtful learning. It is to these ends that this chapter outlines concerns and suggestions for schools.

The problem solving steps offered in Chapter 11 are applied here as a general framework that might guide schools when considering the steps they might take to improve the thoughtful learning within their institution. Throughout the process, inclusive collaboration should be encouraged. More collective participation throughout the school, contributing to the decision making aspects of the problem, issues and challenge of developing more thoughtful learning is key. This is because, as Werner (1980) observed when explaining failure of a curricular innovation in Alberta:

Ideally, implementation as a minimum includes shared understanding among participants concerning the implied presuppositions, values and assumptions which underlie a program, for if
participants understand these, then they have a basis for
rejecting, accepting or modifying a program in terms of their
own school, community and class situations. To state the aim
another way, implementation is an ongoing construction of a
shared reality among group members through their interaction
with one another within the program.

(Werner 1980: 62)

Clarifying the issue(s), problem(s) or challenge(s)

Managers, decision makers and participants of learning within a school
need to clarify what should be done. Reviewing why thinking skills need
addressing and improving in the school should inform where the focus
might lay. Are the thinking skills desired within particular subject areas?
Or is there a more general intent to improve across all subjects? Is there a
wish to nurture good scientists, mathematicians, artists, writers or
linguists? Do they wish that all students metacognitively ponder before
responding to a question? Do they aspire for all learners to become
autonomous and responsible problem solvers? Do they seek excellence
in their creative areas where innovation and new ideas are celebrated?
Do they wish for finely attuned arguers who can reason logically, analyze
and think critically about any piece of work or information? Do they
wish for students who can engage in Socratic questioning and
subsequent deliberations in any forum? Do they hope that pupils will
muse and reflect over perspective and mood in Monet's work or the
rhythm and tone in Mozart's work? Is the aim, as McGuinness (2005:
107) describes, to focus on the development of 'higher order' thinking
that supports learners 'going beyond mere recall of factual information
to develop a deeper understanding' of subject matter? Should the
classrooms convey quiet, individualized, deep, purposeful thinking
focused in a concentrated way on set tasks or should it celebrate
interactional action and dialogue? Should it encourage discussion,
articulation and animated exchange?

Should teachers model excellent thinking to show the best way to
reach a solution, or should there be more open consideration of a
plethora of strategies to achieve a repost? The nature of thinking that a
school wishes to excel in requires clear description before decisions
about *what* and *how* to implement improvements can be made.

Costa (2001: 555) proposes an evaluative questionnaire that administrators can use to self-assess how thoughtful their schools are. He includes a question: 'are students' thoughtful behaviours celebrated in daily classrooms?' Figure 14.1 suggests actions that could be perceived as thoughtful. The list is not exhaustive; it is intended to be suggestive and to help schools to articulate their aspirations. These thoughtful actions or characteristics (discussed in more depth in earlier chapters) can be grouped as critical, creative, critico-creative, metacognitive and social. Thinking critically relates to scrutiny and examination of any given material or information and informs carefully reasoned decisions, thoughts or actions. Thinking creatively relates to any unique thought or product children might develop or construct that is original to them. Thinking metacognitively relates to reflecting in varying ways at different levels about learning. A social dimension should also been included because they are key skills to nurture and emphasize if schools intend to support thinking through collaboration to become learning communities. Figure 14.1 begins to suggest a range of capabilities, which when developed can provide a child's 'mindware'. Perkins (2004) describes the mental tools that we have as our mindware. In an earlier book he describes an analogy of kitchen utensils to illustrate what mindware is:

> Mindware is the software for the mind – the programs you run in your mind that enable you to do useful things with data stored in your memory. Or to make a more prosaic but equally apt analogy with cooking, mindware is like kitchen ware, the equipment of the mind, the pots and pans, measuring spoons and spatulas, egg beaters and corkscrews that enable people to cook up something compelling out of the information at their disposal. Or to put it yet another way, mindware is whatever knowledge, understanding and attitudes you have that support you in making the best use of your mind.
>
> (Perkins 1995: 13)

The ultimate aim, then for schools, is to help pupils develop the best *mindware* they can. Costa and Kallick (2000) suggest encouraging thoughtful behaviours, which they describe as *Habits of Mind*. A whole-school initiative pursuing integration and application of these could underpin development of more thoughtful dispositions. They present an array of traits, described briefly in Table 14.1 that could be helpful for schools, when contemplating how to focus on cognition and create thinking classrooms in thinking schools. The 16 habits of mind identify and describe intelligent behaviours that pupils can usefully apply in any learning situation.

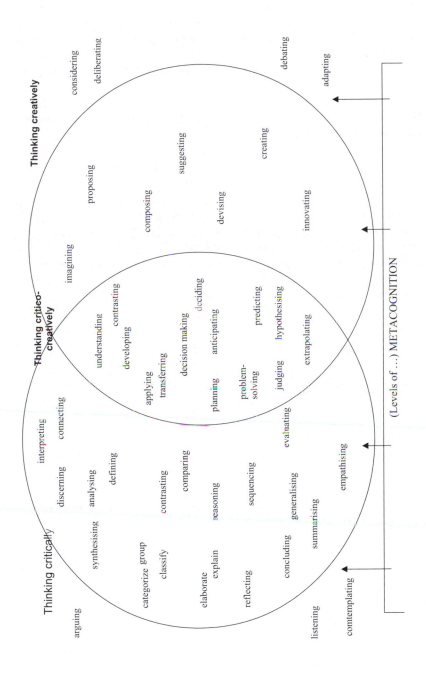

Figure 14.1 Thoughtful acts

Table 14.1 Habits of mind

Habit of mind	Brief description
1 Persistence	This could be described as stick-ability, the tenaciousness to see a task through to completion.
2 Managing impulsivity	Thinking before you act.
3 Listening to others – with understanding and empathy	Listening closely to what is said with the intention of understanding it.
4 Thinking flexibly	Not being constrained in your view of a problem.
5 Thinking about our thinking (metacognition)	This is concerns reflecting and evaluating your own thinking.
6 Striving for accuracy and precision	Aspiring for excellence in an outcome or product.
7 Questioning and posing problems	Knowing what kinds of questions to ask.
8 Applying past knowledge to new situations	Utilizing past experience to help with current problems.
9 Thinking and communicating with clarity and precision	Clearly describing your ideas to others.
10 Gathering data through all senses	Recognizing the sensory pathways to receive information.
11 Creating, imagining, and innovating	Generating creative and innovative ideas.
12 Responding with wonderment and awe	Recognizing the unique value in things and ideas.
13 Taking responsible risks	Daring to be different.
14 Finding humour	Developing funny connections.
15 Thinking interdependently	Thinking together rather than alone.
16 Learning continuously	Recognizing there is always more to learn.

Source: After Costa and Kallick (2000).

What is important in developing thoughtful learning communities?

For schools to develop into thinking communities they need to take account of the programmes of study in the National Curriculum to ensure that content is taught as well as thinking. Thinking has been high on the DfES agenda for some years, especially since, the Leading in

Learning initiative (KS3) emphasized that it should be a whole-school development. As Perkins (1995: 41) explains, smart schools need to ensure that learning is not just a matter of 'accumulating a large repertoire of facts and routines' where the process of learning involves an overwhelming emphasis on factual recall questions and there is little talking about thinking in the classroom. Tests are often comprised of questions requiring right-or-wrong answers and emphasis is on coverage. He represents this as the trivial pursuit theory. Issues for teachers centre around balancing the transmission of knowledge that children must conceivably be given, to achieve in public examinations, *and* engaging in what they perceive as classroom activity that pursues development of lifelong learning and thinking skills (discussed in more detail in earlier chapters).

Just as schools are places of growth for children, they should also be places of growth for teachers and administrators, where the pursuit of intellectual activity and professional collaboration are supported and encouraged. A successful learning organization should enable all members of the school community to collaborate in the processes of goal setting, monitoring and evaluation, creating a dynamic system that changes as the needs and the vision of the community changes. Development of pedagogical approaches and curricular design that can nurture both the content understanding and thinking skills successfully is key. Issues to consider here include whether thinking can be nurtured within content-laden courses. Infusion of thinking, for example, has yet to provide evaluative data to indicate the extent and nature of its impact (McGuinness 2005). Can the timetable constraints be imaginatively reshaped to create thinking opportunities within a school curriculum? Can students' thinking be accelerated (Adey and Shayer 2002) so that prescriptive content of the National Curriculum can be processed more rapidly, thus creating potential space for enhancing and extending thinking through problem solving? As Adey (2004) indicates, critical features required to implement a thinking programme successfully include teacher PD to develop understanding of the underpinning theory or philosophy of the programme and develop familiarity and expertise in using the curricular materials. He also indicates how communication networks, senior management support and the sustained nature of a PD programme, including localized, in situ, coaching as well as centralized training can impact on the levels of success. Supporting professional development that can shift the emphasis in pedagogy to focus on thinking and/or create curriculum time for productive cogitation are issues that require careful planning, preparation and subsequent implementation.

How could we address the issue or challenge?

Understanding that intellect is not a fixed quantity and recognizing that schools can facilitate development of students' thinking in a variety of ways underpins possible curricular and pedagogical approaches. Examples of some simple strategies are:

- Purchasing curricular materials such as the *Thinking Through ...* series. Leat (1998: 2) explains that there are different levels of use of these materials and that teachers need to decide how they would use them to accentuate thinking processes. These materials offer an innovative introduction to the infusion of thinking skills in subject-based lessons.
- Using an established programme, like CoRT or FIE or STS or CA, would mean that teachers have fewer decisions to make about when, where and how to put thinking in place. These programmes, however, require scheduled time, as the lessons are interventional, so curricular space is needed and teachers need PD time to develop appropriate pedagogy.
- In-service training to promote teacher development (detailed in previous chapters) could be provided to the whole school, promoting pedagogical approaches or tactics to inform and educate teachers about the development of thinking. As McGuiness (2005) indicates a generalized thinking skills pedagogy is emerging that involves a metacognitive approach.
- Teaching and learning policies for school development plans can highlight and emphasize the thinking that pupils should engage in. Rewriting policies, however, does not necessarily result in pedagogical changes that influence classroom learning (Stobart and Stoll 2005). Emphasizing that teaching techniques should include explicit modelling, mediating and scaffolding to help students bridge and connect what they learn to new contexts (transfer) greatly enhances the likelihood that students will understand concepts and actively use what they learn. Suggestions about *how* policy intent can be realised in practice are essential to success.

What are all the possible ways this issue or problem could be approached?

All of the above strategies could be implemented in part, in full or in various combinations. Subject-based materials could be purchased (for example, the *Thinking Through* ... series) and integrated into the geography, history, religious education, English and science content programmes (although materials are not yet available for all content areas), so a general thinking programme could also be implemented. Professional development could be provided for the teachers and the school development policy could be amended to articulate the intent to become a learning community. Schools could opt for implementation of a range of subject specific thinking materials (to provide teachers with examples of ways to focus more on thinking in their content area) and consider complementing this with a general thinking programme like STS or CoRT or FIE with pupils who have specific learning difficulties. A school could adopt all the pedagogical strategies that Leat and Higgins (2002), describe as *powerful*, and apply them through all subjects, in an infused way, as the DfES suggests in the Leading in Learning materials. Schools could transfer aspects of an approach or programme, such as de Bono's six hats or only use parts of the CoRT programme, to develop what would work for them. Policy makers could also plan to constrict syllabus content to create time for problem solving and exploration of connections within the secondary curriculum (extending out from the subject area taught), which Kirkwood's (2001a) research study indicated was beneficial in developing thinking of the students involved.

Implementation of only one of the suggestions above is unlikely to result in a whole school change in pedagogy. Development of a paradigm shift (Fullan 2001) whereby all teachers collaboratively support development of a learning community involves careful consideration of curricular design, the nature of pedagogy required and the support that teachers will need to develop this to create appropriate thoughtful cultures within classrooms. The CA approach has been adopted by many schools and has been adapted by overseas countries (including Slovenia, Finland, Holland, Korea and Palestine) Shayer and Adey (2002: 15). The professional development support needed to ensure a new programme is successfully put in place, however, often requires substantial senior management support. Purchase of resources and provision of time and space for teachers to engage in centralized INSET, as well as *in situ* coaching may be key for success. Many whole-school issues require a multifaceted approach to deal with such curricular changes. The DfES (see Figure 14.2) have suggested how such thinking skills development should be implemented. Craft (2000) suggests how many factors can influence the nature and success of professional development.

There are many permutations that schools could apply to augment their approach to thinking skills. The most influential aspects that they could manipulate are likely to be the curricular design, the nature and

Guidance has been provided for school leaders to support the development of thinking skills (DfES 2005) within an educational institution. Initiation and management suggestions are provided to develop and sustain improvement in thinking and learning. The key suggestions include a four-phased development, focusing, developing, establishing and enhancing, at progressive stages of development. At each phase there are different priorities. In Year 7 the focus is to train staff and develop awareness of thinking skills in pupils. It is suggested that a trio of teachers are the leading thinkers. They are trained and more expert in teaching thinking than other staff, their role is to plan a series of three thinking lessons that target prioritized thinking skills. These trios of teachers could work across departments, thus representing perspectives of three different curricular areas, or they could be three departmental members working within similar subject briefs.

The school training manual suggests that all Year 7 will then be involved in three-lesson cycles by the end of the year.

The developing phase in Year 8 involves all departments reviewing thinking skills in their subject and experimenting with one or two strategies in other year groups. By the end of Year 8 there will be a whole school review.

The third phase is centred around establishment, where all Year 9 pupils become involved. At this point new leading thinkers are developing their skills through coaching. The guidance suggests that the extent of collaboration between teachers increases and the portfolio of good practice grows. During this phase there is a whole school review and three more departments develop their trio of lead thinking staff.

The final phase is the enhancing phase, where the manual states that teaching thinking using the strategies is embedded in the practice of all teachers and results in systematic development of thinking skills in all three years of the Key Stage.

Figure 14.2 DfES guidance on thinking skills implementation

content of lesson activities, and the pedagogical tactics or strategies that teachers apply.

Which method would be best and why?

A few years ago a number of reviews (Cotton 1991; McGuinness 1999; Wilson 2000) indicated that a focus on thinking skills improved pupils' performance in a number of ways. Programmes with varied aims and objectives enhanced differing skills, such as FIE, appeared to support improved non-verbal measures of intelligence and inconsistent development of attainment, self-esteem and classroom behaviour. Higgins et al. (2004) systematically reviewed 23 studies and found evidence indicating a positive impact on reasoning and problem solving and attainment. Moseley et al. (2005) also reviewed a substantial number of studies, in post-16 education and developed an integrated model for understanding and learning that focused on information gathering, building understanding and productive thinking (Moseley et al. 2005: 378).

Shayer and Adey (2002) have shown how the CA approach, applied in one subject, for example science, can significantly improve pupils' performance some years later in other content areas. Pupils' attainment in mathematics and English can be improved by up to 20 per cent in their GCSE grades (Shayer 2001). This indicates that the thinking developed in the approach, through metacognitive bridging, is transferable. However, the programme also provides a clear, progressive framework that can support development to achieve high-level abstract thinking. As Dewey (1938) suggests, there should be progressive organization of learning matter for effective education. Thinking programmes should scaffold for successive cognitive experiences that become more complex so that students grow in their capabilities. Ideally they should embrace a wide scope of cognitive skills and a logical sequence (Beyer 2001). McGregor and Gunter (2006) have indicated how implementation of the CA approach can provide an excellent vehicle for departmental or even whole-school professional development to invigorate pedagogic change. Adey (2004) has also shown how the nature and extent of PD can sustain or fail to sustain curricular and pedagogical change.

If school aims are to focus on the process of professional development and/or higher pupil performance and/or redesign of the curriculum, different approaches or programmes provide different kinds of opportunities related to thinking skills (as indicated in earlier chapters).

Is everything in place?

To explore the solution to a problem, all aspects or factors anticipated to impact on the projected solution or approach requires consideration to put them into place.

Implementation of a thinking approach to nurture communities of learning in school may require a number of necessary preparations. Are all participants clear about what is going to change and how the current situation will be modified? As Craft (2000) indicates, everyone involved in a school development needs to be clear about the 'shared goals and vision' of the intended change. Do the teachers recognize that their pedagogy has to refocus? Do the pupils realize that they will be expected to respond differently to questions and learning tasks, reflecting much more on the process by which they reach solutions and being able to describe and explain those processes in cognitive terms? Pragmatic issues related to implementation also need addressing. Managers need to ensure that there are sufficient quantities of (new) materials needed for pupils to work on in classes and probably rearrange teaching schedules and/or room use so that there is adequate time and no resource constraints on the development of thinking.

Is it working? Is it what was anticipated?

This is an application of reflection-in-action, thinking about what has happened thus far. Reflective assessment of the process of change is needed to ensure that what has been planned is progressing as anticipated. Questions that might arise, including, questions about how the implementation is working, may require revisiting the original intent. As Fullan (2001) indicates, planning a new initiative can fail because views 'about what should be changed' often vary inversely with knowledge about 'how to work through a process of change'. Leadership commitment to a particular change requires understanding of the multiple realities of people (Fullan 2001: 96). Understanding of which changes are good indicators of positive progress is needed here. Are the pupils responding positively? Is there formative evidence that they are asking more questions, rather than replying impulsively, becoming more artful and skilful in the ways they think (see Table 14.1) and developing a language to describe their thinking. Is there more discussion in classrooms, more deliberation about alternative perspectives and generally working in a more mutually supportive way? Are teachers focused correctly on the processes of thinking rather than delivering the content and modelling thoughtful behaviour? Is transmission teaching less apparent? Are the anticipated pedagogical changes of shifting to more socially constructive classrooms with appreciation of sociocultural impacts apparent? Is there recognition that cultural changes take time and that successful innovation that requires different teacher behaviours is not immediate? Cobb et al. (1991) found that it might take a teacher 5 months to create a climate in which children showed persistence with problems, became proficient in explaining their ideas to others and successfully collaborated through resolving differences in perspective.

What does the solution look like?

Schools may wish to consider whether the solution that is developing looks like that which they anticipated. Are the structural supports working, for example, the curricular design, the nature of classroom activities and materials. Is the intended ethos of the programme nurtured in the way it is integrated into the curriculum schedule? Is the progression within or beside the curriculum appropriate for the kinds of thinking to be developed? Does the curriculum schedule support timely metacognition and transfer into other subject areas? Are the materials appropriate for the teachers and pupils using them? Is there a positive response to them by both? Have teachers noted that they are successfully changing their pedagogical tactics and have they observed that pupils are responding by thinking, in various ways, more frequently? Is there more evidence of changing pupil behaviours? Are they becoming more intellectual? Is there less implicit agreement, more constructive discussion, more collaboration and more reflection? Have observers of learning in the school noted teachers engaging in insightful practice that supports thoughtful endeavours in the classroom? Costa (2001: 555) suggests that key questions can be used to assess the progress made toward a school becoming thoughtful. Key questions include: Is there a common consensus about what it means to be an effective thinker? Are students' thoughtful behaviours celebrated daily in school? Is growth in thinking skills monitored, assessed and reported?

How far did the approach improve the problem? What else did we need to consider? How could we do it again better?

After a year (or an appropriate period of time), reflection on the impact of the initiative or approach may involve consideration of a number of measures that can indicate success or lack of success. Evaluation may involve both objective and subjective measures of change, improvement or impact. Objective measures may include pupil performance in public examinations or standard intelligence tests. Subjective measures may use questionnaires, focus group discussions or in-depth interviews administered to participants in the school community to assess their perspectives on success. Teachers may have noticed improvements in performance of particular skills, behaviours, or responses to learning tasks, not measured through traditional academic means. Metacognitive reflection about teaching approaches can inform the nature of pedagogic change. Monitoring change and development in pedagogy is important, because different teaching styles accommodate different learning outcomes. As the DfES (2002: 271) indicates, 'teaching thinking and managing discussion well requires a repertoire of teaching strategies and skills. It involves focused intervention as well as effective instruction'.

As Hargreaves and Hopkins (1991) suggest, developments need to take careful account of PD because it is the means to developing the culture of the school, which enables it to become better at responding to change. Investigating recipients' views about changes in the classroom can also provide informative perspectives to improve the school (Ruddock and Flutter 2003). Exploring what pupils' think about thinking is therefore valuable in ascertaining measures of the impact of a curriculum initiative. Examining views about the perceived changes and whether they had improved the community of learning ethos and previous barriers to success could illuminate where future efforts need to focus for other curricular initiatives.

Where else would you use this kind of approach? Where else would this kind of outcome arise?

Schools reflecting on the many ways in which they planned for and supported a curricular change, and subsequently evaluating the impact it had on the nature of thinking and learning, will come to realize the interrelatedness of many factors that can influence initiation in an institution. As Datnow and Stringfield (2000) summarize:

> Our research has documented that reform adoption, implementation, and sustainability, and school change more generally, are not processes that result from individuals or institutions acting in isolation from one another. Rather they are the result of the interrelations between and across groups in different contexts, at various points in time. In this way, forces at the state and district levels, at the design team level, and at the school and classroom levels shape the ways in which reforms fail or succeed.
>
> (Datnow and Stringfield 2000: 199)

Reflecting on action, however, may mean that future developments may be better implemented and planned, because as Fullan (2001: 93) indicates, 'to bring about more effective change, we need to be able to explain not only what causes it but how to influence those causes'.

Conclusion

Smart Schools (Perkins 1992) that nurture thoughtful collaborative learning should recognize that:

- Learning is a consequence of thinking, and good thinking is learnable by all students.
- Learning should include deep understanding, which involves the flexible, active use of knowledge.

With appropriate support teachers can develop and mediate pupil thinking in a tactical and strategic way. Thoughtful pedagogy should encourage thinking to develop understanding in a number of ways. Educators should be supported in becoming thoughtful themselves to support, facilitate and orchestrate strategically scholastic experiences that can lead their pupils on meaningful learning journeys.

Supporting the development of thoughtful citizens for the future requires strategic teaching with cognitive processes providing the mental tools for effective learning and problem solving outcomes in mind.

S	Strategic
T	Teaching is
R	Relevant and realistic
A	Authentic
T	Thoughtful
E	Effortful
G	Gratifying
I	Intellectual and
C	Challenging

Figure 14.3 STRATEGIC thoughtful teaching to develop meaningful learning is . . .

Engaging in motivating games to learn subject content (Leat and Higgins 2002); philosophizing maieutically about life and different social situations (Lipman 2003); creating critical and creative thinking opportunities (Swartz and Parks 1994; de Bono 2000; Fisher R. 2000; Fisher A. 2001); cognitively accelerating to develop high-level abstract thinking (Adey and Shayer 2002) are not sufficient, on their own, to develop discerning citizens of the future. There needs to be a coherent and logical, progressive and applicable teaching plan that connects all subjects in the curriculum. All teachers need to be cognizant of, and actively support, the ultimate aim, which is to enable pupils to *develop* a wide variety of cognitive skills; *apply* and *transfer* their thinking capabilities usefully, from an academic setting to everyday life; and to *enhance* and *extend* their problem solving abilities, for the future.

Key ideas

> The development of thinking can be supported in schools, in a variety of ways, through implementation of a specific programme, curricular materials, adopting a cultural stance or just pedagogic development.

> Curricular design, lesson activities and pedagogy are inter-related factors influencing the nature and extent of thinking in schools.

> Social interactions underpinning collaboration are important in supporting both institutional change *and* the development of cognition in classrooms.

> Teaching to support thinking should be **STRATEGIC**.

References

Abbott, J. and Ryan, T. (2000) *The Unfinished Revolution*. Stafford: Network Educational Press.

Adey, P. (1991) Pulling yourself up by your own thinking, *European Journal for High Ability*, 2: 28–34.

Adey, P. (1997) It all depends on the context doesn't it? The search for general, educable dragons, *Studies in Science Education*, 29: 45–92.

Adey, P. and Shayer, M. (2002) *Learning Intelligence: Cognitive Acceleration Across the Curriculum from 5 Years*. Buckingham: Open University Press.

Adey, P. (2004) *The Professional Development of Teachers: Practice and Theory*. Dordrecht: Kluwer.

Adey, P. and Shayer, M. (1990) Accelerating the development of formal thinking in middle and high school pupils, *Journal of Research in Science Teaching*, 27(3): 267–85.

Adey, P. and Shayer, M. (1994) *Really Raising Standards*. London: Routledge.

Adey, P., Shayer, M. and Yates, C. (1995) *Thinking Science*, 3rd edn. Cheltenham: Nelson Thornes.

Adey, P., Robertson, A. and Venville, G. (2001) *Let's Think! A Programme for Developing Thinking in Five and Six Year Olds*. London: NFERNelson.

Adey, P., Nagy, F., Robertson, A., Serret, N. and Wadsworth, P. (2003) *Let's Think Through Science!* London: NFERNelson.

Adhami, M. (2002) CA in mathematics education in years 5 and 6, in M. Shayer and P. Adey (eds) *Learning Intelligence: Cognitive Acceleration across the Curriculum*. Buckingham: Open University Press.

Adhami, M., Johnson, D. and Shayer, M. (1998) *Thinking Maths: The Cognitive Acceleration in Maths Education Project*. Oxford: Heinmann.

Adhami, M., Shayer, M. and Twiss, S. (2005) *Let's Think Through Maths! Six to Nine Years*. London: NFERNelson.

Ahlberg, A. (1991) *Heard It In the Playground*. London: Puffin.

Alexander, R. (2003) Still no pedagogy? Principle, pragmatism and compliance in primary education. Paper presented at the University of Cambridge Faculty of Education, Cambridge.

Anning, A. (1991) *The First Years at School, Education 4–8*. Buckingham: Open University Press.

Arbitman-Smith, R., Haywood, W.C. and Bransford, J.D. (1984) Assessing cognitive change, in P. Brooks, R. Sperber and C.M. McCauley (eds) *Learning and Cognition in the Mentally Retarded*. Hillsdale, NJ: Lawrence Erlbaum.

Armstrong, T. (2000) *Multiple Intelligences in the Classroom*. Alexandria, VA: Association of Supervisors and Curriculum Development.

Ashman, A. and Conway, R. (1997) *An Introduction to Cognitive Education*. London: Routledge.

Astington, J.W. and Olson, D.R. (1995) The cognitive revolution in children's understanding of mind, *Human Development*, 38: 179–89.

Ausubel, D. (1968) *Educational Psychology*. New York: Holt, Reinhart & Winston.

Ball, D.L. (1993) With an eye on the mathematical horizon: dilemmas of teaching elementary school mathematics, *Elementary School Journal*, 93: 373–97.

Barber, M. (2000) *Thinking for Learning: Teaching Thinking*. Birmingham: Imaginative Minds.

Barnes, J. (ed) (1984) *The Complete Works of Aristotle*. Princeton: Princeton University Press.

Bassey, M. (1999) *Case Study Research in Educational Settings*. Buckingham: Open University Press.

Baumfield, V. (2002) *Thinking Through Religious Education*. Cambridge: Chris Kington.

Bell, T. (2005) The Play SMART research project. Promoting thinking through physical education, *Learning and Teaching in Action*, 1: 35–40.

Bentley, T. (2000) *Learning Beyond the Classroom: Education for a Changing World*. London: Routledge.

Bentley, T. (2003) *Possible Futures: Four Scenarios for Twenty-first Century Schooling*. Nottingham: NSCL

Bereiter, C. and Scardamalia, M. (1989) Intentional learning as a goal of instruction, in L.B. Resnick (ed.) *Knowing, Learning, and Instruction: Essays in Honor of Robert Glaser*. Hillsdale, NJ: Erlbaum.

Beyer, B. (2001) Developing a scope and sequence for thinking skills instruction, in A. Costa (ed.) *Developing Minds: A Resource Book for Teaching Thinking*. Alexandria, VA: Association for Supervisors and Curriculum Development.

Black, P., Harrison, C., Lee, C., Marshall, B. and Wiliam, D. (2003) *Assessment for Learning: Putting it into Practice*. Maidenhead: Open University Press

Black, P. and Wiliam, D. (1998) Assessment and classroom learning, *Assessment in Education*, 5(1): 7–74.

Blagg, N. (1991) *Can we Teach Intelligence? A Comprehensive Evaluation of Feuerstein's Instrumental Enrichment Program*. Hillsdale, NJ : Lawrence Erlbaum Associates.

Blagg, N., Ballinger, M. and Gardner, R. (2003) *Somerset Thinking Skills Course. Handbook*, Reprint of revised edn. Taunton: Nigel Blagg Associates.

Bloom, B.S., Krathwohl, D.R. and Masia, B.B. (1956) *Taxonomy of Educational Objectives: Cognitive Domain*. New York: McKay.

Boole, G. (1854) *An Investigation of the Laws of Thought on which are Founded the Mathematical Theories of Logic and Probabilities*. London: Macmillan.

Boring, E. (1923) Intelligence as the tests test it, *New Republic*, 35–7.

Bricheno, P., Johnston, J. and Sears, J. (2000) Children's attitudes to science: beyond men in white coats, in J. Sears and P. Sorenson, P. (eds) *Issues in Science Teaching*. London: RoutledgeFalmer.

Brittan, D. (2004) Thinking Lessons: New Research Investigates whether Computer Games can Turn Children into Better Learners, *Harvard Graduate*

School of Education News, 1 January. Available at http://www.gse.harvard.edu/news/features/stevens01012004.html

Brooks, J.G. and Brooks. M. (1999) *The Case for Constructivist Classrooms*. Alexandria, VA: Association for Supervisors and Curriculum Development.

Brooks, J.G. and Brooks, M.G. (2001) Becoming a constructivist teacher, in A.L. Costa (ed.) *Developing Minds: A Resource Book for Teaching Thinking*. Alexandria, VA: Association for Supervisors and Curriculum Development.

Brown, A.L. and Ferrara, R.A. (1985). Diagnosing zones of proximal development, in J. Wertsch (ed.). *Culture, Communication, and Cognition: Vygotskian Perspectives*. New York: Cambridge University Press.

Brown, A.L. and Reeve, R.A. (1987) Bandwidths of competence: the role of supportive contexts in learning and development, in L.S. Liben (ed.) *Development and Learning: Conflict or Congruence?* Hillsdale, NJ: Erlbaum.

Brown, G. and Desforges, C. (1979) *Piaget's Theory: A Psychological Critique*. London: Routledge.

Brown, G. and Wragg, E.C. (1993) *Questioning*. London: Routledge.

Brown, R. (1991) *Schools of Thought: How the Politics of Literacy Shape Thinking in the Classroom*. San Fransisco: Jossey Bass.

Bruer, J. (1997) Education and the brain: a bridge too far, *Educational Researcher*, 26(8): 4–16.

Bruner, J.S. (1966) *The Process of Education*. Cambridge, MA: Harvard University Press.

Bruner, J.S. (1986) *Actual Minds: Possible Worlds*. Cambridge, MA: Harvard University Press.

Bruner, J.S. (1990) *Acts of Meaning*. Cambridge, MA: Harvard University Press.

Bruner, J.S. (1996) *The Culture of Education*. Cambridge, MA: Harvard University Press.

Butterworth, M. and O'Connor, M. (2005) *Thinking Through English*. Cambridge: Chris Kington.

Buzan, T. (2000) *Head First*. London: Thorsons.

Campione, J.C., Shapiro, A.M. and Brown, A.L. (1995) Forms of transfer in a community of learners: flexible learning and understanding, in A. McKeough, J. Lupart and A. Marini (eds) *Teaching for Transfer: Fostering Generalization in Learning*. Mahwah, NJ: Erlbaum.

Carroll, J.B. (1993) *Human Cognitive Abilities: A Survey of Factor-analytic Studies*. New York: Cambridge University Press.

Carter, R. (ed.) (1991) *Talking about Geography*. Sheffield: Geographical Association.

Carter, R. (1998) *Mapping the Mind*. London: Seven Dials.

Chen, Z. and Siegler, R. (2000) Across the great divide: bridging the gap between understanding of toddlers' and older childrens' thinking, *Monographs of the Society for Research in Child Development*, 65(2): 5–7.

Claxton, G. (1999) *Wise-up: The Challenge of Lifelong Learning*. London: Bloomsbury.

Cleverdon, J. (2005) In search of inspiration: learning for work, *TES*, 1 July, pp. 2–3.

Cobb, P. (1994) Where is the mind? Constructivist and sociocultural perspectives on mathematical development, *Educational Researcher*, 23(7): 13–20.

Cobb, P., Wood, T. and Yackel, E. (1991) Analogies from philosophy and sociology of science for understanding classroom life, *Science Education*, 75: 23–44.

Cobb, P., Boufi, A., McClain, K. and Whitenack, J. (1997) Reflective discourse and collective reflection, *Journal for Research in Mathematics Education*, 28(3): 258–77.

Coles, R. (1997) *The Moral Intelligence of Children: How to Raise a Moral Child*. New York: NAL/Dutton.

Collins, P.H. (1990) *Black Feminist Thought*. Boston: Unwin Hyman.

Confrey, J. (1995) How compatible are radical constructivism, socio-cultural approaches and social constructivism? in L.P. Steffe and J. Gale (eds) *Constructivism in Education*. Hillsdale, NJ: Lawrence Erlbaum.

Costa, A. (2001) *Developing Minds: A Resource Book for Teaching Thinking*, 3rd edn. Alexandria, VA: Association for Supervision and Curriculum Development.

Costa, A. and Liebmann, R. (1997) *Envisioning Process as Content*. California: Corwin Press.

Costa, A. and Kallick, B. (2000) (eds) *Discovering and Exploring Habits of Mind*. Alexandria, VA: Association for Supervision and Curriculum Development.

Cotton, K. (1991) *Teaching Thinking Skills*. School Research Series (SIRS). Portland, OR: Northwest Regional Education Laboratory. Available at: www.nwrel.org/scpd/sirs/6/cu11.html

Craft, A. (2000) *Continuing Professional Development: A Practical Guide for Teachers and Schools*, 2nd edn. London: RoutledgeFalmer.

Craft, A. (2003) Creative thinking in the early years of education, *Early Years*, 23(2): 143–54.

Crawford, K. (1996) Vygotskian approaches to human development in the information era, *Educational Studies in Mathematics*, 31: 43–62.

Crook, C. (2000) Motivation and the ecology of collaborative learning, in R. Joiner, K. Littleton, D. Faulkner and D. Miell (eds) *Rethinking Collaborative Learning*. London: Free Association Books.

D'Arcy, P. (1989) *Oracy in Action: A Video-based Training Package on Oracy in Secondary Schools*. Swindon: Wiltshire LEA.

Daniels, H. (ed.) (1996) *An Introduction to Vygotsky*. London: Routledge.

Datnow, A. and Springfield, S. (2000) Working together for a reliable school reform, *Journal of Education for Students Placed at Risk*, 5(1): 183–204.

Dawes, L., Mercer, N. Wegerif, R. (2000) *Thinking Together. A Programme for Developing Thinking Skills at KS2*. London: Questions Publishing Company.

De Bono, E. (1973) *CoRT Thinking*. Blandford: Direct Educational Services.

De Bono, E. (1976) *Teaching Thinking*. London: Temple Smith.

De Bono, E. (1991) *Six Action Shoes*. New York: Harper.

De Bono, E. (1993) *Teach Your Child How to Think*. London: Penguin.

De Bono, E. (2000) *De Bono's Thinking Course*. Revised. London: BBC Worldwide Publishing.

De Corte, E. (1999) On the road to transfer: an introduction, *Educational Research*, 31: 555–9.

Desforges, C. and Lings, P. (1998) Teaching knowledge application: advances in theoretical conceptions and their professional implications, *British Journal of Educational Studies*, 46: 386–98.

Dewey, J. (1910) *How We Think*. Lexington, MA: D.C. Heath.

Dewey, J. (1938) *Experience and Education*. New York: Simon & Schuster.

Dewey, J. (1974) In R. Archambault (ed.) *John Dewey on Education: Selected Writings*. Chicago: Univeristy of Chicago Press.

DfEE (Department for Education and Employment) (1999) *All our Futures: Creativity, Culture and Education*. London: DfEE.DfES (Department for Education and Skills) (2002) *Teaching Thinking Module 11*. London: DfES.

DfES (Department for Education and Skills) (2003a) *Key Stage 3 National Strategy. Key Messages About Teaching Thinking*. London: DfES.

DfES (Department for Education and Skills) (2003b) *Twenty-first Century Skills. Realising Our Potential*. London: DFES.

DfES (Department for Education and Skills) (2003c) *Skills for Success. What Skills Strategy Means for Business*. London: DfES.

DfES (Department for Education and Skills) (2004) *Design and Technology. Key Stages 1-4. The National Curriculum for England*. London: DfES.

DfES (Department for Education and Skills) (2005) *Leading in Learning: Developing Thinking Skills at Key Stage 3. School Training Manual*. London: DfES.

Ding, S. and Flynn, E. (2000) Collaborative learning: an underlying skills approach, in R. Joiner, K. Littleton, D. Faulkner and D. Miell (eds) *Rethinking Collaborative Learning*. London: Free Association Books.

Doherr, E. (2000) The demonstration of cognitive abilities central to cognitive behavioural therapy in young people: examining the influence of age and teaching method on degree of ability. Unpublished clinical psychology doctoral dissertation, Univeristy of East Anglia.

Doise, W. (1990) The development of individual competencies through social interaction, in H.C. Foot, M.J. Morgan and R.H. Shute (eds) *Children Helping Children*. Chichester: Wiley.

Donaldson, M. (1987) *Children's Minds*. London: Fontana.

Dowling, M. (1992) *Education 3-5*. London: Paul Chapman.

Doyle, W. (1983) Academic work, *Review of Educational research*, 53: 365-79.

Driver, R. (1995) Constructivist approaches to science teaching, in L.S. Steffe and J. Gale (eds) *Constructivism in Education*. Hillsdale, NJ: Lawrence Erlbaum.

Driver, R., Guesne, E. and Tiberghien, A. (eds) (1985) *Children's Ideas in Science*. Milton Keynes: Open University Press.

Driver, R., Squires, A., Rushworth, P. and Wood-Robinson, V. (1994) *Making Sense of Secondary Science*. London: Routledge.

Driver, R., Leach, J., Millar, R. and Scott, P. (1996) *Young People's Images of Science*. Milton Keynes: Open University.

Duckworth, E. (1987) *Teaching as Research: The Having of Wonderful Ideas*. New York: Teachers College Press.

Duncan, S., McNiven, D. and Savory, C. (2004) *Thinking Skills Through Science*. Cambridge: Chris Kington.

Durkin, K. (1995) *Developmental Social Psychology*. Oxford: Blackwell.

Dyer, H. (1995) Learning logs as ethnographies of Year 1 and 2 children learning at school. Paper presented to the CEDAR conference Ethnographies of Teachers and Students at Work, Warwick, September.

Dyfed County Council (1994) *Improving Reading Standards in Primary Schools Project.* Wales: Dyfed County Council.

Earl, L., Watson, N., Levin, B. et al. (2003) Watching and Learning 3: *Final Report of the External Evaluation of England's National Literacy and Numeracy Strategies.* Nottingham: DfES.

Edwards, D. (1997) *Discourse and Cognition.* London: Sage.

Edwards, J. and Baldauf, R.B. (1983) Teaching thinking in secondary science, in W. Maxwell (ed.) *Thinking: The Expanding Frontier.* Philadelphia, PA: Franklin Institute Press.

Ennis, R. (1986) A taxonomy of critical thinking dispositions and abilities, in J.B. Baron and R.S. Sternberg (eds) *Teaching Thinking Skills: Theory and Practice.* New York: W.H. Freeman.

Ennis, R. (1991) Critical thinking: a streamlined conception, *Teaching Philosophy,* 14(1): 5–25.

Ennis, R. (2001) Goals for a critical thinking curriculum and its assessment, in A. Costa (ed.) *Developing Minds: A Resource Book for Teaching Thinking,* 3rd edn. London: Association for Supervision and Curriculum Development.

Facione, P. (1998) *Critical Thinking: What It Is and Why It Counts.* Available at: http://www.calpress.com/resource.html

Feuerstein, R. (1977) Mediated learning experience: a theoretical basis for cognitive modifiability during adolescence, in Mittler, P. (ed.) *Research to Practice in Mental Retardation,* Vol II . Baltimore: University Park Press.

Feuerstein, R., Rand, Y. and Hoffman, M.B. (1979) The Dynamic Assessment of Retarded Performers: the Learning Potential Assessment Device, Theory, Instruments, Techniques. Baltimore, MD: University Park Press.

Feuerstein, R., Rand, Y. and Hoffman, M.B. and Miller, R. (1980) *Instrumental Enrichment.* Baltimore, MD: University Park Press.

Feuerstein, R., Miller, R., Hoffman, M.B. et al. (1981) Cognitive modifiability in adolescence: cognitive structure and the effects of intervention, *Journal of Special Education,* 15: 269–86.

Fields, J. (1995) Empirical data research into the claims for using philosophy techniques with young children, *Early Child Development and Care,* 107: 115–28.

Fischer, K. and Kaplan, U. (2003) Piaget, Jean, in L. Nadel (ed.) *The Encyclopedia of Cognitive Science,* Vol 1. Basingstoke: Macmillian.

Fisher, R. (1990) *Teaching Children to Think.* Cheltenham: Nelson Thornes.

Fisher, R. (1997a) *Games for Thinking.* Oxford: Nash Pollock.

Fisher, R. (1997b) *Poems for Thinking.* Oxford: Nash Pollock.

Fisher, R. (2000) *Teaching Thinking: Philosophical Enquiry in the Classroom.* London: Continuum.

Fisher, A. (2001) *An Introduction to Critical Thinking.* Cambridge: Cambridge University Press.

Fisher, A. and Scriven, M. (1997) *Critical Thinking: Its Definition and Assessment.* Cambridge: Edgepress and Centre for Research in Critical Thinking, University of East Anglia.

Fisher, P. and Wilkinson, I. (2002) *Thinking Through History.* Cambridge: Chris Kington Publishing.

Flavell J. (1976) Metacognitive aspects of problem solving., in L. Resnick (ed.) *The Nature of Intelligence*. Hillsdale, NJ: Lawrence Erlbaum Associates.

Flavell, J., Green, F.L. and Flavell, E.R. (1995) Young children's knowledge of about thinking, *Monographs of the Society for Research in Child Development*, 60 (1, Serial No. 243).

Fleetham, M. (2003) *How to Create and Develop a Thinking Classroom*. Cambridge : LDA.

Frusco, E.T. (1983) The relationship between children's cognitive level of development and their response to literature. Unpublished PhD dissertation, Hofstra University.

Fullan, M. (2001) *The New Meaning of Educational Change*, 3rd edn. London: Routledge Falmer.

Gallagher, J. and Reid, K. (1981) *The Learning Theory of Piaget and Inhelder*. Austin, TX: Pro-Ed.

Gardner, H. (1983) *Frames of Mind: The Theory of Multiple Intelligences*. New York: Basic Books.

Gardner, H. (1999) *Intelligence Reframed: Muliple Intelliences for the Twenty-first Century*. New York: Basic Books.

Gaukroger, S. (2003) Descartes, René, in L. Nadel (ed.) *The Encyclopedia of Cognitive Science*, vol 1. London: Macmillian.

Gauvain, M. and Rogoff, B. (1989). Collaborative problem solving and children's planning skills, *Developmental Psychology*, 25: 139–51.

Gentner, D. and Stevens, A.L. (1983) *Mental Models*. Hillsdale, NJ: Erlbaum.

Glaser, E. (1941) *An Experiment in the Development of Critical Thinking: Advanced School of Education at Teacher's College, Columbia University*. New York: AMS Press.

Goleman, D. (1995) *Emotional Intelligence: Why It Can Matter More than IQ*. London: Bloomsbury.

Greenfield, P.M. (1984) A theory of the teacher learning activities of everyday life, in B. Rogoff, B. and J. Lave, J. (eds) *Everyday Cognition: Its Development in Social Context*. Cambridge, MA: Harvard University Press.

Greenfield, S. (2002) What is a thought? in H. Swain (ed.) *Big Questions in Science*. London: Jonathan Cape.

Greeno, J. (1991) Number sense as situated knowing in a conceptual domain, *Journal for Research in Mathematics Education*, 22(3), 170–218.

Gruber, H.E. and Voneche, J.J. (eds) (1995) *The Essential Piaget: An Interpretative Reference and Guide*. New Jersey: Aronson

Gunter, B., McGregor, D. and Twist, J. (forthcoming) *SMART Science at KS4*. (Trial materials available from Barry Gunter, Thinking and Learning Ltd 1 Boulton Close, Sandbach, Cheshire, CW11 4GH. Email: barrygunter@thinkingandlearning.co.uk. Tel. (+44) 07981621411.)

Gustaffson, J.E. (1984) A unifying model for the structure of intellectual abilities, *Intelligence*, 8: 179–203.

Gustaffson, J.E. (1988) Hierarchial models of the structure of cognitive abilities, in R.J. Sternberg (ed.) *Advances in the Psychology of Human Intelligence*. Hillsdale, NJ: Lawrence Erlbaum Associates.

Hamaker, A.K. and Backwell, J. (2003) *Cognitive Acceleration through Technology Education: Teacher Guidelines and Pupil Task Pages*. Taunton: Nigel Blagg Associates.

Hamaker, T. Jordan, P. and Backwell, J. (1998) An evaluation of a two-year cognitive intervention for key stage 4 students in the UK, *Journal of Design and Technology Education*, 3(1): 26–33.

Hargreaves, D. and Hopkins, D. (1991) *The Empowered School*. London: Cassell.

Hargreaves, L. and Moyles, J. (2002) How do school teachers define and implement 'interactive teaching' in the national Literacy Strategy in England? Paper presented at the American Research Association Annual meeting, New Orleans, April.

Harland, J., Kinder, K. and Hartley, K. (1995) *Art in their View: A Study of Youth participation in the Arts*. England: NFER

Hartman, H.J. (1998) Metacognition in teaching and learning: an introduction, *Instructional Science*, 26(1): 1–3.

Hass, H. (1980) Appendix B: Experimental research in philosophy for children, in M. Lipman, A.M. Sharp and F. Oscanyon (1980) *Philosophy in the Classroom*. Philadelphia, PA: Temple University.

Hass, A. (1998) *Doing the Right Thing: Cultivating your Moral Intelligence*. New York: Pocket Books.

Hatano, G. and Inagaki, K. (1992) Desituating cognition through the construction of conceptual knowledge, in Light, P. and Butterworth, G. (eds) *Context and Cognition*. Hemel Hempstead: Harvester Wheatsheaf.

Hattie, J. Biggs, J. and Purdie, N. (1996) Effects of learning skills interventions on student learning: a meta-analysis, *Review of Educational Research*, 66(2): 99–136.

Hernstein, R. and Murray, C. (1994) *The Bell Curve: Intelligence and Class Structure in American Life*. New York: Free Press

Hiebert, J., Carpenter, T., Fennema, E. (1997). *Making Sense: Teaching and Learning Mathematics with Understanding*. Portsmouth, NH: Heinemann.

Higgins, S. and Baumfield, V. (2001) *Thinking Through Primary Teaching*. Cambridge: Chris Kington Publishing.

Higgins, S., Baumfield, V., Lin, M. (2004) *Thinking Skills. Approaches to Effective Teaching and Learning: What is the Evidence for Impact on Learners?* London: EPPI-Centre, Social Science Research Unit, Institute of Education, University of London.

Higgins, S., Hall, E., Baumfield, V. and Moseley, D. (2005) *A Meta-analysis of the Impact of the Implementation of Thinking Skills Approaches on Pupils*. London: EPPI-Centre, Social Science Research Unit, Institute of Education, University of London.

Hodson, D. and Hodson, J. (1998) From constructivism to social constructivism: a Vygotskian perspective on teaching and learning science, *School Science Review*, 79(289): 33–41.

Holroyd, C. (1989) *Problem-solving and the secondary curriculum: a review for the Scottish Education Department*. Unpublished.

Hough, L.M. (2001) I/Owes its advances to personality, in B. W. Roberts and R.

Hogan (eds) *Personality Psychology in the Workplace: Decade of Behavior.* Washington, DC: American Psychological Association.

Howe, C. (1997) *Gender and Classroom Interaction: A Research Review.* Edinburgh: Scottish Council for Research in Education.

Inhelder, B. and Piaget, J. (1958) *The Growth of Logical Thinking from Childhood to Adolescence.* New York: Basic Books.

IAPC (Institute for the Advancement of Philosophy for Children) (2002) IAPC Research: Experimentation and Qualitative Information. Available at: www.cehs.montclair.edu/academic/iapc/research.shtml (accessed 1 December 2005).

Jacobs, G.M. (2004) A classroom investigation of the growth of metacognitive awareness in kindergarten children through the writing process, *Early Childhood Education*, 13(1): 17–23.

Johnson, S. (2000) *Teaching Thinking Skills.* IMPACT pamphlet No 8. Oxford: Blackwell Publishing.

Joiner, R., Littleton, K., Faulkner, D. and Miell, D. (2000) *Rethinking Collaborative Learning.* London: Free Association Books.

Joyce, B., Calhoun, E. and Hopkins, D. (1997) *Models of Learning Tools for Teaching.* Buckingham: Open University Press.

Joyce, B. and Showers, B. (1995) *Student Achievement through Staff Development*, 2nd edn. New York: Longman.

Karmiloff-Smith, A. (1991) *Beyond Modularity: Innate Constraints and Developmental Change.* Cambridge, MA: MIT Press.

Kirkwood, M. (2001a) *Thoughts on a deeper level*, TES, 9 September.

Kirkwood, M. (2001b) *Practical ideas for the thinking classroom*, TES, 17 August.

Kirkwood, M. (2005) *Learning to Think: Thinking to Learn. An Introduction to Thinking Skills from Nursery to Secondary.* London: Hodder Gibson.

Kite, A. (2000) *A Guide to Better Thinking.* Slough: NFER Nelson.

Koestler, A. (1975) *The Act of Creation.* London: Picador.

Kozulin, A. (1986) *Thought and Language*, Revised edn. Cambridge, MA: MIT Press.

Kruger, A.C. (1993) Peer collaboration: conflict, co-operation or both? *Social Development*, 2: 35–40.

Kruger, J., and Dunning, D. (1999) Unskilled and unaware of it: how difficulties in recognizing one's own incompetence lead to inflated self-assessments, *Journal of Personality and Social Psychology,* 77: 1121–34

Kuhn, D. (2000) Metacognitive development, *Current Directions in Psychological Science*, 9: 178–81.

Kumpulainen, K., Vasama, S. and Kangassalo, M. (2004) The intertextuality of children's explanations in a technology-enriched early years science classroom, *International Journal of Educational Research*, 39: 793–805.

Kutnick, P. and Rodgers, C. (eds) (1994) *Groups in Schools.* London: Cassell.

Kyriacou, C. (1997) *Effective Teaching in Schools, Theory and Practice*, 2nd edn. Cheltenham: Stanley Thornes.

Lake, M. and Needham, M. (1995) *Top Ten Thinking Tactics.* Birmingham: Questions.

Lambert, E.B. (2000) Problem-solving in the first years of school, *Australian Journal of Early Childhood*, 25(3): 32–8.

Langer, E. (1989) *Mindfulness*. Reading, MA: Addison-Wesley.

Larkin, J., McDermott, J., Simon, D.P. and Simon, H.A. (1980). Expert and novice performance in solving physics problems. *Science*, 208: 1335–42.

Lave, J. (1988) *Cognition in Practice: Mind Mathematics Culture in Everyday Life*. Cambridge: Cambridge University Press.

Lave, J. and Wenger, E. (1991) *Situated Learning: Legitimate Peripheral Participation*. Cambridge: Cambridge University Press.

Leat, D. (1999) Rolling the stone uphill: teacher development and the implementation of thinking skills programmes, *Oxford Review of Education*, 25(3): 387–403.

Leat, D. (2000) *Thinking Through Geography*, 2nd edn. Cambridge: Chris Kington.

Leat, D. (2001) Introduction, in A. Nichols and D. Kinninment (eds) *More Thinking Through Geography*. Cambridge: Chris Kington.

Leat, D. (2005) Introduction, in M. Butterworth and M. O'Connor (eds) *Thinking through English*. Cambridge: Chris Kington.

Leat, D. and Higgins, S. (2002) The role of powerful pedagogical strategies in curriculum development, *The Curriculum Journal*, 13(1): 71–85.

Leat, D. and Lin, M. (2003) Developing a pedagogy of metacognition and transfer, *British Educational Research*, 29: 383–415.

Lee, O. and Anderson, C. W. (1993) Task engagement and conceptual change, *American Educational Research Journal*, 30(3).

Leont'ev, A.N. (1981) The concept of activity in psychology, in J.V. Wertsch (ed.) *The Concept of Activity in Soviet Psychology*. Armonk, NY: ME Sharpe.

Light, P., Littleton, K., Messer, D. and Joiner, R. (1994a) Social and communicative processes in computer-based problem solving, *European Journal of Psychology of Education*, 9(1): 93–109.

Light, P., Littleton, K., Messer, D., and Joiner, R. (1994b). Social and communicative processes in computer-based problem solving, *European Journal of Psychology of Education*, 14: 93–109.

Lipman, M. (1976) Philosophy for children, *Metaphilosophy* 7(1):

Lipman, M. (2003) *Thinking in Education*, 2nd edn. Cambridge: Cambridge University Press.

Lipman, M., Sharp, A. M., Oscanyan, F. (1980) *Philosophy in the Classroom*. Philadelphia, PA: Temple University Press.

Lochhead, J. and Zietsman, A. (2001) What is problem solving? in A. Costa (ed.) *Developing Minds: A Resource Book for Teaching Thinking*. Alexandria, VA: Association of Supervisors and Curriculum Development.

Lowrie, T. (2002) Designing a framework for problem-posing: young children generating open-ened tasks, *Contemporary issues in early Childhood*, 3(3): 354–64.

Lucangeli, D., Galdererisi, D. and Cornoldi, C. (1994) Transfer effects after metacognitive training, *Learning Disabilities, Research and Practice*, 10: 11–12.

MacBeath, J. (1999) *Schools Must Speak for Themselves: The Case for School Self-Evaluation*. London: Routledge.

Mallet, M. (2004) Putting the passion into thinking, *Teaching Thinking*, 13: 12–16.

Marzano, R., Pickering, D. and Pollock, J. (2001) *Classroom Instruction that Works:*

Research-based Strategies for Increasing Student Achievement. Alexandra, VA: Association for Supervision and Curriculum Development.

Mayer, J.D. and Salovey, P. (1993) The intelligence of emotional intelligence, *Intelligence,* 17: 433–42.

Mayer, R. and Wittrock, M. (1996) Problem-solving transfer, in D. Berliner and R. Calfee (eds) *Handbook of Educational Psychology.* New York: Simon & Schuster Macmillan.

McDonald, S. (2005a) Payback time: learning for work, *TES,* 1 July, p. 6.

McDonald, S. (2005b) Water diviners: learning for work, *TES,* 1 July, p. 7.

McFarlane, A.E. (2003) Learners, learning and new technology, *Educational Media International,* 40(3/4).

McGregor, D. (2003) Applying learning theories reflexively to understand and support the use of group work in the learning of science. Unpublished PhD thesis, Keele University.

McGregor, D. (2004) Interactive pedagogy and subsequent effects on learning in science classrooms, *Westminster Studies in Education,* 27(2): 237–61.

McGregor, D. (forthcoming) The influence of task structure on pupils' learning processes: Observations from a series of case studies in secondary science. *Journal of Curriculum Studies.*

McGregor, D. and Gunter, B. (2001a) Changing pedagogy of secondary science teachers, *Teacher Development,* 5(1): 59–74.

McGregor, D. and Gunter, B. (2001b) The CASE for technicians, *School Science Review,* 82(300): 103–8.

McGregor, D. and Gunter, B. (2006) Invigorating pedagogic change. Suggestions from findings of the development of secondary teachers' practice and cognisance of the learning process, *European Journal of Teacher Education,* 29(1): 23–48.

McGuinness, C. (1999) *From Thinking Skills to Thinking Classrooms: A Review and Evaluation of Approaches for Developing Pupils' Thinking.* DfEE Report No. 115. Norwich: HMSO.

McGuinness, C. (2000) Caught in the ACTs, *Teaching Thinking,* 1(2): 48–52.

McGuinness, C. (2005) *Teaching Thinking: Theory and Practice.* London: The British Psychological Society.

McGuinness, C., Sheey, N., Curry, C. and Eakin, A. (2003) *ACTs II Sustainable Thinking in Classrooms: A Methodology for Enhancing Thinking across the Curriculum.* Materials available from Professor C. McGuinness, School of Psychology, Queen's University, Belfast, Northern Ireland.

McKeough, A., Lupart, J. and Marini, A. *Teaching for Transfer: Fostering Generalization in Learning.* Mahwah, NJ: Lawrence Erlbaum Associates.

Mercer, N. (1995) *The Guided Construction of Knowledge: Talk Amongst Teachers and Learners.* Clevedon: Multilingual Matters.

Mercer, N. (2000) *Words and Minds: How We Use Language to Think Together.* London: Routledge.

Mercer, N., Wegerif, R. and Dawes, L. (1999) Children's talk and the development of reasoning in the classroom, *British Educational Research Journal,* 25(1): 95–111.

Milne, A. A. (1928) *The House at Pooh Corner*. London: Methuen & Co.

Moll, L.C. (ed.) (1990) *Vygotsky and Education: Instructional Implications and Applications of Sociohistorical Psychology*. New York: Cambridge University Press.

Morgan, N. and Saxton, J. (1991) *Teaching, Questioning and Learning*. London: Routledge.

Moseley, D., Elliot, J., Gregson, M. and Higgins, S. (2005) Thinking skills framework for use in education and training, *British Educational Research Journal*, 31(3): 367–90.

Moyles, J. R. (1994) *The Excellence of Play*. Buckingham: Open University Press.

Murphy, P. (2000) Equity, assessment and gender, in J. Salisbury and S. Riddell (eds) *Gender, Policy and Educational Change*. London: Routledge.

Murphy, P. and Spence, M. (1997) The influence of task on social interaction. Paper presented at the Seventh Earli conference, Athens, 26–30 August.

National Advisory Committee on Creative and Cultural Education (1999) *All Our Futures: Creativity, Culture and Education*. Sudbury: DfEE.

Neighbor, R. (1992) *The Inner Apprentice*. London: Kluwer Academic.

Nichols, A. and Kinninment, D. (2001) *More Thinking through Geography*. Cambridge: Chris Kington.

Nickerson, R. (1981) Thoughts on teaching thinking, *Educational Leadership*, October, pp. 21–4.

Nickerson, R. (1988) On improving thinking through instruction, *Review of Research in Education*, 15: 3–57.

Nickerson, R.S., Perkins, D.N. and Smith, E.E. (1985) *The Teaching of Thinking*. Hillsdale, NJ: Lawrence Erlbaum Associates.

Nisbet, J. (1990) *Teaching Thinking: An Introduction to the Research Literature*. Edinburgh: Spotlight 26, Scottish Council for Research Education.

Noble, G. and Poynting, S. (1998) 'Weird science' and 'common sense': the discursive construction of accelerative learning, *Discourse: Studies in the Cultural Politics of Education*, (19)2: 141–56.

Norman, K. (ed) (1992) *Thinking Voices: The Work of the National Oracy Project*. London: Hodder & Stoughton.

Nunes, T., Schliemann, A.D. and Carraher, D.W. (1993) *Street Mathematics and School Mathematics*. Cambridge: Cambridge University Press.

Ofsted (Office of Standards in Education) (2000) *Inspecting Science 11–16 with Guidance on Self-evaluation*. London: HMSO.

Palett, M. and Hamilton, D. (1977) Evaluation as illumination: a new approach to the study of innovatory programes, in D. Hamilton et al. (eds) *Beyond the Numbers Game: A Reader in Educational Evaluation*. Basingstoke: Macmillian.

Parker-Rees, R. (1999) Protecting playfulness, in L. Abbott and H. Moylett (eds) *Early Education Transformed*. London: Falmer.

Parkinson, J. (2002) *Reflective Teaching of Science 11–18*. London: Continuum.

Pearson, P.D. (1985) Changing the face of reading instruction, *The Reading Teacher*, 38(8): 724–38.

Perkins, D. (1991) *Smart Schools: Better Thinking and Learning for Every Child*. New York: Free Press.

Perkins, D. (1992) *Smart Schools: Better Thinking and Learning for Every Child.* New York: Free Press.

Perkins, D. (1995) *Outsmarting IQ: The Emerging Science of Learnable Intelligence.* New York: The Free Press.

Perkins, D. (2000) The eureka effect in A. Costa and B. Kallick (eds) *Discovering and Exploring Habits of Mind.* Alexandria, VA: Association for Supervision and Curriculum Development (ASCD).

Perkins, D. (2004) Knowledge alive, *Educational Leadership*, 62(1): 14–19.

Perkins, D. and Salomon, G. (2001) Teaching for transfer, in A. Costa (ed.) *Developing Minds, A Resource Book for Teaching Thinking.* Alexandria, VA: Association of Supervisors and Curriculum Development.

Perkins, D., Jay, E. and Tishman (1993) Beyond abilities: a dispositional theory of thinking, *Merrill-Palmer Quarterly*, 39(1): 1–21.

Phillips, D.C. and Soltis, J.F. (2004) *Perspectives in Learning.* New York: Teachers College Press.

Piaget, J. (1926) *The Language and Thought of the Child.* New York: Harcourt, Brace.

Piaget, J. (1929) *The Child's Conception of the World.* New York: Harcourt, Brace.

Piaget, J. (1950) *The Psychology of Intelligence.* London: Routledge & Kegan Paul.

Piaget, J. (1951) *Play Dreams and Imitation.* New York: Norton.

Piaget, J. (1973) *To Understand is to Invent: The Future of Education.* New York: Grossman.

Pitri, E. (2001) The role of artistic play in problem solving, *Art Education*, 54(3): 46–51.

Pizzini, E.L., Shepardson, D.P. and Abell, S.K. (1991) The inquiry level of junior high activities: implications to science teaching, *Journal of Research in Science Teaching*, 28(2): 111–21.

Pollard, A. (2002) *Reflective Teaching; Effective and Evidence-informed Professional Practice.* London: Continuum.

Polya, G. (1948) *How to Solve It.* Princeton, NJ: Princeton University Press.

Powney, J. and Lowden, K. (2000) *Young Peoples' Life Skills and Work.* Edinburgh: Spotlight 78, Scottish Council for Research in Education.

Puccio, G.J. and Murdock, M.C. (2001) Creative thinking: an essential life skill, in A. Costa (ed.) *Developing Minds: A Resource Book for Teaching Thinking*, 3rd edn. Alexandria, VA: Association of Supervisors and Curriculum Development.

Rand, Y., Tannenbaum, A.J. and Feuerstein, R. (1979) Effects of instrumental enrichment on the psycheducational development of low-functioning adolescents, *Journal of Educational Psychology*, 71: 751–63.

Resnick, L. (2001) Making America smarter: the real goal of school reform, in A. Costa (ed.) *Developing Minds: A Resource Book for Teaching Thinking.* Alexandria, VA: Association of Supervisors and Curriculum Development.

Riggio, R.E., Murphy, S.E. and Pirozzolo, F.J. (eds) (2002) *Multiple Intelligences and Leadership.* Mahwah, NJ: Lawrence Erlbaum Associates.

Riley, J. and Reedy, D. (2005) developing young chidlren's thinking through learning to write argument, *Journal of Early Childhood Literacy*, 5(1): 29–51.

Roberts, M. and Erdos, G. (1993) Strategy selection and metacognition, *Educational Psychology*, 13(3 and 4): 259–66.

Robinson, K. (2001) *Out of Our Minds: Learning to be Creative*. Oxford: Capstone.

Rogoff, B. (1990) *Apprenticeship in Thinking: Cognitive Development in Social Context*. Oxford: Oxford University Press.

Rommetveit, R. (1985) Language acquisition as increasing linguistic structuring of experience and symbolic behaviour control, in J.V. Wertsch (ed.) *Culture, Communication, and Cognition: Vygotskian Perspectives*. Cambridge: Cambridge University Press.

Rose, C. (1997) *Accelerated Learning for the Twenty-first Century*. London: Piatkus.

Roth, W.M. (1995) *Authentic School Science: Knowing and Learning in Open-Enquiry Science Laboratories*. Dordrecht: Kluwer Academic Press.

Roth, W.M. and Robbie, C. (1999) Lifeworlds and the 'w/ri(gh)ting' of classroom research, *Journal of Curriculum Studies*, 31(5): 501–22.

Rudduck, J. and Flutter, J. (2003) *How to Improve Your School: Listening to Pupils*. London: Continuum.

Sarason, S. (1982) *The Culture of the School and the Problem of Change*. Boston: Allyn & Bacon.

Sasserville, M. (1994) Self esteem, logical skills and philosophy for children, *Thinking*, 4(2): 30–2.

Schoenfeld, A. (1985) *Mathematical Problem Solving*. New York: Academic Press.

Schon, D.A. (1983) *The Effective Practitioner: How Professionals Think in Action*. New York: Basic Books.

Schwanenflugel, P.J., Stevens, T.P. and Carr, M. (1994) Metacognitive knowledge of gifted children and un-identified children in early elementary school, *Gifted Child Quarterly*, 41(2): 25–35.

Scottish Executive Education Department (2000) Creating our future ... Minding our past. Scotland's National Cultural Strategy. Available at: www.scotland.gov.uk/nationalculturalstrategy/docs/cult-00.asp

Scribner, S. (1986) Thinking in action: some charactertistics of practical thought, in R. Sternberg and R.K. Wagner (eds) *Practical Intelligence: Nature and Origins of Competence in the Everyday World*. Cambridge: Cambridge University Press.

Selley, N. (2000) Wrong answers welcome, *School Science Review*, 82(299): 41–4.

Selley, N. J. (2001) Alternative models for dissolution, *School Science Review*, 80 (290).

Sharan, S. (1980) Co-operative learning in small groups: recent methods and effects on achievement, attitudes and ethnic relations, *Review of Educational Research*, 50: 241–7.

Shayer, M. (1993) Piaget: only the Galileo of cognitive development? Comment on Niaz and Lawson on genetic epistemology, *Journal of Research in Science Teaching*, 30(7): 815–18.

Shayer, M. (1997) Piaget and Vygotsky: a necessary marriage for effective educational intervention, in L. Smith, J. Dockrell and P. Tomlinson (eds) *Piaget, Vygotsky and Beyond: Future Issues for Developmental Psychology and Education*. London: Routledge.

Shayer, M. (1999a) Cognitive acceleration through science edcation II: its effects and scope, *International Journal of Science Education*, 21(8): 883–902.

Shayer, M. (1999b) *GCSE 1999: Added-value from Schools Adopting the CASE Intervention.* London: Centre for the Advancement of Thinking.

Shayer, M. and Adey, P. (1981) *Towards a Science of Science Teaching.* Oxford: Heinemann Educational.

Shayer, M. and Adey, P. (1992) Accelerating the development of formal thinking in Middle and High School Students II: Post project Effects on Science Achievement.

Shayer, M. and Adey, P. (1993) Accelerating the development of formal thinking in middle and high school students IV: three years on after a two-year intervention, *Journal of Research in Science Teaching*, 30: 351–66.

Shayer, M. and Adey, P. (2002) *Learning Intelligence: Cognitive Acceleration Across the Curriculum.* Buckingham: Open University Press.

Shayer, M. and Beasley, F. (1987) Does instrumental enrichment work? *British Educational Research Journal,* 13(2): 101–19.

Shayer, M., Adhami, M. and Robertson, A. (2004) *Let's Think Through Maths! Developing Thinking in Mathematics with Five and Six Year Olds.* London: NFERNelson.

Simon, C. (1979) Philosophy for students with learning disabilities, *Thinking,* 1(1): 21–34.

Siraj-Blatchford, I. and Sylva, K. (2004) Researching pedagogy in English pre-schools, *British Educational Research Journal,* 30(5): 713–30.

Skinner, B.F. (1953) *Science and Human Behavior.* New York: Macmillian.

Skinner, B.F. (1968) *The Technology of Teaching.* New York: Appleton.

Slavin, R. (2004) What works? *Educational Researcher,* 33(1): 27–8.

Smethurst, R. (1995) Education: a public or private good? *RSA Journal,* 143(5465): 33–45.

Smith, F. (1994) Performance in solving physics problems, *Science*, 208: 1335–42.

Smith, A. (1998) *Accelerated Learning in Practice: Brain-based Methods for Accelerating Motivation and Achievement.* Stafford: Network Educational Press.

Smith, A. and Call, N. (2000) *The ALPS Approach: Accelerated Learning in Primary Schools,* Revised edn. Stafford: Network Educational Press.

Spearman, C. (1904) General intelligence, objectively defined and measured, *American Journal of Psychology,* 15: 201–9.

Spearman, C. (1927) *The Abilities of Man.* London: Macmillan.

Statt, D.A. (1998) *The Concise Dictionary of Psychology,* 3rd edn. London: Routledge.

Sternberg, R. (1983) Components of human intelligence, *Cognition,* 15: 1–48.

Sternberg, R. (1985) Toward a triarchic theory of human intelligence, *Behavioural and Brain Sciences,* 7: 269–87.

Sternberg, R. (1997) *How Practical and Creative Intelligence Determine Success in Life.* New York: Pume.

Sternberg, R. (1999) *Thinking Styles.* Cambridge: Cambridge University Press.

Sternberg, R. (2003) *Wisdom, Intelligence and Creativity Synthesized.* Cambridge: Cambridge University Press.

Sternberg, R. and Bhana, K. (1996) Synthesis of research on the effectiveness of intellectual skills programs: snake oil remedies or miracle cures? *Educational Leadership,* 44(2): 60–7.

Sternberg, R. and Wagner, R. (1982) Understanding intelligence: what's in it for education? Paper submitted to the National Commission on Excellence in Education, Washington, DC.

Sternberg, R., Conway, B., Ketron, J. and Bernstein, M. (1981) People's conceptions of intelligence, *Journal of Personality and Social Psychology*, 41: 37–55.

Stobart, G. and Stoll, L. (2005) The Key Stage 3 strategy: what kind of reform is this? *Cambridge Journal of Education*, 35(2): 225–38.

Swanson, H. L. (1990) Influence of metacognitive knowledge and aptitude on problem solving, *Educational Psychology*, 82(2): 306–14.

Swartz, R. (2001) Infusing critical and creative thinking into content instruction, in A. Costa (ed.) *Developing Minds: A Resource Book for Teaching Thinking*, 3rd edn. Alexandria, VA: Association of Supervisors and Curriculum Development.

Swartz, R. and Fischer, S.D. (2001) Teaching thinking in science, in Costa, A. (ed.) *Developing Minds A Resource Book for Teaching Thinking*. Alexandria, VA: Association of Supervisors and Curriculum Development.

Swartz, R.J. and Parks, S. (1994). *Infusing the Teaching of Critical and Creative Thinking into Content Instruction*. Pacific Grove, CA: Critical Thinking Books & Software.

Swartz, R., Fischer, and Parks, S. (1998) *Infusing the Teaching of Critical and Creative Thinking Into Science*. Pacific Grove, CA: Critical Thinking Books and Software.

Swartz, R., Fischer, S., Parks, S. et al. (2000) *Infusion: Blackline Graphic Organiser Masters*. Available from PO Box 448, Pacific Grove, CA, 93950-0448, US.

Taggart, G., Ridley, K., Rudd, P. and Benefield, P. (2005) *Thinking Skills in the Early Years: A Literature Review*. London: NFERNelson.

Tharp, R. and Gallimore, R. (1988) *Rousing Minds to Life: Teaching and Learning and Schooling in Social Context*. Cambridge: Cambridge University Press.

Thorndike, E.L. (1911) *Human Learning*. New York: Pentice Hall.

Thornton, M.C. (1980) Piaget and mathematics students, in Fuller, R.G. (ed.) *Piagetian, Programmes in Higher Education*. Lincoln, NE : ADAPT Program.

Thurstone, L.L. (1935) *The Vectors of the Mind*. Chicago: University of Chicago Press.

Tight, M. (1996) *Key Concepts in Adult Education and Training*. London: Routledge.

Tishman, S. and Perkins, D. (1997). The language of thinking, *Kappan, 78*(5): 368–74.

Tobin, K. (1984) Effects of extended wait time on discourse characteristics and achievement in middle school grades, *Journal of Research in Science Teaching*, 21(8): 779–91.

Torrance, E.P. (1974) *Norms and Technical Manual for the Torrance Tests of Creative Thinking*. Bensenville, IL: Scholastic Testing.

Trickey, S. and Topping, K.J. (2004) Philosophy for children: a systematic review, *Research Papers in Education*, 19: 335–80.

Tudge, J.R.H. and Rogoff, B. (1989) Peer influences on cognitive development: Piagetian and Vygotskian perspectives, in M.H. Bornstein and J.S. Bruner (eds) *Interaction in Human Development*. Hillsdale, NJ: Erlbaum.

Von Oech, R. (1986) *A Kick in the Seat of the Pants*. New York: Warner.

Vygotsky, L.S. (1978) *Mind in Society: The Development of Higher Psychological Processes*. Cambridge, MA: Harvard University Press.

Vygotsky, L.S. (1981) The genesis of higher mental functions, in J.V. Wertch (ed.) *The Concept of Activity in Soviet Psychology*. Armonk, NY: Sharpe.

Vygotsky, L.S. (1986) *Thought and Language* (A. Kozulin ed.), Revised edn. Cambridge, MA: MIT Press.

Watkins, C. (2001) Learning about learning enhances performance, *National School Improvement Network (NSIN) Bulletin*, 13: 1–7.

Watson, R. and Wood-Robinson, V. (1998) Learning to investigate, in M. Ratcliffe (ed.) *The ASE Guide to Secondary Science Education*. Cheltenham: Stanley Thornes.

Wegerif, R. (2002) *Literature Review in Thinking Skills: Technology and Learning*. A report for NESTA Futurelab, Report no. 2.

Wegerif, R. and Mercer, N. (1997) A dialogical framework for investigating talk, in R. Wegerif and P. Scrimshaw (eds) *Computers and Talk in the Primary Classroom*. Clevedon: Multilingual Matters.

Wegerif, R., Littleton, K., Dawes, Mercer, N. and Rowe, D. (2005) Widening access to educational opportunities through teaching children how to reason together, *Westminster Studies in Education*, 14: 143–56.

Wellington, J. (1989) *Skills and Processes in Science Education. A Critical Analysis*. London: Routledge.

Wenger, E. (1998) *Communities of Practice: Learning, Meaning and Identity*. Cambridge: Cambridge University Press.

Werner, W. (1980) Implementation: the role of belief. Unpublished paper, Center for Curriculum Studies, University of British Columbia, Vancouver, Canada.

Wertsch, J.V. (1985) *Culture, Communication and Cognition: Vygotskian Perspectives*. Cambridge: Cambridge University Press.

Wheeler, E.R. and Wheeler, R.E. (1995) *Modern Mathematics for Elementary School Teachers*. New York: Brooks/Cole Publishing Company.

Wilks, S. and Yates, C. (2002) Interim evaluation of Wigan ARTs project. Summary Report, May.

Williams, S. (1993) *Evaluating the Effects of Philosophical Enquiry in a Secondary School*. Matlock: Derbyshire County Council.

Wilson, V. (2000) *Can Thinking Skills be Taught?* Edinburgh: Spotlight Report 79, The Scottish Council for Research in Education. Available at: www.scre.ac.uk/soptlight/spotlight79.html

Witschonke, C. (2006) Harry Potter casts his spell in the classroom, *Middle School Journal*, 37(3): 4–11.

Wood, D. (1980) Teaching the young child: some relationships between social interaction, language and thought, in D. Olson (ed.) *The Social Foundations of Language and Thought*. New York: Norton.

Wood, D. (1998) *How Children Think and Learn*, 2nd edn. Oxford: Blackwell.

Wood, D. J. and Middleton, D. (1975) A study of assisted problem solving, *British Journal of Psychology*, 66: 181–91.

Wood, D., Bruner, J.S. and Ross, G. (1976) The role of tutoring in problem solving, *Journal of Child Psychology*, 17: 89–100.

Yates, C. and Gouge, K. (2002) Creating a cognitive acceleration programme in the arts: the Wigan LEA ARTS project, in M. Shayer, M. and Adey, P. (eds) *Learning Intelligence*. (Materials available from Wigan Arts Advisory and Support Service, The Professional Development Centre, Park Road, Hindley, Wigan WN2 3RY.) Wigan: Wigan Arts Advisory and Support Service.

Zessoules, R. and Gardner, H. (1991) Authentic assessment: beyond the buzzword and into the classroom, in V. Perrone (ed.) *Expanding Student Assessment*. Alexandria, VA: Association for Supervision and Curriculum Development.